Restoring Japan's Economic Growth

ADAM S. POSEN

Restoring Japan's Economic Growth

INSTITUTE FOR INTERNATIONAL ECONOMICS
Washington, DC
September 1998

Adam S. Posen, *Research Fellow,* was from 1994 to 1997 an economist in the International Research Function of the Federal Reserve Bank of New York. In 1993-94, he was Okun Memorial Fellow in Economic Studies at the Brookings Institution, and in 1992-93 he was a Bosch Foundation Fellow in Germany. He is the author of several works on monetary policy and political economy.

INSTITUTE FOR INTERNATIONAL ECONOMICS
11 Dupont Circle, NW
Washington, DC 20036-1207
(202) 328-9000 FAX: (202) 328-5432

C. Fred Bergsten, *Director*
Christine F. Lowry, *Director of Publications*
Brett Kitchen, *Director of Marketing,*
   Foreign Rights

Library of Congress Cataloging-in-Publication Data
Posen, Adam Simon
Restoring Japan's Economic Growth /
   Adam S. Posen
p. cm.
Includes bibliographical references, index.
   1. Fiscal policy—Japan. 2. Japan—
   Economic policy—1989- 3. Japan—
   Economic conditions—1989- I. Title.
HJ1394.P67   1998
336.3'0952—dc21   98-29813
                                        CIP

ISBN 0-88132-262-8

This is preeminently the time to speak the truth, the whole truth, frankly and boldly. Nor need we shrink from honestly facing conditions in our country today. This great Nation will endure as it has endured, will revive and will prosper. So first of all, let me assert my firm belief that the only thing we have to fear is fear itself—nameless, unreasoning, unjustified terror which paralyzes needed efforts to convert retreat into advance . . .

Values have shrunken to fantastic levels; taxes have risen; our ability to pay has fallen; government of all kinds is faced by serious curtailment of income; the means of exchange are frozen in the currents of trade; the withered leaves of industrial enterprise lie on every side; farmers find no markets for their produce; the savings of many years in thousands of families are gone.

More important, a host of unemployed citizens face the grim problem of existence, and an equally great number toil with little return. Only a foolish optimist can deny the dark realities of the moment.

Yet our distress comes from no failure of substance. We are stricken by no plague of locusts. Compared with the perils which our forefathers conquered because they believed and were not afraid, we still have much to be thankful for. Nature still offers her bounty and human efforts have multiplied it. Plenty is at our doorstep, but a generous use of it languishes in the very sight of the supply. Primarily this is because of rulers of the exchange of mankind's goods have failed through their own stubbornness and their own incompetence, have admitted their failure, and have abdicated . . .

Our greatest primary task is to put people to work. This is no unsolvable problem if we face it wisely and courageously . . . There are many ways in which it can be helped, but it can never be helped merely by talking about it. We must act and act quickly.

Finally, in our progress towards a resumption of work we require two safeguards against a return of the evils of the old order: there must be a strict supervision of all banking and credits and investments, so that there will be an end to speculation with other people's money; and there must be provision for an adequate but sound currency . . .

Franklin Delano Roosevelt
First Inaugural Address, 4 March 1933

Contents

Tables

Figures

Preface

Japan is the world's second largest economy and largest surplus and creditor country. Hence, the Institute has devoted extensive and continuing attention to Japanese economic performance, United States-Japan bilateral economic relations, and the impact of Japanese economic policy on the international economy. Our previous publications on these topics include C. Fred Bergsten and William R. Cline's *The United States-Japan Economic Problem* (1985, revised in 1987), Bela Belassa and Marcus Noland's *Japan in the World Economy* (1988), C. Fred Bergsten and Marcus Noland's *Reconcilable Differences? United States-Japan Economic Conflict* (1993), and Yoko Sazanami, Shujiro Urata, and Hiroki Kawai's *Measuring The Costs of Protection in Japan* (1995).

These Japanese economic issues have now become even more critical in light of the Asian financial crisis and Japan's decline from six years of subpar growth into outright recession. An economically weakened Japan, with a sharply declining yen and large trade surpluses, promotes global instability and deprives the rest of East Asia of necessary investment capital and export opportunities. This in turn intensifies the burden of maintaining an open world trading system, uninterrupted financial linkages, and support for the multinational programs necessary for recycling capital back to Asia—in short, the maintenance of an open world economy—on the United States at a time when our domestic political support for that openness is already being severely challenged. For the longer term, the failure of the Japanese economy to right itself in the 1990s, after several decades of spectacular performance in which it was frequently held up as the economic model for East Asia and elsewhere, raises a fundamental question: "What went wrong?"

In this study, Research Fellow Adam Posen assesses the role of macroeconomic policy in explaining the poor performance of the Japanese economy in the 1990s and its potential role in restoring Japan's economic growth. The analysis demonstrates that there was nothing inevitable about Japanese economic decline in the aftermath of the bubble economy and that the government's combination of fiscal austerity and financial laissez-faire converted a normal cyclical downturn into a deep and persistent stagnation. The Japanese economy suffers from numerous structural inefficiencies which, if reformed, could raise the long-run Japanese economic growth rate—but such factors are not the proximate cause of Japan's slow growth in the 1990s.

Rather than a decline in potential, the problem in Japan has been a failure of the economy to grow at the rate of which it remains capable. Claims that fiscal stimulus was tried and failed in Japan are shown to be false. Serious fiscal stimulus was attempted on only one occasion, in September 1995, and strong growth followed the next year. By contrast, misguided contractionary fiscal policies, notably the consumption tax increase of April 1997, slowed the economy. Moreover, the aging of Japanese society has little to do with appropriate responses to today's crisis, and the current debt position of the Japanese government is far less worrisome than some analysts suggest. Posen argues that the current economic situation in fact presents an ideal opportunity for expansionary fiscal policy to be effective.

Posen offers a program for Japanese economic recovery that combines sizable fiscal stimulus, in the form of permanent income tax cuts, with stabilization of price expectations by means of a 3 percent inflation target and a cleanup of the Japanese banking system. Together, these measures can restore confidence in Japan and thereby induce reinvestment in yen-denominated assets by Japanese and foreign savers. Financial reform will likely have some short-run contractionary effects, as insolvent banks are closed and there is a transitional credit contraction, adding powerfully to the case for linking it with substantial fiscal stimulus. Such a program does not require wholesale reform of the Japanese economy or a lengthy and painful transition in order to reap its benefits. In essence, restoring Japanese economic growth is a matter of policy choice.

This study concludes an Institute trilogy that addresses the Asian (and increasingly global) crisis of 1997-98. Morris Goldstein's *The Asian Financial Crisis: Causes, Cures, and Systemic Implications* (June 1998) delved into the origins of the problem and recommends both direct crisis responses and needed reforms for the international financial architecture. Marcus Noland, Li-Gang Liu, Sherman Robinson, and Zhi Wang's *Global Economic Effects of the Asian Currency Devaluations* (July 1998) assesses the real impact on the world economy of the crisis to date and the likely response of the United States to the resulting sharp rise in its trade deficit. By addressing the critical Japanese dimension of the issue, this study completes a comprehensive Institute appraisal of both the current problem and what can be done about it.

The Institute for International Economics is a private nonprofit institution for the study and discussion of international economic policy. Its purpose is to analyze important issues in that area and to develop and communicate practical new approaches for dealing with them. The Institute is completely nonpartisan.

The Institute is funded largely by philanthropic foundations and private corporations. Major institutional grants are now being received from The German Marshall Fund of the United States, which created the Institute with a generous commitment of funds in 1981, and from The William M. Keck, Jr. Foundation, The Andrew W. Mellon Foundation, and The Starr Foundation. The GE Fund provides partial support for our research on Asian issues. A number of other foundations and companies also contribute to the highly diversified financial resources of the Institute. About 18 percent of the Institute's expenditures in our latest fiscal year were financed by contributors outside the United States, including about 12 percent from Japan.

Partial funding for this project was provided under our new Akio Morita Studies Program, a program of studies on topics of central interest to the United States and Japan. The program was created in 1997 to honor our distinguished former Director and now Honorary Director, Akio Morita, the cofounder and former CEO of Sony. The Program is funded by the Sony Corporation, the New York Community Trust—the Peter G. Peterson Fund, and Mr. David Rockefeller.

The Board of Directors bears overall responsibility for the Institute and gives general guidance and approval to its research program—including identification of topics that are likely to become important to international economic policymakers over the medium run (generally, one to three years), and which thus should be addressed by the Institute. The Director, working closely with the staff and outside Advisory Committee, is responsible for the development of particular projects and makes the final decision to publish an individual study.

The Institute hopes that its studies and other activities will contribute to building a stronger foundation for international economic policy around the world. We invite readers of these publications to let us know how they think we can best accomplish this objective.

C. FRED BERGSTEN
Director
August 1998

Acknowledgments

I gratefully acknowledge the support of many people inside and outside the Institute for International Economics in bringing this project to fruition. This book has benefited in part or whole from comments and suggestions from C. Fred Bergsten, Barry Bosworth, Richard Cooper, I.M. Destler, Benjamin Friedman, Morris Goldstein, Edward Graham, Roger Kubarych, Kenneth Kuttner, Isamu Miyazaki, Marcus Noland, J. David Richardson, and participants in an external study-group meeting sponsored by the Institute on 9 July 1998. Erika Wada and Hiroko Ishii provided research assistance across language barriers and a wide variety of sources. Masao Nishikawa of the Embassy of Japan kindly assisted in the acquisition of necessary data. Denise Groves, Adela Jabine, and Erin Sullivan made possible the completion of the manuscript under deadline pressure. The Institute's publications department—Brigitte Coulton, Kara Davis, David Krzywda, Helen Kim, and Christine Lowry—made possible the transformation of the manuscript into a book under similar deadline pressure. The opinions and arguments expressed herein are solely my own, and I am solely responsible for any errors that remain.

Introduction

Economic historians will look back at the 1990s and be struck by the change in relative performance of the world's two major economies. For two decades, the United States had feared economic decline and Japan had led the industrial democracies in rate of growth, even long after catching up to the American level of technology and wealth. Then, in the aftermath of the Japanese asset-price bubble of the 1980s, Japan's economy slowed, stagnated, and finally contracted sharply in 1997-98. Meanwhile, the rest of the Group of Seven (G-7) countries, especially the United States, withstood the initial blows of the Asian financial crisis and recorded outstanding economic performance.

Clearly, something has gone wrong in Japan. Observers, both from within and outside Japan's borders, have offered many combinations of economic diagnoses and policy prescriptions. The coincidence of Japan's turn for the worse with the Asian financial crisis has made proper understanding of Japan's economic plight doubly critical. Because Japan was widely perceived to be the model for the economic miracle in East Asia, the reasons for Japanese economic stagnation in the 1990s will be key evidence in the world's judgment of whether to blame East Asian economic structures for the crisis. The speed and extent of Japan's economic recovery are the most important determinants of the ability of the East Asian economies to come out of the crisis; the extent of Japanese recovery also determines whether the crisis' effects will be contained rather than multiplied and transmitted worldwide.

The long-run meaning and the short-run effects of Japanese economic policies in the 1990s both depend on the answers to two linked questions:

1

How much growth is enough for Japan? How much can Japanese policymakers do to attain that rate of growth? For some, Japan's declining performance is proof that the globalizing economy demands ever-higher standards of liberalization and adherence to the market. The key word for them is "reform," meaning change in the basic structure of Japan's economy. As a result, they believe that Japan cannot grow faster than it has been until changes are made, and policy should be radical and microoriented.

For others, they see in Japan's declining performance the result of interest-group deadlock. They believe that a tightly woven and corrupt economic system is at the root of Japan's declining performance. For these observers, the key word is "crisis," meaning a problem so large that interest group ties are wiped out. They believe that Japan should grow once again only when there has been sufficient pain to destroy old ways, and macroeconomic policy should do nothing to stem the tide until that has happened.

A third group sees in Japan's declining performance the mounting burdens of an aging society. The key word for them is "inevitable," meaning that there are binding fundamental limits to short-run growth. They believe that growth now is constrained by the legitimate concern for the future, and policy should adhere to the necessary macroeconomic austerity to provide for that future. Of course, many would combine some or all of these three views in their own diagnosis and cure for Japan's economic decline.

I maintain a different view: Japan's declining economic performance is the result of the domestic macroeconomic and financial policies pursued by Japanese policymakers. The key word for characterizing Japanese economic policy is "mistaken." The stagnation of Japan in the 1990s was anything but inevitable, and it was misguided macroeconomic austerity and financial laissez-faire—not lack of return on investment or political deadlock—that caused it. In the 1990s, Japanese economic policymakers were presented with the opportunity to fight the last war, the demand-shock-caused depression of the 1930s, and they chose to adopt the strategy that lost that war. As a result, growth in Japan could have been much higher in the 1990s than it was.

Today's policy should be one of active macroeconomic expansion to restore that attainable rate of higher growth. The longer that Japanese policymakers leave their economy in decline, the more attainable wealth they forgo for their citizens and the more they risk provoking financial panic in all of East Asia, which could have effects beyond the power of economic policy to easily reverse.

When one focuses on the immediate policy issues, criticism of current Japanese macroeconomic and financial policies is so widespread that the reasons for it are assumed self-evident. Given the role of mistaken ideas in bringing Japan to this point, it is important, however, to explain in some depth why a shift in Japanese economic policies would be in Japan's own national self-interest. Calls for a switch to "demand-led growth" and for Japan to fulfill its obligations as the world's largest creditor economy have been heard so often and for so long that they sound to some like code words for what the United States wants from Japan. This impression is compounded by the repeated linkage of justified arguments for necessary cleanup of the Japanese banking system with excessive demands for wholesale structural change. Such linkage makes policy demands appear to be the opportunistic resubmission of a long-standing foreign wish list. Moreover, such calls do not address directly the justifications that Japanese policymakers have expressed for their unwillingness to change course. The justifications invoked are indeed mistaken, but must be shown to be based on a misunderstanding of the economics of the current situation in Japan. Finally, analysis should offer an explicit list of appropriate macroeconomic policy responses and their magnitudes rather than merely an exhortation to action. That is what this book will do to address the present urgent policy discussion.

This emphasis on Japan's domestic self-interest is not a matter of cynicism nor of disregard for the external effects of the world's second largest economy. For Japan—or for any other sovereign nation wealthy enough to set its own economic policy—to undertake a shift in its economic policies, its polity must perceive that shift to be in its own interest. History has shown us that major policy choices largely reflect the domestic power of interests and coalitions in a given country. Were domestic interests and coalitions not the dominant source of policy in Japan's East Asian neighbors, for example, their governments would have adapted to global capital flows long before the 1997 crisis. These economies, being smaller and more vulnerable to international pressures, had significantly more to gain from such adaptation than does Japan. Similarly, the lack of international coordination of macroeconomic policies, which produced the sharp swings of the yen against the dollar in the years preceding the Asian crisis, reflected the primacy of domestic concerns in the Group of Three (G-3) countries (though this neglect obviously contributed to international events that have proven domestically damaging in the end). And if this domestic focus is true of any country, it is certainly true of one whose political leadership has been as weakened as that of Japan in recent years.

Yet it is in Japan's self-interest, even narrowly defined to ignore its external environment, to decide that enough is enough. The reality is not only that Japan has been growing painfully slowly for over six years in absolute terms, but that relative to how fast the Japanese economy could have grown even during the 1990s, the shortfall is unprecedentedly large. The Japanese economic situation of the 1990s is the clearest example since the 1930s of one requiring an appropriate *macroeconomic-policy* response. Comparisons to the aftermath of the 1929 crash come cheap in reference to today's Japan, but the most important historical lesson seems to have been lost. The Great Depression taught us that individually rational optimizing decisions can, under certain circumstances, produce suboptimal economic performance in the aggregate. In less abstract terms, national economies can get trapped in bad situations simply because they respond inadequately to fluctuations in aggregate demand. It is mistaken to see in such an event a change in fundamentals. Macroeconomics exists as a field precisely because national economies are more than the sum of their sector-by-sector efficiencies and waste.

Just as the downturn of 1929-30 became the depression of 1933 when policy mistakes allowed matters to worsen, the Japanese crash of 1992 has become the ill-timed recession of 1997-98 because of government shortsightedness that was highlighted by a return to fiscal contraction in 1996-97. Accumulation of excess capacity and unemployment has eaten at the confidence of Japanese consumers and savers. The resultant rise in fear and uncertainty can turn a recession into a depression if left unchecked by policy, even when those fears stem from the immediate situation and nothing more deeply forward looking. In light of the East Asian economic environment of mid-1998, Japanese households and businesses have ample reason for uncertainty even without the contribution of domestic financial instability.

Broad structural reform cannot substitute for macroeconomic policy response when such a severe decline in aggregate demand occurs, even if these approaches might ultimately complement each other over the long run. Calls for a cleanup of the Japanese bad loan problem, similar to those undertaken in numerous other economies of the Organization for Economic Cooperation and Development (OECD) in the 1980s and 1990s, should not be blown up into an urgent need for the type of comprehensive shock treatment undertaken in New Zealand or the transition economies. In the international policy environment of the 1990s—where there has been a general thrust toward fiscal consolidation and liberalizing deregulation running from the signatories of the Maastricht treaty to the adherents of International Monetary Fund (IMF) austerity programs—it is somewhat understandable that certain Japanese policymakers have forgotten that macroeconomic (i.e., fiscal and monetary) stabilization is irreplaceable. It is also understandable that, when the very advocates of fiscal austerity and structural reform elsewhere have asked Japan to engage in fiscal stimulus, it is seen as contrary to Japan's self-interest even if internationally beneficial.

Still, there is a distinction to be made between recognizing opportunities for further liberalization that over long spans of time can improve economic performance—opportunities that always exist in all economies, including even today's much praised US economy—and attributing every downturn in national economic performance to overt structural decline. The only prima facie case to be made for why Japan's economic structure transformed overnight in 1992 from a model to emulate to something horribly damaging to economic performance is the backward inference that macroeconomic policy has been tried since then but has failed to restore growth. I argue in this book that growth has not returned to Japan because Japanese macroeconomic policy has followed a mistaken course, and the appropriate policies have not been tried. In the present Japanese and international economic environment, substituting structural reform for expansionary macroeconomic policy could be harmful, because the usual short-run effect of such reform is to add to unemployment and excess capacity. Such developments would further fuel Japanese investors' and savers' uncertainty and low expectations, even though sustainable higher growth remains attainable today without such reform. There is no pressing need to forgo stimulating aggregate demand and give up the benefits thereof while waiting for the benefits of further deregulation—the current rate of growth is not enough for Japan.

As it happens, such reversal of austerity would benefit East Asia and the rest of the world as well. It is important that this fact not be used to raise domestic political suspicions about Japan's self-interest in changing policy when it is invoked as an additional reason why Japan should change course. More important, however, Japan must understand that ignoring its external environment is not an option. Public comparisons that focus on explicit lending initiatives to show which countries have "done more for Asian recovery" from the financial crisis are a side show. Without Japanese economic growth at its full potential, East Asian recovery is extremely uncertain and depends all too much on exports to the remainder of the G-7. Without East Asian recovery, Japan will lose significant export, investment, and production opportunities and find its domestic fears heightened. Politically, a Japan that fails to act as a regional leader and global partner when so much is at stake—especially when the action required of Japan is a boon not a sacrifice—will be distrusted for a long time to come.

There are many reasons given for the relative austerity of fiscal policy and the neglect of financial and monetary stabilization in Japan in the 1990s. The first half of this book addresses three related claims that have received significant attention: (1) the stagnation of Japanese growth in the 1990s reflects a decline in Japanese economic fundamentals, not aggregate demand, and so a macroeconomic policy response is inappropriate; (2) significant fiscal stimulus has already been undertaken and failed; and (3) fiscal stimulus is unlikely to have the desired short-run effects, and, moreover, any such benefits of fiscal stimulus now will be outweighed by long-run costs caused by Japan's looming social security burdens.

While all of these claims can be linked to real concerns, none stands up to scrutiny as a justification for continued policy neglect. The existence of these claims by Japanese policymakers does indicate, however, that the policies that have been pursued in the 1990s were the result of conscious choice and not political impotence. That is why explanation of the reasons for a policy change are important, both to move matters forward in Japan today and to understand what went wrong in Japan for the longer-run perspective.

With regard to the first claim, I show in chapter 1 that the extent and sources of the output decline in recent years in Japan cannot sensibly be accounted for by a shift in potential growth. While there are significant structural problems in the Japanese economy that, if removed, would increase its long-run growth rate, there was no sharp worsening of these factors in the late 1980s or early 1990s that could be a proximate cause of the slowdown. Therefore, Japanese policymakers' priority should be to make up the shortfall between Japan's current and potential rate of growth. This potential rate is still at least 2 percent a year. In other words, policymakers should use macroeconomic stimulus to respond to the current downturn. There is no need for Japan to settle for today's rate of growth as sufficient in the short run or for the world to wait until Japan goes through years of structural reform to see the Japanese economy to rebound.

With regard to the second claim, I examine in detail in chapter 2 the combination of tax and spending packages undertaken by the Japanese government since 1992 and document that all announced fiscal packages were far smaller than claimed. In fact, many years' budgets acted to reverse the effects of these programs. Total public investment in all seven stimulus packages from 1992 through spring 1998 was 23 trillion yen, or 4.5 percent of GDP. While not a small number, it seems hardly adequate after taking into account that there have been over 7 years of recession with an output loss in excess of 9 percent of GDP and that the claimed total public expenditures was 65-75 trillion yen. As another benchmark, between 1960 and 1992, in the 12 largest OECD economies there were 21 fiscal expansions undertaken that were larger than any single year's Japanese fiscal stimulus since 1992. Even the largest stimulus effort undertaken to date (in 1995) was still short of the full size appropriate to the situation. Yet, the Japanese economy responded with positive growth in 1996 until the 1996 and 1997 budgets contracted demand, indicating that fiscal stimulus does work.

With regard to the third concern, I argue in chapter 3 that most of the usual economic determinants of the effectiveness of fiscal stimulus are actually favorable in Japan today given people's flight from domestic investment. Whether or not Japan is in a "liquidity trap," monetary policy has been ineffective because households' demand for cash has been sharply rising, and both households and businesses have had such low expectations of return on investment that they would rather sit on their available funds. This combination means that the usual crowding-out offset to fiscal-policy interest-rate rises and displacement of private-sector investment will not occur. Once fiscal policy has absorbed enough savings and raised the return on investment sufficiently for interest rates to bite, it will have done its job and the recovery will be in place (and monetary policy can take over).

The long-run aspects of fiscal policy are also discussed in chapter 3. The historical record and the institutional framework of economic policy in Japan indicate that an incremental rise in the Japanese debt-to-GDP ratio in pursuit of such recovery would likely be reversed in better times, and debt would not increase explosively. Additional Japanese debt incurs direct costs too small to be of concern until that time because Japanese *net* debt is the lowest in the OECD and because it has the lowest share of foreign holders and, therefore, raises few concerns of sustainability. Finally, it must be recognized that Japan's old-age problem is so predominantly driven by demographic factors that paying off the *entire* outstanding Japanese government debt would tackle less than 20 percent of the problem. If the Japanese people wish to address the looming social security burden of the country's aging society, they will have to raise the retirement age or the female participation rate in the labor force or the birthrate or immigration. The government should not sacrifice any more of this decade's growth in a false economy that will make no long-run difference.

The second half of this book addresses what should be done to reverse the mistaken economic policies that have been damaging the Japanese economy. Chapter 4 assesses the mounting risks that domestic financial fragility, consumer confidence, and the international environment pose for the already negative growth forecast for Japan. There is a threat of sizable capital flight abroad and financial disintermediation at home, the beginnings of which have already been seen. Significant further withdrawal of capital from the Japanese economy would start a cycle whereby declining confidence, financial fragility, and international tensions would reinforce each other. Such a cycle would put Japan in a policy dilemma with no ready solution: those policies that would support the financial system (lower interest rates, public infusion of capital, easy monetary policy, etc.) would drive the yen further downward, and vice versa.

In addition, as the events of June 1998 illustrated, there is significant potential for a cycle of competitive devaluations and even a protectionist backlash if Japan fails to act appropriately. Such events could be calamitous for East Asia and the world economy as well as for Japan. Policy inaction or gradualism, which appears prudent, may in reality be reckless when such downside risks are present. The existence of such risks also explains why banking reform and monetary stabilization are critical accompaniments to a policy of fiscal stimulus.

Chapter 5 presents my recommended program for Japanese economic recovery. The distinction must be made between changes in major policies sufficient to restore growth on a sustainable basis and those policies—such as a "bridge bank," exchange rate intervention, or small tax cuts—that can constructively prevent panic in the short run but do not ultimately promote the sustainable ongoing recovery that Japan can achieve. Again, the benchmark must be the rate of Japanese potential economic growth, between 2 and 2.5 percent of GDP a year. Staving off recession (negative growth) is insufficient. Until the current output gap is eliminated by reemploying unemployed workers and unused industrial capacity, the Japanese economy can and should grow faster than that rate of potential growth. While the Japanese economy may never regain the lost wealth that was the cumulative cost of the subpotential growth throughout the 1990s, it can seek to restore full use of its current capabilities. Structural reform that will raise the potential growth rate over the long run will, of course, be helpful over the long run, but it would be a mistaken waste of policy attention and political capital to force those issues at this time beyond the critical minimum required to restore financial stability.

The program I propose is focused on changing Japanese savers' and investors' confidence, both by convincingly restoring expectations of above-potential growth and price stability and by removing the incentives to excessive saving, which perpetuate the downturn. There are three legs to the program. First is *fiscal expansion*, which should include:

■ *Fiscal stimulus of 4 percent of GDP before the end of 1998.* Unless the economy is stimulated above potential growth of 2 to 2.5 percent per year, unemployment will continue to rise and capacity utilization will continue to drop. Confidence, and with it consumption and investment, will erode further. A small fiscal-stimulus package may, therefore, be a waste of money, whereas a sufficiently large fiscal package will lead to sustained growth. Given an expected contraction in the Japanese economy of 1 to 1.5 percent of GDP in 1998 and a rate of potential growth of at least 2 percent, fiscal expansion should be greater than the sum of those numbers.

■ *Permanent tax cuts.* Permanent tax cuts are more likely than temporary cuts to be spent and to affect consumer planning. Income tax cuts are better than consumption tax cuts because income tax cuts get money directly to the salarymen, whose rise in precautionary savings is the main problem. Given the inequities of the Japanese tax code, income tax cuts constitute reform as well as stimulus. Either form of permanent tax cut, however, is better than public works spending. Tax cuts reduce distortions in the economy, induce future cuts in public spending (as the Reagan deficits did in the United States), go beyond specific politically favored sectors, provide a clear signal of commitment from the government, and are more credibly permanent.

■ *Fund deficits with short-term government debt.* Issuing short-term government debt rather than the Japanese government's traditional instrument, long-term government debt, has four advantages: (1) It encourages long bondholders to shift into corporate investment; (2) It offers cash hoarders a safe substitute for currency, thereby recycling savings; (3) It forces the government to confront the issue of debt rollover in the near term, when times are better; and (4) It adds liquidity, which is currently lacking, to the Japanese debt market. This infusion of the right form of asset will change incentives and increase the effectiveness of monetary policy.

The second leg of the program is *monetary stabilization* of price expectations against *both* deflation and inflation. For Japanese households to spend and Japanese businesses to invest they need faith in the stability of the purchasing power of their currency. This is also a prerequisite to any lasting revival of Japanese asset prices. The Bank of Japan, therefore, should:

■ *Announce an inflation target of 3 percent for summer 2000.* Deflation is clearly harmful, especially when debt is held by a fragile financial system. Unanchored monetary expansion, however, will simply replace deflationary restraint with inflationary uncertainty. A positive inflation target, enough above zero to be clearly expansionary but finite and public so that it provides a floor on price expectations, would allow the Bank of Japan to offset deflation without launching an inflationary spiral. Such an anchored and transparent monetary policy offers almost all of the advantages of simply inflating by "turning on the presses" without any of its destabilizing risks.

■ *Avoid intentional yen depreciation.* A decline in the value of the yen, like unanchored inflation, increases uncertainty and erodes wealth. Such loss of purchasing power encourages people to take money out of the economy and deters investment. More so than inflation expectations, movements in exchange rates can spiral beyond the intended push. In addition, depreciation is less effective in stimulating the economy than are domestic policies, because a depreciation's benefits are concentrated in particular (export-oriented) sectors. Depreciation also risks a competitive devaluation response by other countries and a protectionist response to further increases in Japan's trade surplus.

The third leg is *financial reform* that follows the model of prior banking-system cleanups in the United States and other OECD economies in the 1980s and 1990s. Japanese financial fragility is no different in nature, just in size, from those prior episodes. As a result, the cleanup program should follow some basic guidelines:

- At a bank closing in the near future, clarify the extent of deposit guarantees by directly paying off individual account holders to the limit *but* no higher and by not paying stockholders or counterparties;

- Put new capital only into solvent banks, and cut off the moral-hazard-driven overlending of those banks that have zero or negative net worth;

- Hire and train a new "Civilian Financial Conservation Corps" of young bank supervisors that, as urgently as any mobilization effort in response to a natural disaster, would identify which banks merit saving (while they are being trained, outside accountant firms can be hired);

- Privatize the Postal Savings system to stop the ongoing government-subsidized run on the Japanese private banking system.

The likely short-run contractionary effects of these necessary efforts to put the Japanese financial system on a sound footing are an additional reason why fiscal stimulus and monetary stabilization must accompany financial reform. Concentrating on the restoration of incentives for Japanese savers to keep their money in solvent Japanese private-sector banks is a somewhat different policy focus than one intent on providing the short-run alleviation of a credit crunch either for Japanese banks or their borrowing businesses. The latter would be a short-run palliative, while the former would ease the credit constraint on a more lasting basis. While a credit crunch is of immediate concern, especially to some viable small businesses in Japan, the underlying and more dangerous problem is the growing disintermediation of funds from the Japanese private-sector banking system. Premature emphasis on public-sector lending cannot substitute for measures of supervisory, deposit insurance, and postal savings reform—especially since public-sector credit is an inefficient substitute for private-sector banking because of differences in incentives, information, and skills.

Whatever policy response the Japanese government undertakes in 1998 and whatever the ultimate outcome, economic decision makers need to know what the Japanese economic decline tells them about their own current and future policies. Chapter 6 considers the broader lessons of Japanese austerity and stagnation in the 1990s. Japanese economic decline was the outcome of a mistaken set of policy choices and not the nearly inevitable failures of a structurally unsound economic system. As a result, both the future prospects for the Japanese economy and the implications of Japan's performance for policy in general are much different from those commonly expressed. Most of all, this episode should remind policymakers worldwide of the importance of countercyclical macroeconomic policy. The failure of demand management to offset 1970s stagflation or to permanently raise the natural rate of unemployment are cautions that such macroeconomic stabilization is not the solution to all problems, nor proof that the problems for which countercyclical policy is the appropriate response do not occur. If anything, the critical role of the financial sector in transmitting the economic contraction in Japan in the 1990s reminds us that stabilization policy is important because an unavoidable cost of financial markets in a world of imperfect information is their propensity to propagate business cycles.

The Japanese economic experience of the 1990s should not be seen as a verdict on the Japanese model, which remains as much a mixture of good and bad qualities as it always was. In fact, the tendency in the 1997-98 Asian crisis' aftermath to attribute economic performance to national economic models is at best misleading and, at worst, distracts policymaking with excessively dramatic all-or-nothing choices. Instead, discussion should focus on more moderate claims about the importance of individual policy decisions and nondecisions in response to specific economic shocks and situations. Such a more accurate focus also would raise the perceived autonomy and accountability of policymakers for short-run economic performance and would diminish their ability to claim responsibility for long-run economic development. In other words, a shift in focus from models to policy decisions would bring public expectations in line with the real influence of policymakers. To whatever extent national models do apply, the Japanese economy is far less like that of its less-developed East Asian neighbors than it has encouraged others to believe during the period of credit taking. Thus, its problems are far more easily resolved. Japan can rapidly, albeit not costlessly, return to economic growth without wrenching social and institutional change. If history shows that the Japanese economy at the end of the 1990s did not return to its potential economic growth because of an unwillingness to change policy, and the Japanese people and perhaps the world economy suffered as a result, responsibility would rest with those policymakers who made the mistake of deciding that too little growth was enough for Japan.

1

Diagnosis: Macroeconomic Mistake, Not Structural Stagnation

Recent calls for Japanese economic stimulus, most notably at the G-7 finance ministers meeting on 15 April 1998, have been pitched in terms of two concerns: Asia cannot recover without greater Japanese growth and import demand, and data indicating that Japan is slipping into recession make the situation more serious than it was when Japan was merely growing slowly. While both of these concerns are valid, they do not address two issues of Japanese economic performance in the 1990s that must come first for Japanese policymakers: First, is macroeconomic stimulus the appropriate response to prolonged Japanese economic stagnation? Second, if stimulus is appropriate, how much growth should be the attainable goal of that stimulus? More detailed discussion of the role and form of fiscal expansion can only be tackled once these issues are resolved.

An inadequate countercyclical policy response to the 1980s asset-price bubble and its burst accounts for most of the Japanese growth slowdown in the 1990s. There appears to be little justification for invoking additional factors such as a wholesale decline in Japanese economic potential or in the competitiveness of the "Japanese model." While there are significant structural problems in the Japanese economy that, if removed, would increase its long-run growth rate, there was no sharp worsening of these factors during this period that could be a proximate cause of the 1990s slowdown. The Japanese growth slowdown, therefore, merits a policy response of macroeconomic stimulus. Properly designed and implemented, that should be sufficient to restore growth. Deep structural reforms, although beneficial for both Japan and the world economy over the long run, are not a necessary response to this short-run crisis.[1] This is because Japanese potential economic growth remains high even in the aftermath of the bubble. Accordingly, the goal of that macroeconomic stimulus should be to make the Japanese economy grow faster than potential—which, I argue, is likely between 2.0 and 2.5 percent annual real GDP growth—until the current output gap is closed by reemploying unemployed workers and unused industrial capacity. An economy in recession is analogous to a plant temporarily deprived of sun and food: the plant, once taken into the greenhouse and fed to make up for its deprivation, will bloom as if nothing had waylaid it.

Why Japanese Slow Growth Merits a Macroeconomic Response

The potential growth rate of the Japanese economy is a benchmark for the extent to which current Japanese slow growth can be dealt with by macroeconomic policy rather than structural reform. If the decline in output in the 1990s could be fully explained as a drop in the potential growth rate of the Japanese economy—where that potential growth rate is the long-run trend rate at which the economy would grow and around which business cycles would fluctuate—then the appropriate fiscal and monetary policy response would be to do nothing. In other words, if the structure of the Japanese economy reset to a slower growth path in the 1990s, the change would represent the best possible result of Japanese markets as presently constituted. The only way to raise growth in that case would be deregulation and wholesale structural reform.

Such a structural change in potential growth would require an explanation, however, and no obvious one is available. While the asset bubble's collapse certainly was damaging to balance sheets throughout the Japanese economy and especially to those of banks, such a shock would not disrupt the fundamental capacity of the economy to grow. The basic financial "infrastructure" of intermediaries and bond and equity markets still exists, and technological capabilities more broadly in the economy were not lost. Certainly, no physical or human capital in the Japanese economy was suddenly destroyed or rendered obsolete during the 1990s (Kobe earthquake aside). As noted, there were no international shocks on par with the combination of the breakdown of Bretton Woods and the first oil shock in 1973, which marks the last great drop in the rate of

---

1. See Bergsten and Noland (1993) and Bergsten, Ito, and Noland (forthcoming) for a discussion of an agenda for Japanese structural reform. It must be noted that most microstructural reforms (such as retail deregulation) are usually accompanied by short-run contractionary effects at the macro level, even as they offer long-run benefits (see the discussion in chapter 6).

productivity growth for the OECD economies (the Asian crisis, remember, followed over five years of Japanese stagnation). McKinsey & Company (1996) and Alexander (1997), among others, persuasively argue that Japan had a sharp decline in its relative and absolute rate of return on capital *around 1980*. While this implies that Japanese potential growth is at a lower *level* than it might have been, or many assume, it is not evidence of structural change since that time.

If a shock is not to blame, then what has gradually changed either in the Japanese economy or in its environment to knock it from its previous status as a fast-growing economy, if not a model economy? In terms of its external environment, improvements in the United States' or other countries' competitiveness should not affect Japan's ability to grow, unless Japan were being shut out of multiple strategic industries that offer special rents and growth spillovers. That would be a situation hardly consistent with either Japan's continuing success at exporting high-value-added products or with the research evidence on the limited number of such truly strategic industries. It is difficult to imagine that a complex industrialized economy such as Japan's could suffer a decline in its terms of trade that would affect a sufficient range of sectors in the way that a developing economy dependent upon one or a few commodities can be affected—especially without seeing a similar decline in similar countries.

Nor could the much remarked upon burden of rigidities and distortions in the domestic economy, such as the legitimately criticized protection in the Japanese retail sector, have "caught up" with Japan over time. Without government efforts to actively expand rather than merely protect (even zealously) special interests, competitive sectors with a greater real return will grow faster over time and attract more resources, thereby shrinking the burden of protection as a share of the economy.[2] For all the complaints about inertia on the part of Japanese policymakers in the 1980s and 1990s, the reality is not that they have *increased* regulation and inflexibility, but simply that they have not deregulated as quickly as is desirable. The government's Strategic Impediments Initiative has had real if small effects, there was financial deregulation a decade prior to this year's "Big Bang," and some government construction contracts have been opened to more competitive bidding. As a result, the number of distortions in the Japanese economy has shrunk. For example, agricultural employment is down to 3 percent of the workforce, and more discount retail opportunities are

---

2. An additional effect is that many special interests benefit from remaining small, excluding new entrants, and maintaining the ability to coordinate action on their own behalf (see Olson 1971). A classic illustration of this phenomenon of a shrinking burden even in the face of entrenched interests is the protection of coal mining in Western Europe, where the benefits to miners (and their unions) have remained steady or increased over time, while mining with all its public costs has continuously declined as a share of GDP.

available to Japanese consumers than ever before. Structural reform certainly offers further opportunities for efficiency gains, but an insufficient pace of reform cannot be the cause of the current growth slowdown.

It is better to think about Japanese macroeconomic performance from the viewpoint of fundamentals. A country's economic growth normally comes from three sources: growth in the stock of physical capital, growth in the stock of human capital (either the size of the available labor force or the skill and education of that workforce), and growth in the productivity with which labor and capital are used (known as "total factor productivity" [TFP] and thought to track technological progress). For a country's potential growth rate to shift, either its accumulation of physical or human capital must slow or its rate of TFP growth must decline.[3] Demographic and educational factors are slow to change, especially for mature societies such as Japan's. The only aspect of growth in the stock of human capital in the 1990s to change noticeably in Japan is a rise in the employment/population ratio (Haltmaier 1996), but this is hardly of size to account for the shortfall and is more sensibly understood as a response to temporarily declining income growth. Meanwhile, capital accumulation has slowed only slightly since the 1980s, as savings rates have remained high (even if returns to investment remain low).

Productivity growth is calculated as the residual of growth in per-worker income after growth in per-worker physical and human capital have been accounted for. Following Bosworth and Collins (1996), the average annual contribution to growth of each of these factors is calculated for Japan during the periods 1984-1990 and 1990-1994.[4] Assuming a constant capital share of 0.35 in production, the cumulative growth in TFP during 1984-1990 was 9 percent, and it declined to just under 4 percent in 1990-94 (i.e., a difference on the order of 0.5 percent a year). If the capital share is allowed to rise with capital's share of income during the investment boom, which averaged 0.42 in 1984-1990, the productivity numbers change very little. Ultimately, there is no drop in TFP growth of a magnitude sufficient to justify a significant downward revision of Japanese potential growth. The observed drop is nowhere close to comparable to the generalized drop in productivity growth seen in 1973 in the

---

3. Recent economic theories of "endogenous" growth emphasize that some factors have positive externalities for growth beyond their direct usage. To some extent, these are captured by the weighting of the labor force for its quality; another source featured in these models is technological progress embodied in capital. As discussed in Bosworth and Collins (1996) and Young (1995a, 1995b), however, there is little empirical support for this claim as a major source of growth. In any event, such spillovers from capital investment would be far more likely to accrue to an economy that is in a state of technological catch-up than to one at the cutting edge of many industries such as today's Japan.

4. All data are taken from World Bank *World Data* and from Penn-World Tables as in Bosworth and Collins (1996).

industrialized countries or to the drop in Japan around 1980 previously mentioned. It is, in fact, within the range of the usual variation of productivity with the business cycle.

Given the determinants of cross-country differences in long-run growth rates, Japan's potential growth rate should remain high in the 1990s. The neoclassical growth model predicts that economic growth is driven by two fundamental forces: convergence of low-income countries to the higher-income countries' level (through the diffusion of capital and technological knowledge) and determinants of countries' ability to accumulate and make use of productive factors at whatever initial income level. The latter include such factors as schooling and life expectancy (which affect the level of human capital), government consumption and inflation (which affect the accumulation of investment capital), and the rule of law and respect for property rights (which affect labor and capital productivity, as well as technological progress). Lower fertility actually increases per capita economic growth because when a population is growing, a portion of the economy's investment is used to provide capital for new workers rather than more capital per worker, and *per capita* growth is what we are concerned with when we speak about productivity and economic welfare. None of these growth fundamentals changed in Japan in the 1990s from their relatively positive score in international comparison.

Taking all these factors into account, a recent study makes a long-run forecast of 3.2 percent annual real economic growth for Japan from 1996 to 2000 (Barro 1997, 43). While this estimate is somewhat imprecise, it is consistent with what would be generated by any mainstream cross-national growth regression, and the average growth forecast for the remaining rich OECD members, based on these fundamentals, is 0.8 percent lower.[5] This high growth rate obtains even taking into account the fact that, given Japan's current high income and position at the technological frontier, convergence is working against Japan. In fact, the estimated effect of convergence in the panel regression estimated comes in part out of Japan's rapid catch-up in the 1950s and 1960s. This number is almost certainly an overestimate, and more realistic estimates of the level of potential growth are generated later in this chapter. Nonetheless, taking the long view reminds us that it is difficult to find anything in 1990s Japan that could justify a significant negative *change* in the level of Japanese potential growth.

What Has Happened to Japanese Economic Growth?

The movements of Japanese macroeconomic aggregates and the order in which they moved tell the story of an economic decline caused by fiscal

---

5. The 95 percent confidence interval on forecasts made from this regression is 2.0 percentage points in each direction. By "rich OECD countries," I mean that Mexico and Turkey are excluded from this average.

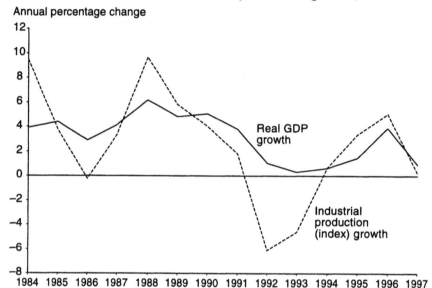

Figure 1.1 Real GDP and industrial production growth, 1984-97

Annual percentage change

Real GDP growth

Industrial production (index) growth

Note: Both are annual growth based on the calendar year.

Sources: For GDP, Economic Planning Agency of Japan, http://www.epa/go/jp.
For industrial production, Ministry of International Trade and Industry of Japan, http://www.miti.go.jp.

austerity and financial laissez-faire. The basic message here is that investment bust and government inaction led to most of the decline. Consumer
and inventory factors followed these downward, which is inconsistent
with a story of structural change.

Since the bursting of the asset-price bubble, economic growth in Japan
has stagnated. From 1992 to 1997, annual real growth in Japanese GDP
has averaged 1.4 percent—a number biased upward by the 3.6 percent
burst in 1996.[6] Industrial production actually declined sharply in 1992-
93 and again in 1997, and has not yet returned to its 1991 level (see figure
1.1). While some slowdown in economic performance was likely after
the strong growth seen during the 1988-91 boom (when GDP grew by
an average of 4.9 percent annually), the present downturn exceeds the
normal depth and duration of a business cycle in Japan and elsewhere.
The downturn is particularly striking given that the two major external
influences on the Japanese economy—the yen/dollar exchange rate and

---

6. Leaving out 1996, growth averaged only 0.9 percent. This higher growth rate in 1996
can be largely attributed to the effects of a one-time policy mix cut short, rather than a
return to a recovery track, as discussed in chapter 2.

Table 1.1 Real GDP annual growth, 1992-97 (percentages)

	Japan	United States	Europe[a]
1992	1.0	2.7	1.0
1993	0.3	2.2	-0.3
1994	0.6	3.5	2.9
1995	1.5	2.0	2.4
1996	3.9	2.4	1.8
1997	0[b]	3.8	2.6[c]
1992-97	1.2	2.8	1.7

a. United Kingdom, Germany, France, Italy, Netherlands, and Spain.

b. The source is *Monthly Finance Review*, February 1998, Ministry of Finance of Japan.

c. This is a predicted value, as of October 1997.

Sources: Japan and United States: *International Financial Statistics, IMF; Stat USA*, US Department of Commerce; Europe: *IMF World Economic Outlook*, May and October 1997.

the price of oil—have been relatively sedate if not entirely benign.[7] The Japanese macroeconomic performance has been poor in comparison to that of the United States (2.6 percent average annual real GDP growth from 1992 to 1997) and even of the slow-growing European economies (the combined average annual real GDP growth of the United Kingdom, Germany, France, Italy, Netherlands, and Spain was 1.7 percent from 1992 to 1997), as shown in table 1.1.

Looking more closely at the development of Japanese GDP and its components from 1984 to 1997, the boom and bust in growth can be largely accounted for by a major swing in nonresidential investment (see table 1.2). In the years of particularly strong economic growth, from 1987 to 1990, this investment growth accounted for 2.0 percent a year in GDP growth on average; the share of investment in real GDP climbed from 13 percent in the early 1980s to an average 19 percent share during the boom. When investment declined in real terms to 7.2 percent of GDP in 1992 and 10.4 percent in 1993, as compared to an average rate of growth of 12 percent a year from 1987 to 1990, it cumulatively took 3.3 percent off GDP in those two years. While private consumption growth declined between the late 1980s and the 1990s, dropping from an average annual contribution to GDP growth of 2.7 percent in 1987-1990 to 0.7 percent in 1992 and 1.0 percent in 1993, this effect takes a back seat to the swing in investment. Private consumption continued to show positive growth rather than contraction until 1997. This leading role for investment is consistent with the standard story that macroeconomists tell of the Japa-

---

7. While it is true that the yen appreciated 20 percent versus the dollar between January and April 1995, by historical standards this was not an unprecedented swing, and it was more than fully reversed by September 1995. The US economy, on the opposite end of this currency fluctuation, has not shown major ill effects from it.

Table 1.2 Contribution to growth of GDP of components, 1984-97 (percentages)

Fiscal year	Private consumption	Residential investment	Nonresidential investment	Private inventory	Government consumption	Public investment	Public inventory	Net exports	GDP
1984	1.5	0.0	1.5	0.2	0.2	-0.3	0.1	0.8	4.1
1985	2.1	0.1	1.7	0.1	0.1	-0.5	0.0	0.5	4.1
1986	2.3	0.5	0.5	-0.3	0.5	0.4	0.1	-0.8	3.1
1987	2.4	1.3	1.2	0.1	0.2	0.6	-0.1	-1.0	4.8
1988	3.3	0.3	2.6	0.5	0.2	0.0	0.0	-0.8	6.0
1989	2.5	0.1	2.1	0.0	0.2	0.1	0.0	-0.6	4.4
1990	2.4	0.3	2.1	-0.1	0.2	0.3	0.0	0.3	5.5
1991	1.6	-0.7	0.5	0.3	0.1	0.5	-0.1	0.7	2.9
1992	0.7	-0.2	-1.4	-0.7	0.2	1.1	0.0	0.6	0.4
1993	1.0	0.2	-1.9	0.0	0.2	1.0	0.0	-0.1	0.5
1994	0.9	0.4	-0.4	-0.2	0.3	-0.1	0.1	-0.3	0.6
1995	1.9	-0.4	1.2	0.2	0.3	0.7	0.0	-1.0	2.8
1996	1.7	0.7	1.5	-0.1	0.1	-0.2	0.0	-0.4	3.2
1997	-0.7	-1.1	0.4	0.2	0.0	-0.5	0.0	1.5	-0.3

Note: The 1997 figure is the average of the first three quarters of FY 1997. The contribution of each GDP component is calculated as the change in the component divided by the initial level of GDP, that is, $(C_t - C_{t\text{-}1})/GDP_{t\text{-}1}$.

Source: Economic Planning Agency, http://www.epa.go.jp.

nese economic slowdown in the 1990s.[8] Easy monetary policy and a rising yen in the mid-1980s contributed to a rise in stock and, with a lag, land prices in Japan. The rise in equity and property values (and, thus, in corporate cross-shareholdings) provided ample collateral for cheap borrowing, which fed further asset demand. The secular rise in asset prices, without signs of inflation in the rest of the economy, led to the Ministry of Finance's reluctance to instruct the Bank of Japan to raise interest rates. United States pressure for low interest rates also contributed to that reluctance. Starting with a 75 basis-point rise in May 1989, however, the Bank of Japan did tighten monetary policy sharply, raising its instrument interest rate by a total of 450 basis points in only 14 months.[9] Stock prices fell quickly and far from a December 1989 peak and, with a four-month lag, so did land prices, albeit not as far.

This asset-price decline reversed the borrowing cycle, as everyone's collateral lost value, banks tightened lending, and borrowers faced rising debt burdens as a proportion of their capital. The contraction of credit and expansion of debt fed back into a decline in aggregate demand, which put further downward pressure on asset values. As a result, Japanese economic growth peaked in the second quarter of 1991, shortly after stock prices peaked. The Bank of Japan kept real interest rates high for an extended period, not lowering nominal rates again until after real estate prices began to decline in spring 1990. Although the effects of tighter money on equity markets is almost immediate, there is a long lag, on the order of two years, between monetary easing and its effects on real economic growth. Therefore, the Bank of Japan's delay in allowing interest rates to fall exacerbated the situation.[10] This contractionary cycle can be seen in the real declines in investment in 1992-94 shown in table 1.2 and in the resultant GDP stagnation.

In summary, the recent course of Japanese economic growth is the result of an overly lengthy investment boom, followed by a proportionately sharp backswing after the bubble burst. Such a bubble and investment response is hardly an unusual process for any market economy in which banks and collateralized lending play a role.[11] The savings and

---

8. For longer narratives largely along these lines, see Bordo et al. (1997), Fisher (1996), Kiyotaki and West (1996), Miller (1996), and Miyazaki (1997).

9. Other monetary policy measures that acted to restrain credit growth included a ceiling on banks' real estate lending imposed in April 1990 and the enforcement of the Basle capital accord minimum starting in March 1993.

10. The Bank of Japan should not be heavily criticized for this policy timing. As has been seen worldwide in the 1990s, monetary policymaking is extremely difficult in the face of asset-price inflation.

11. Kiyotaki and Moore (1997) give a formal model of "credit cycles" amplified through the use of land as collateral, building on a long-standing macroeconomic literature on debt deflation.

loan crisis in the United States and the accompanying overhang of consumer and business debt, the real estate property bust in the late 1980s in the United Kingdom, and the 1990s banking crises in France, Spain, and the Nordic countries are several recent examples of such events driving business cycles on a smaller though sizable scale.[12] In addition, this story of a credit boom and bust driving the recent Japanese business cycle does not require invoking such additional factors as the inefficiency of the Japanese "economic model" or rampant corruption of financial supervision (though the latter certainly did not help matters in 1990s Tokyo, as it did not in 1980s Arizona and Texas). Clearly, this interpretation recognizes the importance of bad loans to the banking system and of harm to balance sheets throughout the economy. If anything, it assumes that such swings in credit, frequently in response to monetary policy, are a major contributing factor to business cycles in Japan and elsewhere.[13] While the accumulation of these financial burdens has contributed to the persistence of the current downturn, that is not evidence that this decline in corporate and household wealth represents a change in Japanese economic fundamentals. Rather, it should be seen as the standard response of the economy to a credit contraction on a larger scale. Kiyotaki and West (1996) and Fisher (1996) estimate models of Japanese investment based on pre-1990s data and find that investment in the early 1990s responded to movements in output and in interest rates in a sensible way, consistent with their predictions.[14] Stated more generally, even severe economic downturns can arise out of the aggregation of individually rational financial decisions with no "real reason" or exogenous shock to blame. This recognition emphasizes the desirability of responding forcefully to movements in aggregate demand, because inefficiencies (such as adverse selection of investment projects) increase during downturns; if business cycles instead reflected real economic shocks, then any policy response would imply working against the proper functioning of markets.

Returning to the movements of GDP components shown in table 1.2 underscores the interpretation that it was a credit boom and bust that

---

12. Fisher (1996, 327) reports that Bank of Japan Governor Yasushi Mieno "sent delegations to the United States and the United Kingdom to investigate how their financial authorities dealt with the property collapses in London and the savings and loan crisis" in the months before interest rates were raised.

13. Much work in macroeconomics in the last decade has focussed on this idea of the importance of the "credit channel"; Bernanke and Gertler (1989) and Bernanke, Gertler, and Gilchrist (1998) summarize this literature.

14. "[O]ne does not have to give pride of place to extraordinary asset price movements to tell a coherent story about the behavior of investment" (Kiyotaki and West 1996, 278); "The fact that endogenous [monetary] policy as estimated from past data accounts for a considerable portion of the fall in output (and investment) is also consistent with the view that the recent recession is not anomalous relative to historical experience" (Fisher 1996, 337).

was allowed to drag on for too long that led to the low-growth 1990s in Japan, and not a shift in fundamentals. Only nonresidential investment and private consumption show meaningful variation, as already discussed. Except for 1991, when land prices tumbled following the earlier equity-price collapse, and 1997, when a spring tax increase cut into housing demand, growth in residential investment never moved sufficiently to be of importance in explaining GDP. Inventories have long been insignificant as a source of business cycles in Japan (see West 1992) and, in these data, continued to play almost no role in the 1990s.[15] As can be seen, the contribution of net exports to Japanese GDP growth did fluctuate in the 1990s, but in no apparent relationship to the multiyear trends in GDP growth. Sensibly, year-to-year swings in Japanese net exports are largely determined by movements in exchange rates (e.g., the large surpluses during the strong dollar years of the 1980s and the decline in the surplus in 1995 following the appreciation of the yen against the dollar).

If the Japanese economy were going through a fundamental transformation in this period—or, as some argue, refusing to transform itself as the international economy changed around it—movements in these other components would explain a greater share of the GDP growth slowdown. Failure to plan properly or rapid forced sectoral change should precipitate a rise in inventories, which should *precede* and lead to the main decline in GDP, as companies take time to adapt or consolidate. Declining general international competitiveness or a terms-of-trade shock to certain Japanese exports should show up as a trend decline in net exports. A radical shift in consumers' savings patterns should have produced significantly underpredicted swings in consumption and a commensurate alteration in the demand for housing (as a store of value)—again, *ahead* of the subsequent decline in GDP. None of these sequences or shifts occurred.[16] None of this argument denies that much of the investment in Japan in the 1980s was wasteful or at least low returning. However, there was no worsening of this return to investment. McKinsey & Company (1996) and Alexander (1997) show that these low returns date back to 1980 and that they did not sharply decline further in the 1990s.

Figure 1.2 plots the annualized quarterly change in three measures of the Japanese price level. There was a clear downward trend in inflation based on the consumer price index (CPI) from January 1991 to the end of 1995, with the monthly rate dipping into outright deflation on 11

---

15. This pattern may reflect the early and wide adoption of "just in time" inventory management in Japan, because, until recently, variations in inventories played a much larger role in US business cycles.

16. Starting in the second half of 1997, consumption finally did decline rather than slow, as noted, and inventories did build up in a significant way, thus lagging the main developments in GDP, and, therefore, understandable as the result of persistent stagnation due to a lack of aggregate demand.

Figure 1.2 Inflation, 1984-97

Annual percentage change

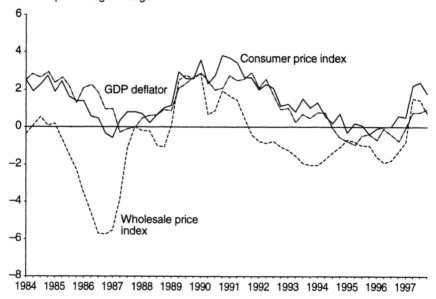

Note: The figures are calculated based on CPI and WPI end of quarter/over quarter.

Source: Economic Planning Agency, http://www.epa.go.jp.

occasions since January 1994. Movements in the wholesale price index (WPI) and the GDP deflator, two alternative measures of the price level, show even greater tendencies to deflation in recent years. The upward shift in inflation in April 1997 in all three series is associated with the rise in the consumption tax from 3 to 5 percent (after one year, this one-time effect on the price level will drop out, and actual inflation should be thought of as the measured level minus that jump).[17] These price movements tracked the path of GDP growth seen in figure 1.1, which is consistent with interpreting this as a decline in aggregate demand. Had there instead been a structural decline in the Japanese economy, say in the relative prices of traded versus nontraded goods or in the productivity of workers, the likely result would have been inflation, because Japanese purchasing power would have declined.

Meanwhile, the paths of government consumption and public investment, the remaining components in table 1.2, did exert significant influ-

17. Moreover, in Japan, as in all industrialized economies, measured inflation is biased upward from true inflation, because the basket of goods priced takes too little account of improvements in quality and substitutions for more expensive goods as prices change. Depending on the size of this measurement error, a CPI inflation rate of 1 or even 2 percent could represent actual price deflation.

ence on the course of Japanese GDP in the 1990s through their conspicuously inappropriate variation. Government consumption, which includes the unemployment and social welfare transfers expected to automatically move in the opposite direction of the business cycle, grew no more quickly than during the 1980s boom and contributed little to growth. Public investment did move countercyclically with large announced stimulus packages in 1992, 1993, and 1995—but not on a par with the size of the slowdown—and even turned contractionary in 1994, 1996, and 1997.[18] This pattern of fiscal austerity in response to a severe decline in aggregate demand is ultimately the story of what has happened to Japanese economic growth.

How Much Growth Should Japan Try to Achieve?

To get a sense of Japanese economic performance in recent years, it is best to focus on estimates of how much short of potential Japanese growth fell. Taking slow growth as given, or fixating on whether Japan is in actual recession (negative growth), misses the point. An output gap is the amount that GDP growth falls below potential, or the sustainable long-run trend in a given year. The cost of a recession may be thought of as the lost wealth of the cumulative below potential growth, the negative output gaps, during that recession.

To estimate an output gap requires some assumptions about the potential growth rate. Luckily, one need not assume either that one can discern directly the inherently unobservable potential growth rate of the economy or that whatever the recent average growth rate was is the true potential rate. In the short run, an economy that runs below potential generates slack, that is, capital and labor resources being underutilized. The logic of supply and demand says that excess capacity should put downward pressure on factor returns (such as wages) and, therefore, on inflation. The converse, that when an economy has a falling rate of inflation there remains slack in the economy, can be used under appropriate circumstances to identify output gaps statistically.[19] To the extent that prices and wages are sticky downward (i.e., resist nominal declines) as inflation nears zero, such an estimate will *understate* the magnitude of the output

---

18. A detailed analysis of these packages and their impact is given in chapter 2.

19. Of course, the statement "If there is an output gap, then there is declining inflation" is not logically equivalent to the converse. There are other reasons why inflation might decline, such as an increase in the counterinflationary credibility of the central bank or an appreciation of the domestic currency. In 1990s Japan, however, neither of these factors would appear to be driving prices. Furthermore, there are statistical measures in any situation that can be used to control for these other factors.

Figure 1.3 Output gap, 1984-97

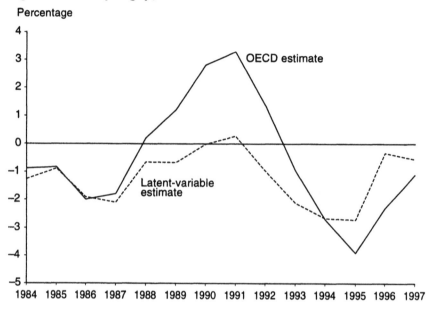

Percentage

Source: Economic Outlook, November 1997, OECD; author's calculations.

gap in the economy, because stability of the inflation rate will falsely imply that potential output has declined to absorb most of the slack.

This caveat is highly relevant to the current Japanese situation because disinflation continued during the 1996-97 period of a declining value of the yen and prolonged loose monetary policy from the Bank of Japan, both of which normally would lead to rises in the inflation rate (see figure 1.2). Thus, the path of prices was consistent with the interpretation that price pressures diminished as slack in the economy accumulated. The absence of any second-round effects on inflation via the passing on of the 1997 indirect-tax rise (i.e., that one-time shift in the inflation level followed by a change in the trend of inflation) is further indication of the lack of pricing power in the slack Japanese economy.

It is possible to be more rigorous about determining the existence and magnitude of an output gap in Japan. Figure 1.3 plots output gaps for Japan estimated by two different methods.[20] The OECD figures are from their "production function" approach, which decomposes potential output into its technology, labor, and capital components, and estimates full-employment levels of each (this is consistent with the discussion of sources of growth given above). This bottom-up approach requires certain

---

20. See Haltmaier (1996) and Laxton and Tetlow (1992) for discussions of the various methods in current literature.

assumptions about factor markets, such as what constitutes the NAIRU (the nonaccelerating inflation rate of unemployment, or the full-employment level of unemployment) and the potential labor-force participation rate.[21] The latent variable approach, following Kuttner (1994), uses a statistical method to derive estimates of potential output that are consistent with observed inflation rates.[22] In short, the two output-gap series shown provide a comparison between estimates of potential output where the former is structural but requires ad hoc decisions to pick up changes, and the latter is statistical but highly adaptable to current conditions. The output gap should be smaller under the latent-variable approach, because it allows more for a recent run of slow growth to represent a change in potential growth; it is also more likely to perceive problems of price- and wage-stickiness near zero inflation as an indication of drop in potential.

For purposes of this paper, and the discussion of the current Japanese macroeconomic situation, the message is clear. Both methods indicate that sizable output gaps existed in the Japanese economy beginning in 1992 or 1993. Surprisingly, by the latent-variable estimate, the solid growth of 1988-91 was not in excess of potential; this is consistent with an estimated drop in the potential output growth rate from over 4.5 percent in 1988 to between 1.5 percent and 2 percent after 1992.[23] The OECD output gap shown in figure 1.3 is based on 2.6 percent average potential annual growth since 1991.[24] On both measures, even the strong growth in 1996 is not enough to close the gap in that year, and above-potential growth would be necessary to reemploy all the resources underutilized in the Japanese economy at present. Thus, even allowing for an unprecedented and, as discussed above, difficult to justify short-run decline in Japanese potential annual economic growth on the order of 2.5 percent, the performance of the economy was still poor in terms of aggregate demand. Structural explanations are insufficient to account for the growth decline.

Implications for the Current Policy Discussion

The implications of recent poor Japanese economic performance being the result of insufficient demand may seem obvious. However, if Japanese policymakers have fully comprehended this point, then their response

---

21. See OECD (1994) for a detailed discussion of their methodology.

22. See the appendix for a discussion of its implementation on recent Japanese data.

23. This amount is so out of step with the evolution of productivity in any other country or time period as to be difficult to believe except as a statistical artifact (see the appendix).

24. The latest version of OECD Economic Surveys: Japan (OECD 1997c, 15) changes this to 3.25 percent from 1988-93 and 2 percent per year since then. The current Japanese Economic Planning Agency estimate of average potential growth in 1990-96 is 2.7 percent.

has been insufficient. Japan is not only growing more slowly than in the glory days of the 1960s and 1970s or than during the recent bubble years, it is falling short of the rate at which it can grow *now* by a larger amount than it has *ever* fallen short of its potential in the postwar period. The cost of this forsaken growth can be seen by adding up the cumulative four-year output gap, using either method, for every four-year period, starting in 1971-74: either the 1993-1996 or the 1994-97 observations are the largest (most negative) under both the latent-variable and OECD estimates. Because the output gap by construction represents movements in output that reflect aggregate demand rather than structural factors, this is simply national wealth forgone. That is not to say that all of the output gaps of the 1990s were avoidable through fiscal and monetary fine-tuning. No one would suggest that any government could ever smooth out all business-cycle fluctuations or that output-gap measures, however estimated, provide a precise metric of how much and when to offset.

Yet discussions that implicitly or explicitly compare the benefits of counteracting such a pronounced shortfall in Japanese national income to a program of saving money in pursuit of any other policy goal have a difficult time justifying the former, because the cumulative cost of growth forgone is so large having been allowed to persist for so long. Let us assume that any discretionary policy response to the Japanese downturn would only have begun in 1994, since the first two years could have been perceived as a normal downturn, perhaps even a desirable offset to the preceding boom. The cumulative output loss from 1994 to 1997 is 6.26 percent of GDP by the latent-variable estimate and 9.80 percent by the OECD estimate (if the benchmark forecast of 3.2 percent for long-run Japanese growth that is based on the fundamentals were used, it would be percentage points higher still). It should also be remembered that, when a given year's output gap is closed, above-potential growth until the slack is taken up would not be accompanied by any meaningful rise in inflation. No economic policy option—not deregulation, nor fiscal consolidation, nor even saving for the burdens of an aging society—comes close to having this large a direct impact on national economic well-being in such a short span of time as this cost of unrestored growth.

From the viewpoint of national welfare, there is nothing special economically about the Japanese economy entering into recession, that is, having below-zero growth. The benchmark to measure performance is the shortfall from potential. As a result, stimulus attempts that are solely intended to be sufficient to keep growth nonnegative are setting far too paltry a goal. Concerns that negative growth has additional destructive effects beyond the obvious distance from potential growth—such as inducing a financial crisis or a cycle of increasing consumer reluctance to spend—are more directly related to deflation and accumulation of bad assets than to negative growth per se. In any event, they only add to the urgency with which stimulus must be undertaken. They do not, however, indicate either that macroeconomic stimulus would be insufficient or that it is enough to merely prevent meltdown.

2

Fiscal Policy Works When It Is Tried

If the current Japanese stagnation is indeed the result of insufficient aggregate demand, what should be the policy response? Fiscal stimulus would appear to be called for, especially in a period following extended overinvestment that has rendered monetary policy extremely weak. Yet the statement is often made that fiscal policy has already been tried and failed in Japan. Claims are made of variously 65 to 75 trillion yen spent in total stimulus efforts since 1991, even before the currently announced package.[1] Both the Japanese experience of the late 1970s of public spending as a "locomotive" to little-lasting domestic benefit, and the worldwide praise for government austerity in the 1990s, have predisposed many observers to dismissing deficit spending as ineffective, if not wasteful. Could there really have been this much stimulus effort having so little effect?

The reality of Japanese fiscal policy in the 1990s is less mysterious and, ultimately, more disappointing. The actual amount injected into the economy by the Japanese government—through either public spending or tax reductions—was 23 trillion yen, about a third of the total amount announced. This limited quantity of total fiscal stimulus was disbursed in insufficiently sized and inefficiently administered doses, with the exception of the 1995 stimulus package. That package did result in solid growth in 1996, demonstrating that fiscal policy does work when it is tried. As on earlier occasions in the 1990s, however, the positive response to fiscal

---

1. For example, a 66 trillion yen number is given in *Bloomberg News*, 23 January 1998, while a 72 trillion yen number is given in "Hashimoto's Response," *Wall Street Journal*, 25 March 1998.

stimulus was undercut by fiscal *contraction* in 1996 and 1997. On net, the Japanese fiscal stance in the 1990s was barely expansionary, and it is the *net* injection of stimulus into the economy that determines the minimum result.[2] In fact, the repeated reversals of fiscal direction and revelations of gaps between announced and implemented policies make even this near-zero net injection an overstatement.

I begin this chapter by establishing certain institutional patterns of the Japanese fiscal system that predispose economic policy to being less countercyclical than that of most other industrialized nations. Even controlling for these factors, discretionary fiscal policy in 1992-97 was barely countercyclical on average, rather than working to make up for these institutional patterns. I then chart the course of total Japanese government revenues and expenditures since the bubble burst, demonstrating that the actual discretionary fiscal response was limited, despite the apparently rising government-debt levels. The one large and effective stimulus package, from 1995, is analyzed in detail, as are the 1996 and 1997 budget measures that reversed its beneficial effects. In summary, Japanese fiscal policy in the 1990s should be seen as a failure of mistaken fiscal austerity and not of fiscal policy per se. The Japanese government got what it paid for in the 1990s—one good year of growth and little else.

Starting from a Cyclical Disadvantage

The Great Depression offered many important lessons for macroeconomic policy. One of the clearest and least controversial is that there is a role for government revenues and expenditures to automatically move in the opposite direction of the business cycle—taxes should fall as the economy slows, and public spending (through unemployment benefits and other social assistance) should rise. This "leaning against the wind" to stabilize economic fluctuations should take place irrespective of any discretionary fiscal policy added to it in times of more severe downturn. The fact that such stabilizers are automatic, however, does not mean that they are equally effective or ambitious in all countries. Before assessing the impact of Japan's announced additional stimulus packages, the overall baseline must be established for Japan.

Total Japanese government spending does not reveal obviously countercyclical tendencies. As noted in the previous chapter, except when it rose by 0.5 percent of GDP in the relatively strong growth year of 1986, government consumption rose by between 0.1 and 0.3 percent every year

---

2. This is a statement based on analysis of the actual amounts spent by the Japanese government and does not rest on any assumptions about "fiscal multipliers" (i.e., the likely ripple effect on the economy of a given stimulus). The ultimate effectiveness of fiscal policy once undertaken, and its long-run costs and benefits, are discussed in the chapter 3.

from 1984 to 1996 (see table 1.2), irrespective of the macroeconomic environment. In 1997, despite the slowing of Japanese growth to an unprecedented negative level, government consumption actually added nothing to growth. Public investment, if anything, moved somewhat procyclically in the last decades, adding over half a percent to GDP growth during the boom in 1987 and 1991, and shrinking in 1994, 1996, and 1997. Of course, these growth numbers include *both* the discretionary and automatic stabilization responses. Since it is impossible to imagine a scenario where the automatic stabilizers would ever go in the *wrong* direction—tax revenues rising as the economy slows or social spending declining as unemployment rises—absent a policy change, this time path of public investment implies that Japanese discretionary fiscal policy was sufficiently procyclical (i.e., in the direction of the downturn) to more than outweigh the appropriate built-in stabilization effects in those years.

The response of the government balance (i.e., the amount of deficit spending) to year-to-year fluctuations in GDP may give a better perspective on the limited countercyclical role of Japanese fiscal policy. Table 2.1 presents a comparative analysis of six of the G-7 governments' changes in fiscal policy with the cycle at the central and local levels.[3] For each country, the average share of government revenue in GDP is reported, as is the estimated coefficient of cyclical stabilization (β_2). This estimate comes from an ordinary least squares regression of changes in annual government (central, subnational, and combined) balances on that year's revenues, the previous year's government balance, a time trend, a constant, and the year-over-year real GDP growth rate, where β_2 is the coefficient on GDP growth.

Several matters are apparent among the six countries considered. First, the Japanese central government's response to cyclical swings in GDP growth is significantly less than that in Germany or the United States (less than 60 percent as much), and the total government response is less than half of that in Canada or the United States. This pattern is true even controlling for the time trend of rising US government deficits in the 1980s and early 1990s and even including the supposedly large Japanese fiscal-stimulus measures of 1992, 1993, and 1995.

Second, in fiscal terms, Japan looks more like the federal states in Canada, Germany, and the United States and less like the centralized British or French states, with subnational governments taking in about a third of total government revenue. Local-government stimulus must take on some of the burden for countercyclical responsiveness in Japan

---

3. Bayoumi and Eichengreen (1995) perform a similar analysis using data through 1990 and a different econometric technique. I am grateful to Tam Bayoumi for discussion of their methods. The other member of the G-7, Italy, is not included because such regressions were not stable over the sample period.

Table 2.1 Government cyclical stabilization, 1970-95

	Central government (including social security fund)			Subnational government			Central/subnational government revenue	Combined government		
	REV/GDP[a]	β₂	t-stat for β₂	REV/GDP[a]	β₂	t-stat for β₂		REV/GDP[a]	β₂	t-stat for β₂
Canada	0.196	0.227**	3.48	0.298	0.106	1.86	0.66	0.388	0.386**	3.846
Germany[b]	0.330	0.504	0.35	0.172	0.191**	3.40	1.92	0.441	0.129	0.315
United States	0.212	0.527***	5.79	0.133	0.060*	2.64	1.59	0.310	0.571**	6.469
France	0.543	0.004	0.28	0.084	0.002	1.15	6.45	0.591	0.003	0.706
Japan	0.243	0.296**	4.32	0.123	0.062	1.74	1.98	0.283	0.201*	2.227
United Kingdom[c]	0.300	0.213	1.70	0.109	0.033	1.44	2.74	0.396	0.241*	2.612

Note: $\Delta BAL/GDP(t) = \alpha + \beta_1(REV/GDP(t)) + \beta_2(\ln(Y(t)) - \ln(Y(t-1))) + \gamma(BAL/GDP(t-1)) + \sigma(t) + \epsilon$.

*(**)indicates significance of coefficients at the 5(1) percent level of confidence. Central and local government figures, which are fiscal-year basis, do not sum to general government figures, which are calendar-year basis.

a. REV/GDP column shows mean of REV/GDP for each country over the entire time period.

b. A dummy variable for Germany is included because after 1991 the government budget is based on a unified government. Dummy variable = 1 if year ≧ 1991, 0 otherwise. It is significant at the 5 percent level of confidence in the local government equation, but is not significant in the central or general government equation.

c. 1995 United Kingdom data are not available; the sample includes data from 1970 to 1994.

Sources: OECD, National Account, Volume II, detailed table, various issues. IMF, International Financial Statistics Yearbook, 1997.

to be effective.[4]

Third, countercyclical responsiveness is not a function of the share of government in the economy. Japan and the United States have the lowest government-revenue-to-GDP ratios of the six economies (i.e., the smallest government sectors), yet they are on nearly opposite ends of the ranking for cyclical stabilization. Meanwhile, France—with the largest, most-centralized government sector—has the smallest countercyclical response.

There are some institutional reasons that Japanese automatic stabilization might be less than in some other countries, such as in the United States. In particular, the Japanese labor market is designed to rely on the adjustment of workers and employers to shifts in aggregate demand, rather than having the government share some of the burden. By most estimates, official measured unemployment only captures half the actual number of idle laborers—the other half are often retained on business payrolls, at sometimes 30 percent cuts in salary, even when demand for these firms' products declines (Ito 1992, chapter 8, 1994; Miyazaki 1997). There are microeconomic efficiency arguments for why this can be a rational policy for the Japanese firm, such as the cost of retraining workers when new ones are needed, or the effects on general loyalty and morale (see, for example, Aoki 1989, 1990). At a macroeconomic level, however, this means that while businesses' balance sheets are eroding, they are carrying more labor per unit of production. Had these workers actually been made redundant, the firms' costs would have fallen and the burden of supporting these workers would have been spread over the whole society. In the present system, those idle workers continue to pay withholding taxes to the government and take benefits from their employers rather than from the government. This means that the Japanese government's taxes decline less, and social transfers increase less, in response to the business cycle, than in an economy where the burden of unemployment is shared.

In addition, the government-provided social safety net in Japan is far smaller than that provided in the other G-7 economies. As Ostrom (1997) points out, the Japanese unemployment program is less generous than that of the United States, let alone those in Europe; before-tax benefits as a share of previous earnings are only 9.9 percent, the benefits last only six months, and only 40 percent of the unemployed receive benefits (see OECD 1997b; Layard, Nickell, and Jackman 1994). Social welfare spending is also at the bottom of the OECD as a percentage of GDP. While actual poverty is very rare in the wealthy Japanese society, and there is a great deal of self-insurance through private savings and family networks, this, too, serves to diminish the automatic response of fiscal stabilizers to the business cycle. When unemployment actually increases, as it currently is,

---

4. As discussed later in this chapter, part of the gap in fiscal stimulus in the 1990s arose because Japanese local governments refused to spend on public works anywhere near as much as the national government requested (see Ishii and Wada 1998).

the average rise in public spending is small, while the fall in consumption for those parts of the private sector affected by the downturn is large, effectively deepening the downturn.

In general, the institutional reliance on private self-insurance (such as private business supporting the hidden unemployed) in Japan can account for part of the demonstrated lower government responsiveness to the business cycle. If a significant portion of the society draws down its own resources simultaneously, and that is the part of the society already hit by the downturn, then we would expect a sharper change in national income than when the government spreads out the pain over all of society and smoothes out the expenses over many years.[5] In fact, this lack of a safety net, which encourages self-insurance, may make consumption (saving) more procyclical (countercyclical) than it otherwise would be, causing it to drop (rise) greatly in downturns. Yet even limited automatic stabilization is still countercyclical, and the assessment of limited Japanese stabilization presented here takes into account *all* of the discretionary fiscal policy in the 1990s as well—including *contraction* of total public-sector consumption and investment in 1996 (−0.1 percent of GDP) and 1997 (−0.5 percent). So, despite starting from a prior design that limits countercyclical response, discretionary fiscal policy was sufficiently austere to give the lie to claims of strong fiscal stabilization efforts in Japan in the 1990s.

The Size of the Budget and the Deficit

Another way of establishing the fact that Japanese fiscal policy in the 1990s was, on net, only mildly countercyclical is to recognize that most of the government deficits accumulating during the past seven years were the result of the downturn and not of any discretionary response to it. In other words, while large budget deficits were reported in the 1990s, structural deficits that measure what the revenue would be given full employment were much less. The cumulative amount of additional public debt taken on was not excessive either by Japanese historical or by international standards. There is no question that over a span of decades, less public debt is to be preferred to more, but there is also little question that the path of Japanese debt accumulation in the 1990s is consistent with repeated reversals of fiscal stimulus rather than with a sustained break from austerity.

---

5. It is an empirical question whether the gains in, for example, labor-market efficiency from forcing workers to plan ahead and look after themselves ultimately outweigh the losses from larger macroeconomic responses to widely felt negative shocks. The 1996 *OECD Jobs Study* would emphasize the benefits of the former, but the repetition of some aspects of 1930s history in 1990s Japan in the absence of stabilization may turn out to be a counterargument.

Table 2.2 lists the size of recent Japanese government budgets, the number of bonds issued, and the year-to-year change, for 1991 through 1997. A 1965 law requires that public bonds in Japan be split between those issued for purposes of "public investment" (such as infrastructure construction) and those that feed into general revenues (special public bonds). The regular government budget is followed every year by a "supplementary budget" voted on around April, because any amendments offered to the Diet ruling coalition's original budget constitute a no-confidence vote if passed. The sum of these two budgets is the fiscal program for the year. Often, and throughout the 1990s, additional public works spending has been included in the supplementary budget and classified as "public investment."

In a time of minimal GDP growth, the central government budget has remained essentially stable since FY1993, with the combined initial and supplementary budgets fluctuating around 77 trillion yen, or 15 percent of GDP. There is no secular upward trend in government expenditure. As would be expected in a downturn, when tax revenues decline, however, bond issuance has risen as a percentage of total expenditure. From 1994 to 1997, significant numbers of revenue-generating special public bonds were issued; many construction bonds were issued as well. As of the end of FY1997, Japanese government bonds held directly by the private sector totaled 254 trillion yen, or 49 percent of GDP. When those bonds held in the "special account" are included, that is, largely those in the portfolio of the postal savings system, the outstanding bonds total 344 trillion yen or 67 percent of GDP. These are all seemingly large amounts.[6] Yet, as shown in table 2.2, the total amount of new government bonds issued, rather than just rolled over, was 79.4 trillion yen from 1992 to 1997. If the additional deficit spending in this period arising from discretionary fiscal stimulus had been the 70 trillion yen often claimed, then tax revenues would have fallen only 10 trillion yen below expenditures cumulatively in the period of Japan's most extended postwar recession, while automatic government expenditures would have increased as well. This is a patently absurd claim, even allowing for some revenue increase as a result of the government spending. Simple arithmetic proves that no such amount of net stimulus was undertaken. Assuming, quite reasonably, that the government issued only half of the bonds to compensate for a decline in revenues, fiscal stimulus for 1992-97, net of contractionary revenue-enhancing policies, is capped at 40 trillion yen (plus any amount of taxes generated by the stimulus), or less than 60 percent of the headline claims. As we will see, this number is an overstatement as well.

---

6. Whether that amount is large or small is discussed in chapter 3 (remember that the Maastricht criteria on government debt for prospective EMU members was 60 percent of GDP, and most members exceeded that amount in the end without market meltdown).

Table 2.2 Recent budget, 1991-97 (billion yen)

| | General accounting, initial budget plan | | | | | | | | Supplementary budget | | |
| | Total | | Public investment | | Public bonds issued[b] | | Special public bonds | | Total | Public investment | Additionally issued bonds |
Fiscal year	Size	Percentage changes over previous year	Size	Percentage changes over previous year	Size	Bond/total[a] (percentage)	Size	Bond/total[a] (percentage)	(size)	(size)	(size)
1991	70,347	6.2	6,666	6.3	5,343	7.6			266	761	1,387
1992	72,218	2.7	8,097	21.5	7,280	10.1			-728	1,844	2,256
1993	72,355	0.2	8,600	6.2	8,130	11.2			5,083	6,576	8,044
1994	73,082	1.0	11,146	29.6	13,643	18.7	3,134	5.2	349	1,625	2,847
1995	70,987	-2.9	9,240	-17.1	12,598	17.7	2,851	4.8	7,047	4,977	9,434
1996	75,105	5.8	9,618	4.1	21,029	28.0	10,118	15.9	2,666	1,599	1,339
1997	77,390	3.0	9,745	1.3	16,707	21.6	7,470	11.4	na	na	na

na = not available.

Note: Central government account only, not including local government bonds. In 1997, government bonds outstanding are as follows (accumulative figures): Stock of ordinary bonds (including construction and special bond) is 254 trillion yen, or 49.2 percent of GDP. When stock of bonds issued from special account is included, total is 344 trillion yen, or 66.6 percent of GDP. When stock of local government bonds is included, total is 476 trillion yen, or 92.2 percent of GDP.

a. Bond/total represents the share of that year's expenditure financed by issuing bonds.

b. Public bonds include all newly issued government bonds, including special bonds.

Source: Zusetsu Nihon no Zaisei, 1997, Toyo Keizai Shinposya, Tokyo, Japan: 340.

Figure 2.1 Government and structural deficit[a]

Percentage share of GDP

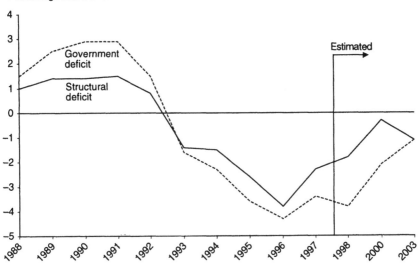

a. This refers to general and central government fiscal balances.

Source: IMF, *World Economic Outlook* 1998.

The way to separate discretionary fiscal stimulus from the additional deficit spending to make up for the revenue shortfall is to recognize that the structural deficit has remained limited in Japan in the 1990s, as one would expect for a government sector that remained stable in size.[7] Japan's potential growth rate is largely unchanged, as argued in the previous chapter, so its long-run capacity to support the same share of government in national income is also unchanged. Figure 2.1 shows that the structural deficit has moved less than appears in the official budget figures, exceeding 3 percent only in 1996. Not coincidentally, that was the one year that followed a large fiscal-stimulus package that was actually implemented. The fact that the structural budget deficit declined in both 1996 and 1997 and was projected to contract again in 1998 (prior to the announcement of the April supplementary budget) indicates that discretionary fiscal policy since the 1995 package has moved in the direction of austerity. The fiscal reversal of 1996-97 was actually opposite and more than equal to the stimulus of 1995 (the structural deficit in 1995 was 2.6

---

7. "The structural budget balance is the budgetary position that would be observed if the level of actual output coincided with potential output. Changes in the structural budget balance consequently include effects of temporary fiscal measures, the impact of fluctuations in interest rates and debt service costs, and other non-cyclical fluctuations in the budget balance" (IMF 1998, 35).

percent of GDP, and in 1997, 2.3 percent). Similarly, whatever discretionary policy there was in 1994 must have been contractionary, as the structural deficit rose only 0.1 percent in 1994 despite the fact that the 1993 stimulus should have given an ongoing increase to the deficit in 1994 because of the momentum of spending (as the 1995 program did to 1996). The total change in the structural deficit since 1992 is 5 percent of GDP, despite claims of 15 percent of GDP spent on stimulus packages. In all, the structural-deficit numbers confirm the start-stop, expand-retrench, fiscal policy indicated by the behavior of the public components of GDP discussed in the previous section.

To get a sense of the magnitudes involved, the highest annual structural deficit in 1990s Japan was 3.8 percent of GDP in 1996. This was comparable to or less than the highs of the United States (3.4 percent), Germany (4.0 percent), France (3.6 percent), the United Kingdom (4.4 percent), and Canada (4.6 percent) for the decade. However, none of these other countries suffered as great a recession, and so they had less justification for deficit spending. Table 2.3 puts recent Japanese fiscal expansion efforts in a longer-term comparative perspective. I identify a list of episodes of large discretionary fiscal impulses from a sample of 13 OECD countries from 1960 to 1992. Following Alesina and Perotti (1995), if a country in a given year has a Blanchard-measure fiscal impulse of greater than 1.5 percent of GDP, where that impulse is defined as the difference between an unemployment-adjusted measure of the primary deficit and the previous year's deficit, that impulse is classified as a major fiscal expansion.[8] In 28 episodes, deficits rose by more than 1.5 percent of GDP in a given year, that is, by more than any year-over-year increase in the Japanese structural deficit in the 1990s.

Obviously, not all of these increases in deficits were salutary. No country would want to use the history of Italian fiscal policy or the widespread stop-go budgetary policies of the 1970s as a model for fiscal policy. But even in the 1990-92 period, when fiscal probity was the order of the day among the many conservative majority parliaments, there were seven such major fiscal expansions. The important perspective is that there is indeed precedent for one-year fiscal stimulus packages on an even larger scale than Japan has undertaken in the 1990s. This leaves aside the Japanese government's net reversals of the more limited packages already undertaken. Claims made by Japanese officials that the scale of Japanese

---

8. See Blanchard (1993) for details. This measure is obviously analogous in intent to the year-to-year change in a more carefully constructed and country-specific structural deficit series, but it facilitates cross-national comparison. Alesina and Perotti (1995) point out in their broader study that using any of three other measures of changes in the budgetary position of the government to capture its fiscal stance produces an essentially unchanging list of expansionary episodes in their larger sample.

Table 2.3 Major fiscal expansions in OECD countries

Country	Year	Rise in deficit (GDP share)	Rise in expenditure (GDP share)	Cut in revenue (GDP share)	Real GDP growth (percentage) Same year	Year − 1	Source of deficit
Australia	1975	3.4	4.7	−1.3	2.3	2.0	
	1976	0.9	1.2	−0.3	4.1	2.3	
	1991	1.6	1.9	−0.3	−1.5	1.4	Tax Cut and Expenditure
	1992	3.0	1.3	1.7	2.3	−1.5	Tax Cut and Expenditure
Austria	1967	2.7[a]	0.9	0.5	2.8	5.1	
	1975	2.4	3.1	−0.7	−0.4	3.9	
Belgium	1975	2.5	5.2	−2.7	−1.5	4.3	Expenditure
	1981	4.3	5.2	−0.9	−1.0	4.1[c]	
Canada	1975	2.0	1.4	0.5	2.6	4.4	
	1982	3.2	2.6	0.6	−3.2	3.7	Expenditure
	1991	0.5	0.7	−0.2	−1.8	−0.2	Expenditure
France	1975	3.0	3.1	0.0	−0.3	3.1	Expenditure
	1981	2.2	3.0	−0.7	1.2	1.6	Both
	1992	2.5	0.7	0.3	1.2	0.8	
Germany	1974	2.0	2.0	0.1	0.1	4.7	
	1975	3.0	3.1	−0.2	−1.2	0.1	
	1990	1.6	0.2	0.7	5.7	3.7	Unification
Italy	1965	1.7[b]	2.1	−0.4	3.3	2.8	
	1971	1.7[b]	2.3	−0.5	1.9	5.3	
	1972	0.8[b]	0.0	0.9	2.9	1.9	
	1975	5.6	6.2	−0.4	−2.1	4.7	Expenditure
	1981	0.5	−0.1	0.6	0.5	3.5	Expenditure

continued next page

Table 2.3 Major fiscal expansions in OECD countries *(continued)*

Country	Year	Rise in deficit (GDP share)	Rise in expenditure (GDP share)	Cut in revenue (GDP share)	Real GDP growth (percentage)		Source of deficit
					Same year	Year − 1	
Japan	1975	3.4[a]	1.6	1.9	2.9	− 0.6	Tax cut
Netherlands	1975	2.9	4.8	− 2.2	− 0.1	4.0	
	1987	1.3	1.8	− 0.9	1.4	2.8	Tight fiscal policy
Spain	1982	0.5	2.8	− 2.1	1.6	− 0.2	Tight fiscal policy
Sweden	1974	1.8	1.9	0.0	3.2	4.0	
	1977	1.3	3.9	− 2.8	− 1.6	1.1	
	1979	2.4	− 0.9	3.2	3.8	1.8	
	1991	2.6	0.6	2.0	− 1.7[c]	1.4	Expenditure
United Kingdom	1971	2.5	0.3	2.2	2.0	2.3	
	1972	2.1	0.5	1.6	2.4	2.8	
	1990	0.8	2.2	− 1.4	0.4	2.2	Expenditure
	1991	1.7	2.3	− 0.1	− 2.0	0.4	Expenditure
	1992	4.0	2.7	1.0	− 0.5	− 2.0	Expenditure
United States	1967	0.6[b]	1.8	− 1.9	2.6	5.9	
	1975	3.3	2.7	0.5	− 0.8	− 0.6	

a. Without grants and lending, minus repayments.
b. Without grants.
c. Data are not consistent with earlier data.

Sources: IMF, *International Financial Statistics, Government Finance Statistics* (various years); OECD, *Economic Surveys, Economic Outlook* (various years).

fiscal expansion in 1995 or proposed for 1998 is extraordinary, or likely to have negative effects if exceeded, are simply unsupportable.[9]

The Reality of Japanese Stimulus Packages

Since Japanese fiscal policy has been barely countercyclical on net in the 1990s, what gives rise to the popular perception that a great deal of money has been spent in stimulus efforts? There is a two-part answer. First, all announced Japanese fiscal programs hugely overstate their stimulative content, usually by a factor of 2 or more. Second, the stimulus package implemented in the second half of 1995 and the early part of 1996 was indeed large, though not unprecedentedly so. In fact, the 1995 package was not only large, but also effective. It led to GDP growth of 3.6 percent in 1996 when most forecasts were for a full point lower, even when made after the package's announcement. As noted in the previous section, however, the combined contractionary policies of 1996 and 1997 completely offset the positive effects of the 1995 package. Since the contractionary policies have been consistently announced with far less fanfare than the expansionary packages, if with any notice at all, it is not surprising that this fact has been overlooked.

The recurring tendency for overstatement of Japanese government fiscal packages is demonstrated in table 2.4. Of the seven stimulus measures announced prior to this year, the one in September 1995 topped the list of actual stimulus at less than 60 percent of the headline amount; the other six injected into the Japanese economy less than half the amount claimed, and three had no direct stimulative content whatsoever. This is because for fiscal stimulus, it is actual deficit spending—either through increased public spending or tax cuts—that adds to demand. This amount is captured in the *mamizu*, or "clear water," the total of new public investment projects in announced stimulus packages. Had tax cuts played a significant role in fiscal packages prior to this year's, they too would have been a source of real stimulus worth counting.[10] The total packages

---

9. "This [1998 supplementary budget] is the largest package we have ever implemented. I haven't heard of any package like this in the rest of the world that amounts to an impact of between 2 to 3 percent of GDP. I would argue against any criticism of this package as being too small. It may be too big" (Eisuke Sakakibara, vice minister of finance, quoted in *Nikkei Weekly*, 27 April 1998. See also "Japan's Cabinet Backs Revival Plan," *The Washington Post*, A13, 25 April 1998). Sakakibara's claim was made based on the 1998 stimulus package of 16 trillion yen, or 3 percent of Japanese GDP (as argued at the end of this chapter, the actual stimulus is likely to be less than 1.5 percent of GDP, and smaller still in effect).

10. The pattern, however, has been to announce the number of tax code revisions included in a given fiscal package, even when the total change in effective taxes has been negligible. The 1998 package does include noticeable tax cuts on the order of 4 trillion yen, or 0.75 percent of GDP. Because these are temporary—their partial reversal in 1999 is already announced—they are likely to have much less than that effect. I provide more detail on this subject later in this chapter.

Table 2.4 Announced stimulus packages in the 1990s

	3/31/92	8/28/92	4/13/93	9/16/93	2/8/94	4/14/95	9/20/95
Economic situation							
Exchange rate, yen/dollar[c]	132.92	123.26	113.40	104.45	108.66	104.15	103.25
Discount rate (percentage)	3.75[a]	3.25	2.5	1.75	1.75	1.75	0.5
Nikkei 500 stock price (yen)	19,799	18,000	20,919	20,502	20,660[b]	16,304[b]	18,198[b]
Total package announced	390	10,700	15,230	6,418	6,020	4,800	12,810
Mamizu	0	4,240	5,082	1,500	0	2,700	8,000
Mamizu share							
of total package	0.0	39.6	33.4	23.4	0.0	56.3	62.5
of GDP[d]	0.0	0.9	1.1	0.3	0.0	0.6	1.6
Public investment incentives	0	2,100	4,210	1,268	5,710	na	0

na = not available.

Note: *Mamizu* is calculated as total public investment minus spending in the following year, purchase of land for future public works, and other asset transfers, and represents the amount that potentially increases GDP. *Private investment incentives* are announced government lending programs, which do not directly increase GDP. They do not include local government-processed expenditures.

a. Discount rate was reduced from 4 to 3.75 on 1 April 1998.

b. This is the price at the end of the day, while others are the monthly average.

c. These are the end of the day rate.

d. This refers to fiscal year-based GDP.

Sources: Nihon Keizai Shimbun, various issues; Masao Nishikawa, "Keizai Seisaku (Economic Measure)" *Nihon Keizai Jiten (Japan Economic Dictionary)* 1996, Nihon Keizai Shimbun, Tokyo, Japan; *International Financial Statistics*, various issues; Holt's Stock Market Report, gopher://wuecon.wustl.edu:671/11/holt; Federal Reserve Board Home Page, http://www.bog.frb.fed.us.

announced, however, always include many measures that are not *mamizu*, which have no direct effect on GDP growth.

"Private investment incentives," which are loan programs offered by government-affiliated institutions to the private sector, are one important example of such "pumping up" of the announced packages. There is a long history of government-directed lending in postwar Japan intended to serve public ends. It is made primarily through the Fiscal Investment and Loan Company (FILP) and the Japan Development Bank and uses Postal Savings funds recycled by the government.[11] Such lending may or may not be productive, but its predominant effect is on the *allocation* of funding among various investment projects, not on the total *level* of investment in the economy. If the postal savings were not channeled into the particular sectors emphasized by these stimulus packages, they would go into government bonds or other safe investments. They would not, however, add any more funds to the economy in the way that bond-financed public investment would. Especially in a period such as the 1990s when monetary ease, which has a far more direct effect on private investment than does government lending, has not been able to overcome the drag on investment demand of excess capacity and damaged balance sheets, it is difficult to imagine there being even small benefits from more aggressive government lending. Yet, as seen in the last line of table 2.4, such lending constitutes a significant portion of the announced packages.

Other items that have little or no effect on GDP growth but are often included in the stimulus package announcements are front-loading of previously committed public works programs, land and other asset purchases, and direct injections of funding into the financial system. Moving forward public spending already planned just shrinks future spending by an equivalent amount; even if forward-looking businesses and consumers do not take this into account when planning, and therefore discount the initial spending, this front-loading ends up being the stop-go stance of Japanese fiscal policy in miniature, with no net gain. Government purchases of assets have no direct effect on GDP because they simply reshuffle who owns what without creating any income or wealth. If I sell my house, and I get something close to fair market value for it, I put in my bank account the same amount that I transfer from my real estate assets when I complete the transaction. Put differently, no one believes that when a government privatizes a firm or service it is engaging in fiscal contraction by selling a public asset, and that is just the same transaction in reverse. Discussion of the merits of injecting public money into the financial system is given in chapter 5, but the essential point is that while the balance sheets of banks and the level of the Nikkei stock index will

---

11. See Bergsten and Noland (1993, chapter 3) and Noland (1993) for discussion of the FILP and other lending programs.

influence the *response* of the economy to a given policy, their repair is not strongly stimulative in and of itself without growth in the economy more broadly.

The actual size of the Japanese fiscal-stimulus packages in the 1990s should be thought of as their public investment content, which ranged from zero to 1.6 percent of GDP (in September 1995) and anywhere from zero to 56 percent of the announced figures. The total amount spent was 23 trillion yen, or 4.5 percent of a year's GDP. While a not insignificant amount of money, it is not a terribly large amount spread out over six-plus years of recession, with a total cost in wealth forgone of 8 to 10 percent of GDP (as argued in chapter 1).[12] The reasons for the repeated overstatement of these packages' actual simulative effect are difficult to fathom. As mentioned at the start of this chapter, a surprising number of the Japanese public and the foreign press have gained the false impression that total public investment has been very sizable in the 1990s, rather than the 23 trillion yen actually spent from 1992 until this year. Unlike in the case of monetary policy, however, a fiscal-policy surprise adds nothing to its effectiveness. The more sophisticated observers in financial markets and in Japanese and foreign governments know to mark down announcements of fiscal-policy stimulus by around half, depending on the details of the *mamizu* and tax measures.[13] Meanwhile, the OECD has gone so far as to suggest in print that there should be greater transparency in Japanese fiscal accounting (see OECD 1997c, 76).

One sensible albeit conspiratorial-sounding interpretation would be that repeated overrepresentation of fiscal stimulus is the result of an effort by the Ministry of Finance to be seen as acceding to political pressures to do something for the economy in the short run, while discrediting the effectiveness of countercyclical fiscal policy in the long run. As recounted in Sakakibara (1991), Schick (1996), and elsewhere, since the introduction of a ceiling on ministry spending requests for the 1961 budget, the Ministry of Finance's role in Japanese budgeting has been to establish budget totals at the start of the process, leaving the details of spending within those totals up to the Liberal Democratic Party (LDP) politicians and their interest-group constituents. The Ministry of Finance officials have been ideologically committed to opposing "lax" fiscal policy due to the future aging of the population and the memory of how long it took to bring

---

12. Figure 3.6 shows that the structural deficit increased by 5 percent over 1992-1996 (from a 1 percent surplus in 1992 to 4 percent deficit in 1996). Thus, the *net* effect of all tax and spending changes not explicitly counted in this 23 trillion yen of public expenditure was 0.5 percent of GDP. In other words, net discretionary fiscal policy is well summarized by these public-spending packages, minus whatever negative effect small rises and falls in taxes have.

13. See, for example, Feldman's (1998) analysis of this year's announced spending packages.

down the deficits that originated in the late 1970s (see, for example, Schick 1996, 31-48).[14] The Ministry of Finance also maximizes its power (or fulfills its role, depending upon one's interpretation) by casting the fiscal situation in as grim a light as possible. It calls attention to the Japanese government's gross debt and interest payments rather than their net levels, underestimates future tax revenues at the time of setting the regular budget, slows the disbursement of supplementary budget funds (since those budgets are passed with less initial input from the Ministry), counts as part of stimulus packages public works spending already programmed in multiyear investment plans, and, of course, consistently publishes the cumulative announced stimulus packages as if they were the actual amount of fiscal expansion. The ultimate significance of this active disinformation program is that by the time the Ministry of Finance completes its efforts, even the levels of stimulus given in the *mamizu* line of table 2.4 probably *overstate* the actual amount put into the economy.

The Plan That Worked Until Stopped

The Japanese government took two economic measures in 1995: "Emergency Measures for Yen Appreciation and the Economy" in April and "Economic Measures Toward Steady Economic Recovery" in September. Both were prompted by the sharp appreciation of the yen versus the dollar and the fall of the *Nikkei* stock average below 20,000 for the first time since 1992, with the expected negative effects on economic growth.[15] In both cases, the measures were adopted through supplementary budgets passed by the Diet (and, thus, outside the Ministry of Finance's general spending ceilings). The April measure consisted of a 2.7 trillion yen increase in actual government spending and a 0.1 trillion yen (800 yen, or less than $8 per capita) tax cut. The situation continued to worsen, prompting the Bank of Japan to cut its discount rate from 1.75 percent, where it had been held since mid-1993, to 0.5 percent by the time of the second supplementary budget of 20 September. The monetary effort was sufficient to reverse the yen's spike upward to 80/dollar, but any real economic effects of the rate cut would not be felt for at least a year.[16] A

---

14. Balassa and Noland (1988, chapter 6) argue that the unwillingness of the Ministry of Finance to countenance serious fiscal expansion was a primary reason for excessive monetary stimulus in the mid-1980s. The economic logic of this austerity stance is discussed in chapter 3.

15. A number of private-sector forecasters, including Dai-Ichi Life, Daiwa, Nippon Research Institute, Sanwa, and Salomon, forecast real GNP growth of 1 percent or less for 1995 at the time of the September package announcement.

16. As discussed in chapters 3 and 4, because the limited-interest elasticity of investment and other spending in the Japanese economy declined further in 1996 and 1997, this monetary loosening had little effect.

fiscal stimulus of such small magnitude would hardly be expected to reverse the momentum of declining expectations, especially since it was oversold as always, with the claimed total stimulus being 4.8 trillion yen.[17]

The September package, however, was a unique event in Japan in the 1990s. It was the only package to exceed both 50 percent of its announced level and 1 percent of GDP (see table 2.4). In fact, with a *mamizu* of 8 trillion yen in actual spending for the second half of FY1995 and into FY1996, it exceeded 1.6 percent of GDP.[18] Unlike the April 1995 package, the September package included a planned 6.9 trillion yen of prefectural and municipal government expenditure (2.3 trillion of which actually was a transfer from the central government and should not be counted twice). Pumping up the announced total, in typical fashion, were 3.23 trillion yen for "promotion of efficient land use," 520 billion yen for "expansion of loan programs of the housing loan corporation," 1.23 trillion yen for "acquisition of land for public works projects," and 1.29 trillion yen in lending "measures for small- and medium-size firms," all of which have no stimulative effect.

As shown in the first two columns of table 2.5, the total additional expenditure in the central government supplementary budget amounted to a little over 7 trillion yen. The increases were primarily in public works spending (4.98 trillion), education and science (0.72 trillion), and a difficult to trace "miscellaneous" category (1.10 trillion). Tax revenues declined by 3.05 trillion yen from the initial budget forecast as well, because of declining economic activity, not tax cuts. As summarized by the then head of the Economic Planning Agency, Isamu Miyazaki (1997, 289), "The effect should be measured after deducting loans by government financial institutions, funds for individual projects by local governments and government spending for the efficient use of land. . . . Even when these are excluded, however, the total magnitude exceeds 8 trillion yen, which is believed to be sufficient to boost nominal GDP by about 2 percent over the next 12 months if these spendings [sic] are implemented properly."[19]

---

17. In fact, the previous announced fiscal package of the Japanese government, in February 1994, purported to inject 6 trillion yen into the economy but actually was 95 percent "private investment incentives" (i.e., loans, and a *mamizu* of zero). This was hardly an auspicious precedent for Japanese households to react to a package announcement and on which build confidence.

18. Though, of course, the package was claimed to be "worth a total of 14.22 trillion yen, the largest measure ever in terms of working expenditures" (Ministry of Finance, *Monthly Finance Review*, October 1995, 23).

19. The reference to "if these spendings [sic] are implemented properly" should be taken to mean if the Diet-legislated spending were fully implemented, rather than stalled or spread over a longer period by Ministry of Finance action. Some commentators have suggested that a contributing factor to the 1995 package's success was the presence of a strong Economic Planning Agency minister in the person of Isamu Miyazaki, who openly kept track of the actual amount spent.

Table 2.5 Japan's budget plans, 1995-97 (millions of yen)

	FY1995 Planned expenditure			FY1996 Planned expenditure			FY1997 Planned expenditure		
	Initial budget	With supplementary budget	Difference	Initial budget	With supplementary budget	Difference	Initial budget	With supplementary budget	Difference
Social security	13,924,412	14,548,037	623,625	14,287,943	15,000,360	712,417	14,550,145	15,460,100	909,955
Education and science	6,076,461	6,801,870	725,409	6,226,955	6,311,342	84,387	6,343,566	6,288,400	−55,166
Debt service	13,221,300	12,856,803	−364,497	16,375,197	16,083,851	−291,346	16,802,329	16,268,100	−534,229
Pensions and others	1,726,552	1,726,206	−346	1,659,022	1,658,681	−341	1,597,259	1,597,000	−259
Tax grants to local governments	13,215,395	12,302,115	−913,280	13,603,826	13,944,993	341,167	15,480,975	15,481,000	25
National defense	4,723,610	4,733,996	10,386	4,845,479	8,489,085	3,643,606	4,947,517	4,953,600	6,083
Public works	9,239,759	14,216,406	4,976,647	9,618,359	11,217,544	1,599,185	9,744,659	10,525,300	780,641
Economic cooperation	1,035,114	1,028,254	−6,860	1,071,486	1,078,999	7,513	1,088,486	1,096,300	7,814
Small businesses	185,691	639,262	453,571	185,523	204,450	18,927	186,517	255,900	69,383
Energy	681,862	711,983	30,121	692,283	696,206	3,923	686,017	680,700	−5,317
Foodstuff control	272,318	272,260	−58	270,484	310,380	39,896	269,194	308,000	38,806
Transfer to the individual investment special account	1,281,226	1,281,226	0	171,541	171,541	0	171,541	171,500	−41
Miscellaneous	5,053,420	6,149,255	1,095,835	5,061,826	685,000	−4,376,826	5,171,799	5,297,300	125,501
Reserves	350,000	200,000	−150,000	350,000	5,358,798	5,008,798	350,000	171,500	−178,500
Emergency stabilization fund				685,000	200,000	−485,000			
Adjustment to previous budget		566,335	566,335					150,000	150,000
Total	**70,987,120**	**78,034,006**	**7,046,886**	**75,104,924**	**77,771,231**	**2,667,257**	**77,390,004**	**78,533,200**	**1,143,196**

(continued next page)

Table 2.5 Japan's budget plans, 1995-97 (millions of yen) (continued)

	FY1995 Planned revenue			FY1996 Planned revenue			FY1997 Planned revenue		
	Initial budget	Budget with supplement	Difference	Initial budget	Budget with supplement	Difference	Initial budget	Budget with supplement	Difference
Tax and stamps	53,731,000	50,681,000	−3,050,000	51,345,000	51,736,000	391,000	57,802,000	56,266,000	−1,536,000
Income tax	21,348,000	19,564,000	−1,784,000	19,338,000	18,995,000	−343,000			
Corporate tax	13,695,000	12,714,000	−981,000	13,548,000	13,986,000	438,000			
Administrative fees, charges, nonindividual sales	14,569	14,569	0	14,670	14,670				
Enterprise and property income	18,926	19,282	356	21,737	21,737				
Sales of land and intangible assets	304,044	304,044	0	326,956	326,956				
Miscellaneous[a]	4,318,796	4,373,661	54,865	2,348,201	2,380,365	32,164			
Japanese government bonds	12,598,000	22,032,000	9,434,000	21,029,000	22,368,000	1,339,000	16,707,000	18,458,000	1,751,000
From previous year	1,786	609,450	607,664	19,360	923,503	904,143			
Total	**70,987,120**	**78,034,006**	**7,046,886**	**75,104,924**	**77,771,231**	**2,667,257**	**77,390,004**	**78,533,200**	**1,143,196**

Note: All figures are in millions of yen.

a. Miscellaneous includes revenue from public land, Bank of Japan horse racing association, automobile registration, foreign exchange local government share of public investment, public university tuition, licensing fees, etc.

Source: *Ministry of Finance Statistics Monthly* 5, no. 529, 1996, Ministry of Finance, Tokyo, Japan.

Table 2.6 Economic forecasts, 1992-98

FY	OECD[a]	IMF[b]	EPA[c]	Consensus[d]	Actual
1992	2.4	2.2	3.5	2.4	1.5
1993	2.3	0.3	3.3	1.4	0.1
1994	0.5	0.7	2.4	0.6	0.6
1995	2.5	1.8	2.8	1.4	0.9
1996	2.0	2.7	2.5	2.4	3.6
1997	1.6	2.2	0.1	1.6	0.9
1998	1.7	1.1	1.9	0.1	na

na = not available.
Notes:
a. OECD forecasts are taken from December of the previous year's issue of *Economic Outlook*.
b. IMF forecasts are taken from the May *World Economic Outlook* of the same year (except 1998, which is taken from December 1997 issue).
c. EPA forecasts are made in December for the following fiscal year (April-March).
d. Consensus forecasts are the average of private-sector April forecasts for the same calendar year.

Source: OECD *Economic Outlook*, various issues; IMF *World Economic Outlook*, various issues; Economic Planning Agency; *Keizai Hakusyo (Economic White Paper)*; Consensus Forecasts.

In the end, the September 1995 stimulus package did add significantly to economic growth in 1996.[20] Not only was the actual real GDP growth of 3.6 percent significantly higher than the 0.9 percent recorded in 1995, it was at least 0.9 percent higher than the growth forecasted for 1996 by all of the major international institutions and the financial consensus (see table 2.6). This stimulative effect can largely be attributed to the fiscal package, although the decline in the yen also stemmed the decline in net exports (by −1 percent of GDP in 1995 and by −0.4 percent in 1996). There clearly were no crowding-out effects on nonresidential investment, which rose strongly in 1995 (by 1.2 percent of GDP) and 1996 (1.5 percent), while interest rates continued to drop. Despite the list of measures that were included in the September package announcement as a means of "overcoming imminent problems" (which included "giving vitality to the security market" and "coping with the problem of nonperforming assets held by financial institutions") and "accelerating structural reform of the economy" (including "further promotion of deregulation"), there was actually no meaningful progress made on any of these fronts.[21] There was no other source of positive impetus to the Japanese economy in late 1995 and early 1996 that can be identified *except* discretionary fiscal policy.

20. The package was actually passed by the Diet on 18 October, and then implemented.

21. The quoted categories and subcategories of measures are taken from the "contents" list of the package (Ministry of Finance, *Monthly Finance Review*, October 1995, 25).

It must be pointed out, however, that there were tax factors outside the September 1995 package at work during this period. The Ministry of Finance had managed to get a consumption tax of 3 percent introduced in April 1989. This was part of an ongoing effort to switch from direct to indirect taxes so that any given amount of government revenue could be collected with minimum distortionary costs (an effort recommended and, to a lesser degree, shared throughout the OECD in the 1990s). In November 1994, the upper and lower houses of the Diet passed a temporary personal income tax cut of 5.5 trillion yen to be paid for by increasing the consumption tax to 5 percent starting 1 April 1997. Despite the clearly temporary nature of such an explicit one-for-one fall and rise in taxes over such a short time period, it had an immediate effect on aggregate demand. Private consumption (presumably brought forward by consumers) rose by 1.9 percent of GDP in 1995 and 1.7 percent in 1996, versus only 0.9 percent in 1994. As also might be expected, such a clear change in the form of taxation caused a shift in spending pattern as well as timing—the promised tax rise included an exemption that spending on residential construction would be taxed at 3 percent for the duration of the project, so long as the contract was signed by September 1996. Residential investment grew by 0.7 percent of GDP in 1996, the highest rate since 1987, after contracting in 1995. Despite the fact that the Diet debate over the consumption tax in November 1994, as well as during the lower-house election campaign of October 1996 (when the issue was reopened), centered on the Ministry of Finance's loudly enunciated justification for the eventual tax rise in terms of future social security costs, this temporary tax cut had real effects. In fact, the measure was intended to be revenue neutral, with some small long-run benefits by decreasing distortions, but it proved stimulative nonetheless.

In contrast, the 1996 budget and supplementary budget were contractionary. The combined planned expenditure of 77.77 trillion yen was slightly less than the 78.03 trillion yen of 1995, but it was a smaller fraction of a larger economy because the 1995 package did lead to growth. Revenues included essentially the same amount of taxes (51.73 trillion yen) and government bond issuance (22.37 trillion yen) as in 1995.[22] Table 2.5 shows that, hidden in the 1996 budget was a switch of 5.16 trillion yen into "reserves" (i.e., money not spent during the fiscal year), mostly from public works (3 trillion yen cut from 1995 to 1996). The planned budget for 1997 continued this pattern, slightly decreasing the same level of nominal expenditures (to 77.39 trillion yen) and cutting public works a further 1.5 trillion yen. On 1 April 1997, the contraction was compounded when the planned consumption tax rise from 3 to 5 percent was implemented.

---

22. Figures for the proportion of bonds rolled over for years after 1995 are not available at the time of this writing.

By the end of 1997, private consumption had declined by 0.7 percent of GDP and residential investment had dropped by 1.1 percent; combined with the contraction in public investment and flat government consumption, these domestic factors took 2.3 percent off Japanese GDP. Had net exports not grown by a remarkable 1.5 percent of GDP after the yen declined sharply—the largest contribution of net exports to the nation's GDP growth in two decades—the Japanese economy would have experienced not only negative growth of 0.3 percent of GDP, as it did, but an outright decline of historic proportions. This reversal from the solid growth of 1996 can only be attributed to the Japanese government's fiscal policy, including carrying through the consumption tax rise regardless of the consequences, because just as in 1995-96, no other significant factors changed during this period. The Asian financial crisis did not harm the Japanese economy in this period, given that net exports increased, no increases in distortionary regulation or special interest protection were passed by the Diet, and the financial system's fragility was if anything reduced by the year-plus of solid growth (though essentially unchanged). Fiscal policy works to expand the economy as well as contract it, when that is misguidedly tried.

Is Fiscal Stimulus Being Tried Today?

The "Comprehensive Economic Measures" stimulus package of 24 April 1998 is seen by many as the latest in a series of fiscal-stimulus efforts. While this statement is partially mistaken—the only real fiscal stimulus was undertaken (successfully) in September 1995—the package of spring 1998 proposed by the Hashimoto government is indeed expansionary. Unsurprisingly, it is far less expansionary than claimed at the time of announcement. The headline number given is 16 trillion yen, of which only 12 trillion yen, at most, are purported to be actual spending and tax measures. As usual, 4.3 trillion yen of the 16 trillion headline number consist of asset reshuffles (2.3 trillion yen for land acquisition and "creation of land demand for the drastic redevelopment of cities") and government lending (2 trillion concentrated in small- and medium-sized business lending, largely an automatic rise proportionate to the increase in postal-savings deposits), neither of which increase aggregate demand (Economic Planning Agency of Japan 1998).

Another 1.5 trillion yen of the remaining 12 trillion is a central government "request [to] local governments to increase their independent public works without financial support from the central government"—a request unlikely to be fully met without a direct transfer of funds from the central government, which would mean a cut in spending elsewhere. As documented in Ishii and Wada (1998), local (i.e., prefectural, city, town, and village) governments spend on average about 65 percent of total government revenue, and the national government can only request, not force, these subnational governments to increase their public works spending in line with the announced packages. The local governments have repeatedly exercised this right of abstension, as their debt has mounted; from 1992-1996, "the local governments spent 3.7 trillion yen less than their initial budget. That is, the local governments not only failed to spend [the 6 trillion yen of solo local public works announced] in the supplementary budgets, but also spent less than their initial plans. This means that the local governments reduced capital spending by about 10 trillion yen" (Ishii and Wada 1998, 6-7).

There is claimed to be 7.7 trillion yen in total public works spending in the April 1998 package. On the spending side, this leaves 3.6 trillion yen of public works (and 200 billion yen of "disaster restoration works"), which do not require local government matching or solo action. This expenditure is to be concentrated in "information and communications and science and technology," "special projects for environment and new energy," and "social welfare, medical treatment, and education" ("Doubts Raised About Japan's economic Stimulus Program," Sandra Sagawara, *Washington Post*, D3, 5 June 1998). This would be a *mamizu* of 0.7 percent of GDP, less than half of the 7.7 trillion announced and, sadly, in line with all prior fiscal-stimulus packages. It is this 3.8 trillion yen of spending that passed the Diet in June 1998. The missing 2.4 trillion to bring the total up to the claimed 7.7 trillion is the expected local government contribution to joint spending projects. While this full amount is unlikely to be spent, even including it brings the total public spending package up to about 1.2 percent of GDP.

The tax side of the "Comprehensive Economic Measures" is a bit more complicated to assess, but it also ends up having much less stimulative effect on the Japanese economy than advertised. Between the consumption tax increase of April 1997 and the announcement of the current package a year later, one significant discretionary fiscal-policy act was implemented. In December 1997, an income tax reduction of 2 trillion yen was legislated, half of which was paid in February 1998 as a tax return from federal income tax and half of which will be paid from July to December 1998 as a local tax rebate.[23] This amounted to about 65,000 yen (about $480) for an average household of 2 adults and 2 children. The "implementing additional and continued special tax cuts" listed in the April 1998 package counts fully an additional 2 trillion yen temporary tax cut, which "will reduce tax payments by 29,000 yen per year [per] individual taxpayer and 14,500 yen per dependent . . . from August 1, 1998."

---

23. The December 1997 measure also included business and financial tax code changes that, while arguably improving the tax system's efficiency, only amounted to a negligible cut in taxes of 650 billion yen and so can be left aside for purposes of this fiscal-stimulus discussion.

Even this meager stimulus on the tax side is being undercut by its temporary nature. Another tax cut of 2 trillion yen is promised for FY1999, but that means that, *on net*, taxes will *rise* by 2 trillion yen next year because these are fixed lump-sum cuts rather than cuts in tax rates, and there was a total cut of 4 trillion yen in 1998. In other words, Japanese households are being told that they will pay 130,000 yen (typically) less in taxes this year than last year, but will pay 65,000 yen more in taxes next year than this year. Logic would have taxpayers smooth out their income by spreading the benefits of this year's cut over the next year and beyond and, thus, save much of the cut. The de facto temporary cut in consumption taxes in 1995 stimulated activity to a greater degree because it induced a shift in the composition and timing of spending in a way that a temporary income tax cut does not. The Japanese government acknowledges this reality by stating that the multiplier on income tax cuts is 0.46 within one year (Government of Japan 1998b), but this is misleading because it is the temporary nature of the cut that limits the multiplier effect below one.

Thus, the April 1998 stimulus package does not reflect the lessons of 1995, that is, that fiscal policy only works when it is tried. With a public works injection of 3.8 trillion yen from the central government (6.2 trillion yen, if we make the unrealistic assumption that all local governments will pay their full share of joint projects) and a temporary tax cut of 2 trillion yen, this year's package is an insufficient improvement on other fiscal stimulus packages undertaken in Japan in the 1990s: it consists of less than 60 percent of the amount announced in the headline (16 trillion yen), it totals a share of GDP (between 1.1 percent and 1.6 percent, depending on local government participation) below the appropriate size to make a difference to confidence, and it is structured to emphasize wasteful public construction projects and inefficient temporary tax changes. As is set out in chapter 5, a program of fiscal stimulus in which the stated amount equals the actual, in which that amount is sufficient to raise the growth rate above potential (meaning, as argued in chapter 1, above 2.0 to 2.5 percent of GDP) so that there is visible reemployment of excess labor and capacity, and in which the stimulus primarily takes the form of permanent income tax cuts, is a fiscal policy that would work.

The danger of the April 1998 package as passed by the Diet in June is not only that it will fail to restore growth to the Japanese economy in 1998—a matter of some urgency given the mounting downside risks to the Japanese and world economies discussed in chapter 4—but that it will also contribute to the myth that fiscal expansion in Japan has been tried and failed. Possible future claims by the Ministry of Finance and certain members of the LDP leadership that 12 or 16 trillion yen (rather than the true 8 trillion or less) was spent in 1998 to little or no avail could be used to support further fiscal contraction in 1999 or 2000. Similar contractions undertaken both openly and by hidden means in 1994, 1996, and 1997, with reference to announced but unimplemented spending, had destructive effects. Future government packages must recognize that when the Japanese government paid for fiscal stimulus in 1995, it got economic growth, and that when it mistakenly pursued fiscal austerity in most of the remainder of the 1992-97 period, it got economic contraction.

3

The Short and Long of Fiscal Policy

Fiscal stimulus, like any other economic policy, is subject to cost-benefit analysis. Even if there is evidence that fiscal stimulus had a significant positive effect on Japanese growth when it was tried in late 1995, there remain two concerns: First, would current circumstances, such as financial fragility and consumers' thrift, diminish or offset short-run effects of additional stimulus undertaken now, that is, would any fiscal expansion be effective? Second, would the long-run costs of additional public spending and, therefore, of adding to the outstanding stock of public debt, outweigh the short-run benefits of additional growth now? These concerns have been widely expressed by Japanese policymakers, with the long-run issue invoked frequently as a justification for the austere policies documented in the previous chapter.[1] Both, however, rest on fundamental misconceptions of the current economic situation in Japan and of the determinants of savings and growth.

In essence, the effectiveness of the 1995-96 fiscal expansion was to be expected, because Japan not only has underutilized productive capacity, as evidenced by its unprecedentedly high unemployment rate and falling

---

1. On both aspects, the statements of LDP Secretary-General Koichi Kato have been prominent and representative. As reported in the *Nihon Keizei Shimbun* ("Permanent Tax Cuts Not Effective in Stimulating Economy," 6 May 1998), Kato "questioned the need for permanent income tax cuts, insisting that previous cuts have just boosted national savings, and further tax cuts more likely would end up there as well. . . . [He] underlined worries about future pension costs and said that while some temporary slowdown in the pace of fiscal consolidation is warranted, Japan still must pursue its longer-run interest in a more fiscally conservative way."

price level, it has also diminished demand for investment. The recent sharp rise in Japanese households' propensity to save is an additional reason why stimulus is called for, rather than a sign that fiscal policy will be ineffective. There are signs of emerging panic among consumers—a serious matter indeed, as discussed in the next chapter—but that is actually something that expansionary government policy can reverse rather than encourage, and it is not indicative of a systematic "Ricardian" offsetting response by the private sector to government spending. Finally, the connection between the long-run burdens of an aging society in Japan and the optimal policy of today is far more tenuous than often held. The direct long-run costs of a marginal increase in total government debt are few, and the current benefits are potentially very large.

In this chapter, I recap the likely short-run determinants of fiscal-policy effectiveness and show how the current Japanese situation seems to be as favorable as possible. I then examine Japanese savings behavior and argue that, both historically and during the 1990s, fiscal policy had little effect on it. As a result, fiscal stimulus sufficient to improve growth expectations should stop the precautionary rush to savings rather than increase it. This would, in fact, be a rational response on the part of the Japanese public, because—as a clarification of certain basic facts about the influence of government debt on long-run Japanese growth prospects reveals—neither the direct effects of government debt nor the necessary adjustments to equalize generational distribution pose as much a constraint on the present or are as important for the future as is often stated.

The Most Appropriate Situation for Fiscal Stimulus

When the government injects money into the economy, through deficit-increasing tax cuts or public spending, it increases aggregate demand. In older macroeconomics textbooks, much was made of the "multiplier effect"—public money would go into the private sector, where individuals would spend a portion and save a portion (which banks would lend), and of that spent portion, the individuals receiving the money would spend a portion and save a portion, and so on, summing up to a net expansionary effect on GDP some multiple (greater than one) of the original fiscal stimulus. In more recent times, it has been fashionable to play down the size of multipliers. Deficit spending potentially "crowds out" private investment by increasing demand for savings and driving up interest rates; some of the remaining fiscal stimulus can leak abroad in the form of increased imports because an interest rate rise should lead to an appreciation of the home currency. Some of the initial spending is on imports, in any event. Additionally, to the extent that fiscal stimulus is viewed as temporary, some portion of the population will save much of the increase in cash that comes their way so as to smooth out the benefits over their lifetime.[2] All in all, there is a seemingly daunting list of reasons to limit faith in the effect of fiscal expansion under normal conditions.

Yet, while all of these are theoretically plausible effects, the actual magnitude of these offsets to fiscal policy depends on the contemporary context and the public's attitude at the time of the stimulus effort. In fact, most of these offsetting factors have proven to be small in the current Japanese context. For the September 1995 fiscal expansion, we have already seen that the rate of growth of both investment and net exports rose, and interest rates fell, while the consumer side of the stimulus was indeed spent rather than bottled up in savings accounts.[3] There would seem to be a prima facie case that successful fiscal expansion is possible in Japan, at least in the short run while there is underutilized capacity (as though the Reagan fiscal expansion of 1982-83 in the United States was not demonstration enough of the general case).

Ultimately, the short-run effectiveness of fiscal expansion depends on the availability of savings in the economy to finance the expansion. When an economy has excess capacity and limited demand for new investment, newly issued government debt has little with which to compete for the supply of capital. The indicators of room to expand in this sense are the interest rates in the economy. When the supply of capital grows scarce, its price is bid up, and government spending crowds out private investment, which cannot pay the higher interest rates. The fiscal impulse, of course, tells only part of the story, because monetary policy also affects interest rates. Monetary policy can accommodate fiscal expansion by moving to offset whatever rise in interest rates the issuing of government debt causes. This possibility is generally overlooked if not actively opposed in most policy discussions today, because a central bank engaging in such accommodation must purchase the government bonds by printing money—this is generally referred to as the *monetization of deficits*, and it is the primary source of sustained rises in inflation and inflation expectations. That potential rise in inflation, however, is a cost like any other to be weighed against

---

2. This life cycle response to changes in income should not be confused with the "Ricardian" response to changes in government spending. The relevance of these aspects of savings behavior is discussed in the next section.

3. When banks have weak balance sheets they may be expected to take in deposits more to build up reserves than to lend. That would further diminish the effect of fiscal stimulus to the extent that savings are recycled by the banking system. The private banking system is no longer as important to the transmission of fiscal policy in Japan as it was even a few years ago, however, reflecting regulatory changes as well as the natural adaptation of the nonfinancial sectors of the Japanese economy to a persistently weak banking system. This also reflects, however, a worrisome trend toward disintermediation from that weakened banking sector, which presents a mounting risk to the Japanese economy in a different way. I discuss these points in chapter 4.

the benefits of monetary accommodation, and it depends upon the current level of inflation and inflation expectations.

Even then, there is no one-to-one correspondence between interest rates and investment, because the degree of interest sensitivity of investment will vary. Moreover, investment demand depends not only upon interest rates but also upon the expectations of aggregate demand growth in the economy. If the expansionary effects of fiscal stimulus on national income stimulate investment demand more than whatever induced rise in interest rates diminishes it (either because there is so much capital available that interest rates do not rise or because the investment response to the change in demand outweighs the response to the change in interest rates), then fiscal stimulus crowds investment *in*. So, the appropriateness and effectiveness of expansionary fiscal policy depend on a number of factors.

In the Japanese economy of 1998, all of these factors are not only favorable for the effective use of stimulative fiscal policy, they also explain why fiscal stimulus must be undertaken before monetary or financial-sector efforts. The Japanese economy currently suffers from a dire case of the paradox of thrift. Individual Japanese consumers have decided in large part that they must save a greater share of their income, and individual businesses looking at their balance sheets and income projections have made a similar decision.[4] Yet, if everyone and every business simultaneously attempts to build up their cash positions by cutting back spending, no one is better off. The 100 yen I do not spend at the barber when I skip a haircut gives the barber reason not to spend 100 yen to eat out at lunch. In turn, the fellow at the *soba* (noodle) stand has 100 yen less income and 100 yen less available to buy this book from the Institute for International Economics, and so on. Normally, this cycle of saving, which results in contraction of spending and in further saving, can easily be dealt with. Positive developments in the economy restore people's and businesses' confidence that national spending will rise so that they can spend. Failing self-correction through swings of the business cycle or a positive shock, expansionary monetary policy provides people with more cash balances and restores aggregate demand. So long as expectations for the economy, particularly for the return on investment, are above some minimum level, declines in interest rates will prompt investment and satisfy individuals that a sufficient supply of cash is available.

When expectations for the returns to investment in an economy drop too low—as arguably they have in today's Japan—declines in interest rates no longer stimulate investment and any increase in the money supply is hoarded by cash-hungry individuals. This is because fearful citizens react to negative predictions of future income growth and to a general

---

4. The grounding of this rise in saving based on precautionary motives is discussed in the next section.

increase in uncertainty with a greater desire for liquidity. The interest rate paid to savers, which is the premium people are paid for giving up liquid cash and tying up their savings in investments instead, must rise to pry cash loose. At the same time, as overcapacity builds up and securities are sold off to raise cash (perhaps as part of a market panic that is not entirely justified), the rate of return on investment declines. If the difference between the rate of return on capital (its marginal product) and the rate of interest required to clear the money market (the liquidity premium) widens—say, because the perceived risk-adjusted return on capital drops faster than monetary expansion lowers the rate of interest on savings—investment demand declines and there is too much saving for the economy to absorb.[5] In such a situation, aggregate demand will be below capacity even with declining or zero short-term nominal interest rates.

Asset markets will reinforce this development because holders of government bonds will then fear a capital loss in their holdings if interest rates rise (as they must, eventually, if nominal interest rates are at zero and/or if the economy begins to rebound). These bond holders will also sell bonds for cash, contributing to the liquidity premium and the wedge between the market interest rate and the return on investment. This not only further diminishes the interest elasticity of investment, it also weakens the link between shifts in the money supply and interest rates that are prompted by monetary policy. Such a situation, where interest rates become insensitive to monetary policy and investment becomes insensitive to interest rates, all because expectations concerning the long-run return on capital drop without regard for policy, is what Keynes called the *liquidity trap* (see Keynes 1936, chapter 17).[6]

What does this hypothetical instance of the paradox of thrift have to do with today's Japan and the practical relevance of fiscal policy? Everything. There is strong evidence that monetary policy is ineffective in moving the money supply and investment in Japan at present. Despite negative long-term real interest rates for a year and negative short-term rates for over 18 months (see figure 3.1), investment has steadily declined since the end of the 1995 stimulus (as discussed in the previous chapter). Aggressive expansion since mid-1995 of the narrow money supply, in part through yen depreciation, has not resulted in a commensurate expansion of credit; as seen in figure 3.2, the M1 measure of the money supply has been growing at a double-digit rate on average for over two years, while the M2 measure has grown at less than half that rate (normally, the broader aggregate will grow at a faster rate than the narrower, as can

---

5. Krugman (1998a) offers a formal model along these lines.

6. Tobin (1987, chapter 1) and Skidelsky (1992) give good discussions of Keynes' use of the concept.

Figure 3.1   Real interest rate, 1984-98

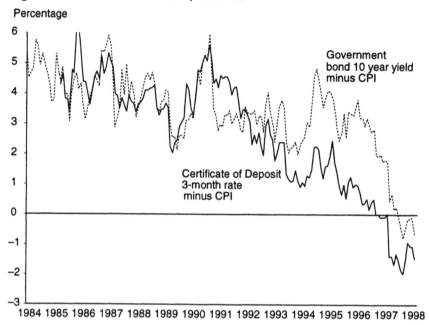

Source: Economic Statistics Monthly, Bank of Japan.

be seen in M2 versus M1 growth through 1991, because it includes the narrower aggregate as a component of it). The lower rate of growth in M2 than M1 while both short- and long-term interest rates drop is consistent with a hoarding of cash by investors and banks. Figure 3.3 shows the steady rise of cash as a share of M2 plus certificates of deposit outstanding, further underlining the point. After fluctuating between just 6.5 and 7 percent from 1984 to 1993, even during the bubble years and the crash, the cash share is now 25 percent higher, a substantial shift. Saving propensities have been rising in Japanese society in tandem with demand for liquidity. While the annual national-accounts data show only a small rise in private saving through 1996 (for the latest available data, see figure 3.4), the surplus rate, which is based on a monthly survey, has been climbing since 1992 (see figure 3.5), and the quarterly saving rate from the same survey has risen from 25.5 percent in 1992 to 30.4 percent in the first quarter of 1998.[7]

---

7. The surplus rate is defined as disposable income minus living expenditure divided by disposable income, while the savings rate is defined as a residual from other questions about pretax income. The *Family Income and Expenditure Survey* has been collected monthly since 1950, and currently surveys 8,000 households representing 84 percent of the population.

Figure 3.2   Growth in monetary aggregate

Percentage

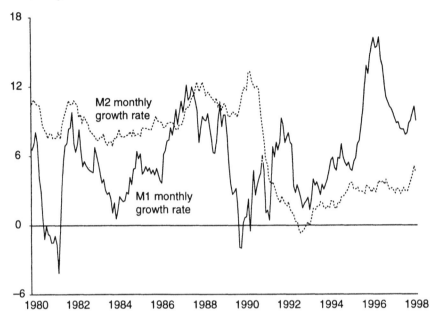

Source: *Economic Statistics Monthly*, Bank of Japan.

The complementary reality of the ineffectiveness of monetary policy caused by the liquidity trap is the near-zero interest elasticity of investment demand. As described by Vickrey (1992) and Tobin (1987), the recycling of savings into the economy can be stymied by a rise in precautionary saving out of fear, that is, a distrust of calculations concerning the future. The key point is that the interest rate that clears the money market need not be the one that brings about full employment. As Tobin (1987, 80) notes, Keynes' "skepticism [regarding the efficacy of monetary policy in a deep recession] arose from his belief that the long-run expectations governing the marginal efficiency of capital are so volatile and unsystematic that central banks might well be unable to offset them by variation of interest rates." The good side of all this is that in Japan today the primary short-run channel offsetting fiscal expansion no longer holds.

It is biased upward by its underrepresentation of younger and low-income households, but the trend should be more accurate than the annual Standard National Accounts (SNA) data (see Matsuoka and Rose 1994, chapter 4).

Figure 3.3 Share of cash in M2 and certificates of deposit, 1984-97

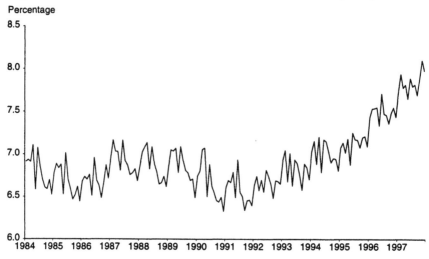

Percentage

Note: Seasonally adjusted by author.

Source: Economic Statistics Monthly, Bank of Japan.

A rise in public spending will not immediately drive up interest rates because there is an oversupply of savings, and, to the extent that it eventually does move interest rates, the effect on investment will be small. Under these circumstances, monetary policy's ineffectiveness constitutes an automatic accommodation of fiscal policy without immediate inflationary consequences. When fiscal expansion eventually creates sufficient demand to raise interest rates and inflation, the goal of policy has largely been attained. At that point, when savings are being employed and the gap between the return on investment and the liquidity premium has been closed, monetary policy can take over from fiscal stimulus to the extent necessary.

It is precisely under these dire circumstances of an uncertainty-driven lack of propensity to spend, as obtains in Japan today, that fiscal stimulus is called for by Keynes. As Krugman (1994, 31-32) observes,

> So the usual and basic Keynesian answer to recession is a monetary expansion. But Keynes worried that even this might sometimes not be enough, particularly if a recession had been allowed to get out of hand and become a true depression ... [households] may simply add any monetary expansion to their hoard. Such a situation, in which monetary policy has become ineffective has come to be

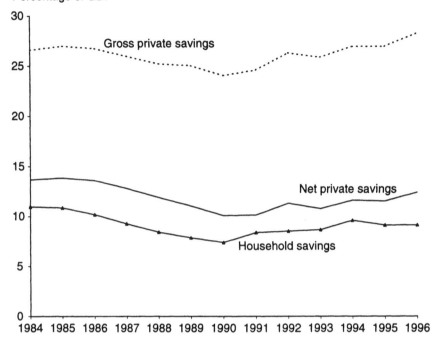

Figure 3.4   Private saving rate, 1984-96

Percentage of GDP

Source: *Economic Statistics Monthly*, Bank of Japan.

known as a "liquidity trap"; . . . The Keynesian answer to a liquidity trap is for the government to spend.[8]

It is for this reason that Krugman's (1998a) call for "turning on the presses" at the Bank of Japan in response to the liquidity trap would not be effective. In his model, printing yen drives down the interest rate in the money market (i.e., saver's liquidity premium) to a potentially negative rate of return on capital. However, that reverses the endogenous and exogenous variables—the binding constraint is the interest rate premium necessary to clear the money market because of people's uncertainty. The goal of policy should be to reduce uncertainty and drive up the return on capital, and monetary policy cannot affect those factors directly when demand for cash is too strong. The liquidity trap possibility had been ignored for years by economists in part because it requires such an ad hoc assumption that the public's fear can cause interest rates to diverge from the fundamental long-run return on capital for an extended period.

---

8. Tobin (1987, 7-8) adds, "What does the *General Theory* itself say about policy? Fiscal policy, long regarded as the main Keynesian instrument, is introduced obliquely as a means of beefing up a weak national propensity to spend in the event monetary policy fails."

Figure 3.5 Seasonally adjusted surplus rate, 1984-98

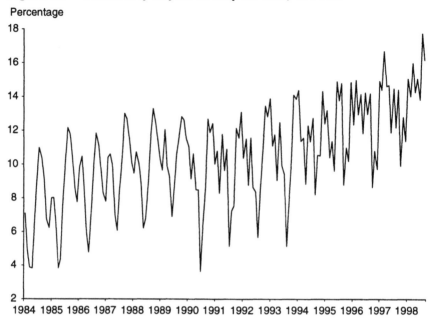

Percentage

Source: Household Income and Expenditure Survey, Management and Coordination Agency.

To base it on rational actors, Krugman (1998a) requires that the return on capital represent the actual return, which is why that becomes the rate that cannot be altered (except by structural change). The point is that individuals' perceptions of an economy's future can have significant implications for the short-run effectiveness of policy, regardless of this perception's relation to the fundamentals. This is a fact that those who observed Japan's bubble economy of the 1980s or who find some plausibility in Radelet and Sachs' (1997) interpretation of the Asian financial crisis as panic driven should not find surprising.

Whether or not the label "liquidity trap" is justified in the case of Japan today, the hoarding of cash, rising savings levels, low interest rates and deflation, and an absence of investment demand—all of which clearly are present—make this the perfect time for expansionary fiscal policy. As Bosworth (1993, 42) summarizes the impact of fiscal policy in an open economy, "The extent of the offset [to stimulus] coming from higher interest rates depends on the interest elasticity of the demand for money," and Japanese money demand appears to be independent of interest rates at present (see figures 3.1-3.5 and the discussion of them earlier in this chapter). On the trade side, if capital mobility is somewhat limited, it is likely that the inflow in capital in response to a fiscal stimulus will fall short of the initial deterioration in net exports, so that the exchange rate will appreciate less than usual. This is the case in Japan today, where the connected lending and ownership of the Japanese economy has made yen-denominated assets difficult to sell in international capital markets because buyers and sellers have asymmetric information about their risks and liabilities. If interest rates do not rise, in any event, the exchange-rate and net-export offset to fiscal expansion will be diminished.[9] In sum, to whatever extent fiscal policy begins to compete for capital, it is reversing the negative expectations and crowding investment in, and until it does so, its expansionary impact will not be offset.

The presumed unwillingness of banks to lend is another aspect of the Japanese economy that might work against the effectiveness of fiscal policy. If people save most of the money that they receive from the stimulus in banks, and if the banks in turn hold on to most incoming deposits due to their limited capital bases, then the money will not circulate widely through the economy. This is more a possibility than a major effect in current practice, however. As will be discussed in chapter 4 on risks to the Japanese outlook, evidence of a sharp credit crunch, that is, banks withholding lending, is limited at best up until very recently, despite press coverage to the contrary. This apparent lack of lending constraint makes sense for two reasons: First, to the extent that Japanese banks have low or negative net worth, they have an incentive to lend *more* rather than less, albeit inefficiently, to high-risk, high-return projects, because the bank management and ownership would share fully in any positive developments but have only what is left (if anything) in net worth to lose.[10] Second, the problem at present in Japan is a lack of investment *demand*, including demand for loans, because firms are carrying too much outstanding nominal debt (built up, along with Japanese asset prices, when their net worth was higher) and prospects appear to be too bleak to justify adding to capacity. Moreover, even with the rising savings rate depicted in figure 3.5, Japanese households are still spending 80 percent of their disposable incomes; so long as any rise in their income due to fiscal stimulus is viewed largely as permanent, which it would have to be if growth is ever to be maintained, that ratio of spending should

---

9. Bosworth (1993, 18) establishes a long-standing pattern in the responses of the yen, based on data from prior to the current situation, that while there is a strong negative correlation between foreign (US) interest rates and the exchange rate, there is no evidence of a positive correlation between the exchange rate and the Japanese domestic interest rates.

10. This is an example of moral hazard, where the incentives created by deposit insurance are perverse for the insurer's (i.e., the public's) interest. Mishkin (1991) gives a summary of how asymmetric information in financial markets leads to various inefficiencies, such as this incentive to "bet the bank" once net worth sharply declines.

continue, and bank deposits would not absorb more than a small portion of the stimulus.

Moreover, the amount of new deposits that banks would want to put aside for improving capital/asset ratios, though large, is finite. Japanese banks have on the order of 780 trillion yen in outstanding assets in total at present, and an (overstated) capital base of 29 trillion yen, for a ratio of 3.7 percent (*Economic Statistics Monthly*, Bank of Japan). While short of the 8 percent required by the Basle capital accord for the capital-to-assets ratio, any rapid build-up of deposits would give the banks greater access to capital markets and more incentive to write off bad loans and lend carefully, further strengthening the banks' positions beyond the direct infusion of deposits. As Keynes wrote to President Franklin D. Roosevelt in 1934, even if banks piling up excess reserves meant that spending $200 million a month would not work to stimulate output, spending $400 million a month would (quoted in Schultze 1992, 211).[11] The imminent danger is not that Japanese banks will sit on deposits and not lend what comes in, but that, if the Japanese public's expectations continue to fall, they will be rapidly deprived of deposits and contract current lending further, as discussed in chapter 4. This is not to say that a cleanup of Japan's sizable bad-loan problem and recapitalization of its viable (and only its viable) banks would not aid matters immensely once fiscal stimulus restarts growth—some ways to do that are part of the program for Japanese economic recovery suggested in chapter 5. But fiscal stimulus need not wait for financial reform in order to be effective, and financial reform without fiscal stimulus is unlikely to address people's low expectations.[12]

Precautionary Hoarding, Not Ricardian Saving

One aspect of the link between the short-run and long-run effects of fiscal policy is the influence of fiscal policy on savings behavior. In the previous section, the maintained assumption was that fiscal policy primarily affects savings through its influence on income growth and expectations thereof. This is consistent with a rising savings rate and cash hoarding in the face of declining interest rates and provides seemingly ample motive for precautionary thrift in today's Japan. An alternative interpretation is that savings rise to offset any fiscal expansion because households see in such a policy future tax rises that they or their heirs will bear. This interpretation is at first glance plausible as well, because both savings and deficits have

---

11. For reference, $400 million was 6 percent of US GDP at the time, so Keynes was illustrating the general point rather than recommending such monthly largesse.

12. In fact, financial reform done properly will likely be contractionary in the short run, which is all the more reason to mitigate its effects with fiscal stimulus (see chapters 4 and 5).

risen with the Japanese recession in the 1990s. Meanwhile, the Japanese government, among others, has repeatedly made fearful reference to the aging society and mounting future burdens, perhaps to raise consciousness of the need for future tax revenues and for younger savers to self-insure. Distinguishing between these two alternative motives for the sharp rise in Japanese saving in the 1990s—the precautionary and the Ricardian—is critical to deciding upon the utility of fiscal expansion.[13] If the rise in savings is precautionary, fiscal stimulus should crowd in investment by encouraging Japanese households to spend, as discussed in the previous section. If the rise in savings is Ricardian, that is, largely driven in offsetting response to government expenditure, further government spending will be neutral and not affect economic growth. While this latter response would lead to an offset of fiscal stimulus, it comes through an entirely different channel than those discussed in the previous section and does not put pressure on interest rates.

Realistically, the question of a Ricardian response to government spending is one of how many obvious additions to outstanding Japanese government debt will be offset by saving today, given the oft-expressed concerns for the aging society, rather than whether savers are or are not fully Ricardian. To the extent that today's individuals view money spent on them or bonds sold to them by the government as a net benefit rather than one they will have to pay back in full in their lifetimes, government spending will raise individuals' wealth or income and, therefore, their consumption.[14] This view can stem from the fact that people's motive to leave bequests for their children—say, sufficient to make up for government-debt increases incurred during their lifetime—is not always strong (or they have no children); it might also be that the discount rate of individuals is higher than that of the government, which will presumably outlive them. In either case, the further off that tax increases can be deferred relative to people's time horizons, the greater the wealth effect of the current issuance of government bonds (and the greater its effects).

Even if households are sufficiently long-lived, and/or have children that they care enough about, to expect to bear some of the taxes for today's government spending, there are several other reasons why Ricardian equivalence would not hold. If the government can borrow at a lower interest rate than can individuals and if some individuals are liquidity

---

13. This theory and the term "Ricardian" are due to Barro (1974). The emphasis here is on the *change* in the rate of savings. Like most economists, I believe that much of savings behavior can be explained by the Life Cycle/Permanent Income Hypothesis. Most of these aspects, however, such as demographics or social security coverage, did not change sufficiently in 1990s Japan to explain the rise in savings.

14. This discussion draws on Blanchard and Fischer (1989, chapter 3); Romer (1996, chapter 2); and Frenkel, Razin, and Yuen (1996, chapter 8).

constrained,[15] then any government tax cuts are equivalent to government borrowing on the individual's behalf, and consumption will rise. Also, individuals have an interest in minimizing the effects of taxes on their economic decisions at any given time, irrespective of the total lifetime (or longer) tax burden that they face. In the words of Vickrey (1992, 305):

> If sales or earnings taxes are the relevant revenues, deficit financing would mean lower tax rates currently with expectations of higher rates in the future. It would then be individually rational for taxpayers to shift expenditure and earning effort toward the present, even with certainty as to future tax rates and full concern for progeny, with a current stimulating effect on the economy. Uncertainties and liquidity constraints would have a further effect on the same direction, in addition to whatever 'debt illusion' there may be in giving more weight to bonds possessed individually as assets than to the debt as a collective liability.

With these many potential reasons, there has been little surprise that evidence supportive of Ricardian equivalence has been difficult to find and certainly insufficient to be considered when governments make financing decisions.[16]

Returning from the general to Japan in particular, the sources of Japan's historically relatively high savings rate have been the subject of intense study. The broad pattern of Japanese savings behavior has been established to include a substantial decline in the national savings rate since the mid-1970s. This decline, which is robust by any means of measurement, stabilized in the late 1980s. This movement, however, goes precisely the wrong way in relationship to Japanese government deficits if Ricardian equivalence were to hold—private savings dropped as government deficits rose to postwar highs in the late 1970s and early 1980s and did not decline while deficits shrank sharply in the late 1980s. In a series of papers, Horioka and various coauthors made more sophisticated tests for the determinants of Japanese savings, holding other factors constant and using a variety of methods (Horioka 1990, 1993, 1995, 1997; Horioka et al. 1996; Horioka and Watanabe 1997). They found substantial support for the idea that a combination of life cycle and precautionary motives could explain much of the variation in Japanese savings behavior over time and across individuals. Importantly, they demonstrated that the rate of savings in Japan is influenced negatively by the retiree/worker dependency ratio and by the extent of social security coverage and positively by the level and growth rate of income. These findings are consistent with life cycle motivations and inconsistent with Ricardian ones. Independently, Bosworth (1993) also demonstrated the significance

---

15. That is, if these people could borrow more against future income or current assets than capital markets typically allow them to, they would do so.

16. See Bernheim (1987) for the standard summary of the original empirical results. Romer (1996, chapter 7) gives a more up-to-date survey along these lines.

of income and demographic factors for Japanese savings behavior, and Cigno and Rosati (1997) showed savings to be a declining function of the level of social security coverage and a positive function of income.

Even more importantly for the current policy discussion, Horioka (1990), Horioka et al. (1996), and Horioka and Watanabe (1997) find direct evidence from government surveys of Japanese savers that precautionary motives have been the most cited motive for savings even prior to recent stagnation. "Precautionary motives [are] defined as motives arising from uncertainties concerning future income and/or expenditures. Examples include saving for income fluctuations, unemployment, illness, accidents, natural disasters, and longevity risk" (Horioka and Watanabe 1997, 538). While answers to survey questions may be unreliable, the bias should run *against* admitting to this motivation, because the option of stating that the motive for saving was to leave bequests to the subjects' children was offered and could have been taken to look good.[17] Horioka (1990) finds that the proportion of households in Japan saving for precautionary motives and the household savings rate have shown parallel movements over time. Accordingly, interpreting the rise in savings in the 1990s as a precautionary response by Japanese savers to a rising likelihood of unemployment or income fluctuation would be well in line with the established patterns of Japanese behavior. Thus, if expansionary fiscal policy can decrease the likelihood of unemployment or the variability of income, it should lead to a decline in savings, which will reinforce aggregate demand further.

Economic research has long acknowledged the role of precautionary motivations for saving, especially in causing short-run fluctuations in the savings rate. Carroll (1997) points out that Milton Friedman's original "permanent income hypothesis" included many references to people's desire for a buffer stock of savings over time. In general, as individuals' risk aversion and income uncertainty (including transitory shocks to income such as recessions) increase, so should savings, and movements of income from the future to the present (such as through a tax cut today) should work in the opposite direction, even if expected lifetime income is unchanged.[18] And Japanese savers are not alone in stating in surveys that being prepared for emergencies and hard times is the most important motivation for saving.[19]

---

17. In fact, very few Japanese savers surveyed claimed to be saving to leave their children money and of those so claiming, a majority were doing so for self-described nonaltruistic reasons (e.g., assuring oneself of a place in the child's home).

18. See Barsky, Mankiw, and Zeldes (1986), Blanchard and Fischer (1989, chapter 6), Caballero (1990), Carroll (1997), and Zeldes (1989) for formal demonstrations of this point.

19. Carroll (1997) cites surveys in the United States that put the precautionary savings motive first among 40 percent of those answering, the most popular response by far.

As a result, Japanese policymakers should recognize two realities. First, Ricardian concerns are not motivating current rises in Japanese saving. Not only will fiscal expansion draw down savings (and increase consumption), but repeated reference to coming government tax burdens will only contribute to a contemporary source of panic without serving any long-run purpose. Second, Japanese savers may be thought of as having some target wealth-to-permanent-income ratio, so that efforts to raise wealth and diminish uncertainty—say by a program of fiscal expansion, stabilization of the price level at above-zero measured inflation, and clean-up of the financial system, as I propose in chapter 5—will reverse the rise in savings to the Japanese public's benefit. The appropriate response to increased Japanese fear about the future is not to validate it by government speech or inaction, because persistent precautionary saving can bring about economic contraction of its own accord (as discussed in the previous section).

Why Today's Deficit Does Not Imperil Tomorrow's Elderly

There is doubt in Japan about whether a rise in the deficit today would be worthwhile, even if fiscal expansion were effective. The aging of the Japanese population, and the mounting social security and health care obligations associated with that trend, are seen as predominant concerns. This is a false opposition. While the rising future burdens of today's and tomorrow's Japanese taxpayers are indeed worthy of serious public concern, they are in no meaningful sense related to the budget decisions of 1998. To make such a link, one would be required to believe either that rising Japanese debt levels are in and of themselves burdening the economy so greatly that a little more debt will be unsustainable, or that the direct costs of an incremental rise in Japanese debt are large enough to outweigh the benefits of fiscal-led expansion, or that the amount of money saved by today's austerity will aid in rectifying the generational imbalance, or that additional deficit spending today is unlikely to be reversed. Yet none of these is the case. The Japanese debt level is currently sustainable, the direct long-run costs of an additional couple of percent of GDP in debt are far outweighed by the benefits, the generational imbalance is so largely dependent upon demographic forces that even a balanced budget this year would not affect it, and there is no historical or institutional reason to think that today's deficit rise would not be reversed in better times. Being realistic about what today's deficit spending implies for Japan over the long run—rather than hiding unfounded assertions behind claims of opposition to "short-sighted" or "spendthrift" behavior— is an act of responsibility.

What matters for a country, like any growing business or household, is whether its *net* debt is growing faster than the country's income. If debt grows faster than national income for an extended period, the government is racking up obligations faster than its ability to pay them. Net rather than gross debt matters because a government's assets can be sold, just as any other property owner can draw down capital to pay off loans. Table 3.1 and figure 3.6 chart the path of Japanese government debt and deficits as a share of GDP. Note that the Japanese government was in surplus in 1987-92, even on structural deficit measures, and that net debt was declining from 1984 through 1992. In addition, after several years of general government deficits in the 1990s, the social security surpluses and assets held in FILP leave a net debt of only 15 percent of Japanese GDP, the lowest level by far in the G-7 (see figure 3.7). To give a sense of scale, 15 percent of a year's national income is only two years' worth of the annual transfer payments from western Germany to eastern Germany made since 1991. The gap between net and gross debt in Japan is clearly the largest in the G-7. If social security trust funds in the United States were not considered, so that gross debt levels were compared, the United States would be on a par with Germany, France, and the United Kingdom; the difference in gross debt between Japan and the G-5 would then essentially come down to the accumulation since 1992. In other words, Japan's poor gross-debt position is an artifact of the current business cycle, so it should be reversible, while its more important net-debt level is a world leader.

One can, of course, keep redefining what constitutes "net" debt—Asher and Smithers (1998) throw in a large number of contingent claims, such as the underfunded pension liabilities of the Japanese economy, and produce catastrophic figures for the outstanding obligations of the Japanese government. There are three problems with such exaggeration. First, precisely because these are *contingent* claims, they are unlikely to come due all at once, and it is unlikely, even over very long periods, that all will have to be paid (no one declares insurance companies insolvent by comparing their assets to what would happen if all policies in force had to be paid simultaneously). Second, this underfunding of contingent claims is true of all OECD economies (see Hutchison 1992). It is difficult to see how capital markets could punish Japan by withdrawing funds or raising risk premiums without doing so largely equally to all the countries and, therefore, to none of them. Third, as discussed below with regard to generational accounting, almost all definitions of contemporary government debt situations misrepresent their countries' long-run social security imbalances, so it makes sense to limit discussion of the current debt snapshot only to those explicit obligations and credits of the government—the standard definition of net debt. And Japanese government net debt is still lower than it was in the early 1980s, while its social security surplus has been rising (see table 3.1).

Table 3.1 Government budget balance as a share of GDP, 1983-96

	Balance (fiscal year)				Net debt (calendar year)	Gross debt (calendar year)	Memorandum		
	General	Central government	Local	Social security			Central government net debt	Local government net debt	Social security net debt (−asset)
1983	−2.9	−4.9	−0.8	2.7	26.0	66.6	na	na	na
1984	−1.8	−4.0	−0.6	2.8	27.1	67.9	na	na	na
1985	−0.8	−3.6	−0.3	3.1	26.7	68.7	na	na	na
1986	−0.3	−3.0	−0.4	3.1	25.7	72.1	na	na	na
1987	0.7	−1.9	−0.2	2.8	21.3	74.5	na	na	na
1988	2.2	−1.1	0.1	3.2	18.1	72.7	na	na	na
1989	2.6	−1.2	0.6	3.2	14.9	70.0	na	na	na
1990	3.5	−0.3	0.3	3.5	9.6	69.1	34.0	8.4	−32.8
1991	3.4	−0.2	−0.1	3.7	5.0	66.7	31.3	7.8	−34.1
1992	0.1	−2.1	−1.1	3.4	4.3	70.0	31.8	9.0	−36.5
1993	−1.4	−2.8	−1.6	3.1	5.3	75.1	33.7	10.6	−38.9
1994	−3.0	−3.7	−2.0	2.7	7.9	82.2	36.5	12.8	−41.1
1995	−3.9	−4.2	−2.6	2.8	13.5	89.7	40.2	15.2	−43.4
1996	−4.1	na	na	na	15.5	94.2	na	na	na

na = not available.

Note: Gross debt includes all financial liabilities. Net debt includes gross debt less all financial assets except corporate shares, as defined by the System of National Accounts, and covers the general government sector, which is a consolidation of central government, local government, and the social security sector. Changes in "net debt" do not equal to the "general government balance" because net debt is based on the calendar year and all balance figures are based on the fiscal year. Moreover, changes in net debt are adjusted for changes in the value of government assets and liabilities (e.g., US Treasury bonds).

Source: Annual Report on National Account, Economic Planning Agency, 1997, http://www.epa.go.jp (17 April 1998).

Figure 3.6 Government debt and deficit as a share of GDP, 1983-96

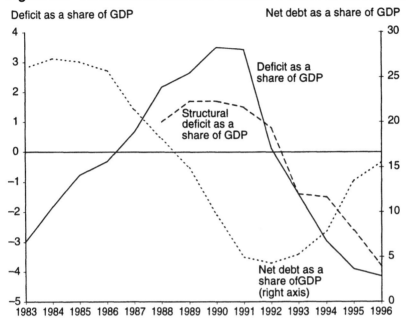

Sources: OECD National Account 1997, OECD; Annual Report on National Account 1997, Economic Planning Agency; World Economic Outlook, May 1998, IMF.

The Japanese economy is growing more slowly in the 1990s than in the early 1980s, which somewhat changes the importance of the same net-debt level (though, as argued in chapter 1, that growth differential is in large part temporary, which minimizes the difference). The key question is whether the nominal rate of interest on the outstanding debt is greater than nominal GDP growth, because so long as income growth exceeds interest payments, debt will decline as a share of GDP. This means that there are two ways to reduce the debt burden: run surpluses or increase the rate of growth of the economy. Either one is equally effective. If fiscal stimulus were to lead to sustained growth, the debt incurred in stimulating the economy would pay off; even if deficit spending simply moves growth forward, there is no reason not to wait to run surpluses to repay the debt until the growth rate is higher. As shown in figure 3.8, until the 1990s, the yield on a 10-year Japanese government bond was below that of the (nominal) rate of growth of the Japanese economy. At any foreseeable growth rate, this beneficial differential will return. There are no obvious signs that Japanese debt growth is on a consistently rising path that is unsupportable by Japanese economic growth.

Next comes the question of the direct costs of budget deficits. When the United States ran exceptionally large full-employment government

Figure 3.7 General government financial liability in 1996

Percentage of nominal GDP

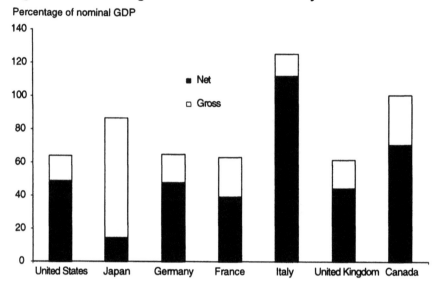

Note: Gross liabilities include all financial liabilities as defined by the System of National Accounts and cover the general government sector, which is a consolidation of central government, state and local government, and the social security sector. Net liabilities include all financial liabilities less all financial assets as defined by the System of National Accounts and cover the general government sectors.

deficits in the 1980s, this became a much studied phenomenon. Perhaps surprisingly, most mainstream macroeconomists were not as terrified by deficits as the popular impression would have it.[20] Buiter and Kletzer (1992) list four reasons why a policymaker or citizen might be concerned about public deficits and debt. First is financial crowding out, the displacement of private investment or an increase in the balance of payments deficit, as discussed in the first section of this chapter. Because Japan is at present below full employment and has a lack of investment demand and a balance of payments surplus, this is hardly relevant. Second is the desire to smooth the collection of taxes over time, to minimize their distortionary effect on savings and investment decisions. As Buiter and Kletzer (1992, 290) point out, "The proposition that balanced budgets are sub-optimal is, however, more robust [to changes in specific assumptions] than the tax smoothing result."

The third reason why policymakers and the public might be concerned about deficits is fear that mounting public debt will persuade the govern-

---

20. Though they all certainly advocated at least a gradual return to budget balance over the business cycle as well as a slowdown in the rate of debt accumulation (see Friedman 1992, 1994; Ball and Mankiw 1995).

Figure 3.8 Yield on government bond and GDP growth, 1984-96

Percentages

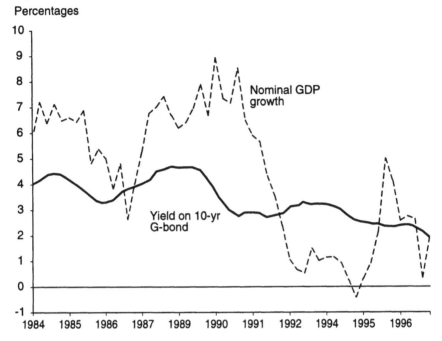

Note: Both data are monthly.

Sources: Economic Planning Agency, http://www.epa.go.jp; Bank of Japan, http://www.boj.or.jp.

ment to monetize the deficit and cause severe inflation in so doing. The idea that the now independent Bank of Japan would ever engage in such behavior is absurd, especially because the burden of Japanese public debt is sustainable. Unless the Bank of Japan aggressively prints money, such monetization and hyperinflation cannot occur.[21] Finally, the Japanese government could go bankrupt, that is, it could partially or wholly repudiate its debt obligations. Such a tactic is in the government's interest only if nominal debt grew faster than nominal national income for an extended period—like a firm, a government's willingness to repudiate debt depends entirely on its net worth and ability to access capital markets. If the government still has enough net assets and credibility to be able to roll over its debt, it has an interest in maintaining its access to credit; the government will choose to go bankrupt only when it has so little to lose that the one-time benefit of debt repudiation outweighs the benefits of continued rollovers. The five years of a Japanese growth rate below bor-

---

21. See chapter 5 for a discussion of why and how a modest positive inflation rate in the current Japanese context would be helpful if implemented.

Figure 3.9 Foreign share of purchases of Japanese public and corporate bonds, 1978-97

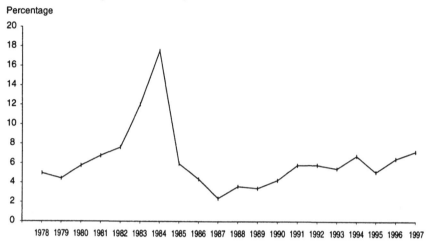

Percentage

Source: Bank of Japan, *Economic Statistics Monthly.*

rowing costs (interrupted in 1996) depicted in figure 3.6 are hardly sufficient to run the Japanese government into insolvency, and, thus, there is
insufficient incentive to repudiate the debt. From the perspective of its
net-debt level, this is a far-fetched hypothetical.

Even if the Japanese government were to remove some of its debt
burden either through direct repudiation or through inflation, the costs
would be lower than in most other countries. This is because its debt is
almost entirely domestically held and is completely denominated in yen.
Government refusal to completely pay off debt in Japan would, therefore,
simply constitute an internal redistributive tax that transferred wealth
from government bondholders to government transfer and spending
recipients; inflation would perform the same redistribution so long as
benefits were indexed. If the central bank accedes, government repudiation faces a hard constraint only if the borrowing was from international
capital markets, particularly in foreign currency. As can be seen from
figure 3.9, outstanding foreign purchases of Japanese debt (public and
private) is very small.[22] There remains the small possibility of a "hard
landing" for the yen if the Japanese government were to pursue an unsustainable course of debt accumulation, which would arise first as a higher
risk premium on yen-denominated borrowing. Starting from a net-debt

---

22. Direct numbers on foreign holdings of Japanese government bonds are unavailable, but
most estimates would put them at around 1 percent of the total outstanding. The foreign
purchases of Japanese bonds spiked up in 1984-85 because of a number of regulatory changes
that eased banks' ability to engage in bond transactions.

level of 15 percent of GDP, however, the government would have to accumulate a lot more debt to make that threat real. While there is some evidence of a "Japan premium" for Japanese banks borrowing in the interbank market, that is directly associated with the information problems and systemic uncertainties of the Japanese banking sector—Japanese government bonds and nonfinancial corporate paper continue to be issued at extremely low rates of interest.

It remains to assess the long-run direct costs to the Japanese economy of carrying government debt, even if the amount is sustainable and unlikely to result in bankruptcy, hyperinflation, or a hard landing. Presumably, government borrowing takes away capital from other purposes once an economy returns to full employment. Thus, even if the debt-to-GDP ratio is stabilized or slowly brought down when the Japanese economy recovers, there is the potential for ongoing losses from the debt that is rolled over. As the IMF (1996, 50) put it in their review of fiscal policy, "Why persistent budget deficits are a problem [is because] . . . government dissaving hurts national saving and lowers future living standards because either investment is reduced or borrowing from abroad is increased, and with it, future obligations to service foreign debt out of future national income." Because Japanese savers are not Ricardian, and the borrowing of a few percent of Japanese GDP is a large enough amount to affect interest rates (given that the Japanese government mostly draws on domestic savings sources), government debt will absorb capital that presumably could earn a higher return if invested in the private sector. Like many effects discussed in this chapter, however, the relevant question is how large is this long-run cost of debt, not whether it exists.

Ball and Mankiw (1995) and Elemendorf and Mankiw (1997) propose a clever thought experiment to put an upper bound on the quantitative importance of a society's debt to its economic welfare—the parable of the "Debt Fairy."[23] Imagine that the Debt Fairy appeared one night, and replaced all of the Japanese government's outstanding bonds with useful private capital of equal face value. This would take care of the entire gross (not net) debt of Japan, about 100 percent of GDP on latest figures. What would be the effect on Japanese economic growth? If the entire gross debt of the Japanese government were replaced, the government would no longer have to pay debt service of under 1 percent of GDP (100 percent of GDP in debt times a real interest rate of below 1 percent—see figure 3.1). Assume that factors of production, like capital, earn their marginal product. The marginal product of capital can be thought of as the capital share of national income divided by the capital/output ratio. In Japan, the capital share of national income is around 0.4, and the

---

23. This was developed with regard to the discussions of the United States deficit in the early 1990s.

capital/output ratio is about 3.6, which together imply a marginal product of capital of 11 percent. Output would be raised by the marginal product of capital times the additional capital stock, or 11 percent of GDP. As discussed in chapter 1, however, there is good reason to doubt that Japanese capital investment is as productive as American, which would reduce this product. Assuming a Cobb-Douglas production function, the marginal product of capital is proportional to the capital/output ratio. Thus, if capital stock rises from 3.6 times output to 4.6 times output, or by 30 percent, while output rises by 11 percent, there is an 18.5 percent drop in the marginal product of capital, to about 9 percent.

This 11 percent gain means that even if the *entire* accumulated government debt of Japan were replaced by useful capital, the lump-sum benefit to the economy would be on the same order of magnitude as the lost output in the Japanese economy just since 1994 (see the cumulative cost estimates in chapter 6). Avoiding the costs of insufficient countercyclical policy in the form of wealth forgone during the mid-1990s could have done just as much for Japanese economic welfare as paying off the total public debt would. If, as McKinsey & Company (1996) and Alexander (1997) argue, the return on capital is much lower than assumed here, the benefits of the Debt Fairy's replacement are lower still. Whatever the rate of return of Japanese capital, this comparison is overly generous to the benefits of debt reduction, because not even fiscal responsibility's strongest advocates in Japan in the 1990s propose anything more than a measured reduction in the debt level, if not just stabilization; the magnitude of the benefits of shifting capital from the public into the private sector declines one for one with the size of that substitution, so the actual benefit of any debt reduction policy would be much lower.

Furthermore, this parable is, by construction, the source of an *upper-bound* estimate on the benefits of public-debt reduction. To the extent that the marginal productivity of capital declines as the stock of capital increases (something that the Japanese experience of the 1980s would certainly seem to illustrate), or that at least some portion of government expenditure went to productive uses that earned returns similar to those on private investment, or that it was interest-sensitive consumption rather than investment that was crowded out—all of which are likely to have held to some degree in Japan or any other economy—the quantitative benefits of replacing government debt with private investment would be lower still. So on any reasonable reading of the data, the long-run cost to output of rolling over total gross Japanese public debt is smaller than that incurred by allowing subpotential growth for even a few years in the 1990s—and the direct cost to the economy of incrementally increasing the public debt by a few percent of GDP to stimulate growth is indeed negligible.

Yet the Japanese public sector appears to need a greater share of national income in the future, not a lower one. Japan is aging, and current

Table 3.2 Summary of expected pension burden

	Pension balance		Dependancy ratio		Pension expenditure	
	2020	2030	2020	2030	2020	2030
Australia	−2.9	−3.8	25.1	33.0	2.9	3.8
Austria	−4.5	−6.8	32.6	44.0	12.1	14.4
Belgium	−5.4	−8.6	31.9	41.1	10.7	13.9
Canada	−2.8	−4.3	28.4	39.1	6.9	9.0
France	−3.9	−5.8	32.3	39.1	11.6	13.5
Germany	−4.8	−9.1	35.4	49.2	12.3	16.5
Italy	−2.1	−7.1	37.5	48.3	15.3	20.3
Netherlands	−2.6	−5.4	33.9	45.1	11.2	12.1
Spain	−3.6	−6.3	30.7	41.0	11.3	14.1
Sweden	−6.2	−7.2	35.6	39.4	13.9	15.0
United Kingdom	−1.1	−1.5	31.2	38.7	5.1	5.5
United States	−0.9	−2.3	27.6	36.8	5.2	6.6
Japan	−5.6	−6.6	43.0	44.5	12.4	13.4

Source: OECD (1997d).

social security surpluses will not be sufficient to pay for today's middle-aged to receive the same benefits that their parents now receive upon retirement. This reality goes without question. Recognizing that retiree/ worker dependency ratios will rise throughout the OECD and especially in Japan (see table 3.2) is not the same thing, however, as putting a number on the problem. Clearly, despite the well-known demographic trend in Japan, interest rates (even real interest rates) remain lower there than elsewhere in the industrialized world. Generational accounting schemes, following the work of Auerbach and Kotlikoff (1987), have been designed to give quantitative estimates of what would be required of today's tax-payers to restore generational equity. The conclusion of the most recent study is that Japan's demographic trend is so substantial that "eliminating official debt would have a minor impact on the Japanese imbalance" (Kotlikoff and Liebfritz 1997, 15).[24]

In Japan, as in all the OECD countries, if no further demographic change took place, 75-80 percent of the current social security imbalance would be removed. This would swamp the influence of any contemporary debt position.[25] If a society truly wishes to rectify its generational inequities with regard to lifetime net social security benefits, it must take on the problem directly. The society can decrease the dependency ratio by allow-

---

24. This again refers to the *entire* Japanese debt, as in the Debt Fairy parable. See also Takayama, Kitamura, and Yoshida (1998) from the same multiauthor NBER research project.

25. "The complete lack of any consistent relationship between nations' generational imbalances and their deficit or debt positions is not surprising given that, from a theoretical perspective, there is no intrinsic connection between the two measures" (Kotlikoff and Liebfritz 1997, 11).

ing immigration, increasing fertility, or, most promisingly for Japan, increasing female labor-force participation. Countries can also reduce benefits and/or raise the retirement age. Any short-run finite increase in government debt, which therefore does not involve a long-run commitment to expanded social security benefits, will not affect this problem. Individuals who wish to protect their own children can, of course, simply leave bequests sufficient to make up for the intergenerational transfers that the social security system gives them. Because Japanese (or for that matter OECD) citizens are not voluntarily making this decision in large numbers, democratic consent would be needed to impose such a move.

An analogy between the Japanese economy and a rice paddy puts the long and short of fiscal policy in perspective. Japanese policymakers, the farmers, have received word that, barring major change in human behavior, global warming is coming in 30 years. When temperatures rise and the water table sinks, the farmers will have to shift a lot of water from other uses if they want to keep growing rice. Meanwhile, a drought has hit this year, independently of the long-run trend. Clearly, the farmers should use the water held in the town reservoir to save this year's rice crop. Holding on to that small store of water for global warming 30 years hence will make no real difference to the problem and would sacrifice this year's crop as well. Similarly, the aging trend in Japan is very real, but withholding the money from the appropriate policies to respond to today's crises only harms the Japanese economy today without doing anything to truly prepare it for its future burdens. It is a false trade-off.

The sustainability of the outstanding level of Japanese government debt, the limited direct cost of its crowding-out investment, and its lack of relevance for the problem of aging in Japan all depend upon the assumption that debt will not grow explosively. Some discussions of government spending in Japan, however, seem to take it for granted that debt accumulation is a slippery slope—if Japan does not reverse its deficit spending in the 1990s, it will open the floodgates. Even though most of the deficits incurred in the 1990s were the result of the economic downturn and not discretionary fiscal expansion (as established in chapter 2), is such a spiraling path of deficits likely to occur in the future? Clearly, those who supported Prime Minister Ryutaro Hashimoto in passing the original law that required deficit reduction by 2003 felt that a long-run commitment was necessary. Japan was not alone in such legal efforts to contain public spending in the 1990s, which may indeed have been part of the impetus. A long literature in economics, going back to the work of Buchanan and Tullock (1965), provides apparent intellectual justification for such fears of government's tendency to grow if unchecked. Finally, the late 1970s and early 1980s in Japan have been seen by some as an immediate historical example of the difficulties in bringing rising budget deficits under control.

Despite this generalized perception, the vision of public-debt accumulation as an explosive process is not supported by the evidence, either in general or with regard to Japan in particular. Institutionally, budget deficits are most likely to rise where there is no centralized coordinator of the budget process, such as the Appropriations Committee in the US Congress (see Schick 1996); they are also more likely to be uncontrolled when a weak or multiparty coalition holds legislative control (see Alesina and Perotti 1995, 1996). In both cases, the impetus for expansion is the same—the need for extensive logrolling and side payments to get any fundamental legislation passed. If the budget process is properly designed and majority party discipline is strong, the tendency to logroll is diminished.

In Japan, the Ministry of Finance serves the coordinating role similar to that of the Appropriations Committee, and the inability of Diet members to amend the General Budget without calling a "no confidence" vote further enforces discipline (see chapter 2). While the LDP in Japan is often referred to as a coalition of factions, it would have to go a long way to reach the levels of intracoalition bargaining and free riding of the true multiparty governments in, for example, Belgium and Italy—countries where lack of government discipline truly did result in accelerating growth of government deficits. Moreover, fiscal laxity generally tends to be politically popular only if the monetary authority is prepared to accommodate the deficits, that is, print money and cause inflation to cover the mounting bills; if rising deficits require significant interest rate increases, or the amount of redistribution involved in the inflation tax becomes so high as to be visible and publicly troubling, deficit spending incurs political costs. This is why the governments of Belgium and Italy were able to significantly reduce their debt levels (albeit from very high starting points) by joining the European exchange rate mechanism. The Bank of Japan provided this type of hard constraint while under the direction of the Ministry of Finance, and its move to independence will only strengthen its ability to hold the line.[26]

Historical precedent as well as institutional structure would seem to justify confidence in Japanese policymakers' ability to restrain future debt accumulation, even if, as I argue they should, they do engage in deficit spending now. Figure 3.6, which shows the time path of Japanese government deficits since 1983, demonstrates how a combination of conscious choice and business cycle swings moved deficits up and down. No institutional change took place within the Japanese government, nor does the timing of the swing fit with the one time that the LDP lost a majority in the Diet. Yet the Japanese government decreased deficits, then ran surpluses, and then fell back into deficit again. There is no suggestion of a correlation of deficit spending with political weakness. The Japanese budget consoli-

---

26. See Ueda (1993) and Cargill, Hutchison, and Ito (1997) for historical analyses of Bank of Japan monetary policies.

dation through the 1980s was achieved slowly, through gradual tightening toward "zero-ceilings" on ministry budget increase requests and through tax revenues increased by bracket creep. Meanwhile, nominal expenditures were eroded by inflation (see Schick 1996, 18-21; Asako, Ito, and Sakamoto 1991).[27] As in the United States in 1998, unexpectedly high growth and tax revenues were the final push to achieving budget balance in 1988 and 1989.[28]

In fact, the general course of Japanese debt and deficits is similar to that of the United States and many other OECD countries, in that it was significantly influenced by variation in the rate of economic growth (that is, cyclical factors), it rose and fell in long slow-moving (not explosive) trends, and, when debt reduction was desired, deficits did eventually decline. Behavior also consistent across Japan, the United States, and post-Maastricht Western Europe was that announcements of budget targets and rules were never strictly met but were good indicators of an ongoing desire to make progress toward greater fiscal restraint.[29] Finally, in keeping with the earlier discussions in this section, none of the OECD countries that experienced multiyear rises in debt prior to reversing the trend— not the 1980s United States, Italy, or even Belgium—suffered calamitous blows to national economic well-being. Deficit spending of explicitly limited size and duration, as advocated for Japan in chapter 5, would incur even less cost.

The costs and benefits of fiscal-policy choices do not end with vague references to long-run concerns or principles of thrift. In the short run, the effectiveness of fiscal policy depends on the economic situation, particularly the distance of the economy from full employment and the readiness of savers and investors to respond to interest rates. Where savings are driven by precautionary motives, as in Japan today, the appropriate fiscal policy response is very different from when savings behavior is in response to long-run government plans. The long-run influence of today's fiscal expansions in any situation is far smaller and less constraining than is frequently assumed, so long as today's expenditures are not part of an explosive expansionary trend. As seen in the historical

---

27. It is worth observing that, as in the 1990s, an announced multiyear target for budget consolidation (a September 1979 commitment to end dependence on the issuance of deficit bonds by fiscal year 1984) was pushed back for several years, to 1990. This relaxation of a budget rule or target did not lead to calamity, and, in fact, the trend toward budgetary consolidation continued slowly but unabated. This is an important example to keep in mind if the Japanese government fully reverses itself on its legal budget balancing target (now for 2005), as recommended in chapter 5.

28. Asako, Ito, and Sakamoto (1991) identify surprise versus planned changes in Japanese government expenditures and revenues for the 1965-1970 period.

29. See Blinder (1987) for a discussion of US budget politics such as Gramm-Rudman-Hollings in the 1980s.

record, and as limited by institutional arrangements, such explosive trends are rare for industrial democracies. The long and the short of fiscal policy for Japan in the 1990s are encouraging about the benefits of a truly expansionary fiscal response to the current downturn. The concerns about fiscal policy usually invoked to argue against such a policy do not hold up to analysis either as relevant or of sufficient magnitude to matter.

4

Mounting Downside Risks: Financial and International

Until now, this book's argument has analyzed recent Japanese economic conditions, how those conditions differ from the economy's potential state of recovery, and what factors would be involved in moving it from the current low state of growth to the higher one. Policymaking, however, should be forward-looking. The question is not just where are we now and where *can* we be now, but what might happen in the future? In other words, it is important to assess the risks to the current situation, both positive and negative, in the absence of policy action. These opportunities or risks might be easily encouraged or prevented by current policy, or they might require a different policy stance, but they should be taken into account either way. As will be discussed, there do not appear to be any developments on the horizon likely to bail out the Japanese economy from its current situation without policy action. In fact, the balance of opportunities and risks buttresses the need for decisive policy action by Japanese policymakers, because without such action the situation may take a significant turn for the worse. In the summer of 1998, with the Japanese people and world financial markets looking for action after the LDP victory in the Diet's upper-house election, those risks may be realized on a timetable faster than the Japanese government's.

There are three primary sources of downside risk to the Japanese economic outlook. First, there could be a collapse of confidence on the part of Japanese households. As discussed in chapter 3, there is evidence of an accelerating rise in precautionary saving by Japanese citizens. This trend has taken a sharp turn for the worse now that the downturn is more likely to directly affect these citizens' fortunes because the fiscal-policy-caused contraction of 1997-98 has taken hold. Through 1996, despite the poor performance of the Japanese economy, such a collapse of confidence did not appear to be occurring; unsurprisingly, as the Japanese labor market situation has eroded, so has consumer confidence.

The second risk is that of outright financial crisis. While the Japanese banking system, and financial system more broadly, has weakened since the bubble burst in 1992, it is only since mid-1997 that the inefficiency that this weakness caused has begun to exert strong effects on the macroeconomy. Just as Japanese consumers lost confidence rapidly only when the risks to their employment and income became obvious, the decline in Japanese banks' ability to intermediate credit became relevant only when their own capital began to erode significantly. Also analogously to the situation with consumers, the lending of Japanese banks has the potential to decline rapidly should certain events come to pass. These two sources of risk have a great potential to reinforce each other, because consumers are also savers, and seeing lending and investment drop because of banking problems, they will seek to remove their money from the banking system; the banking system, in turn, stands most threatened should deposits be withdrawn from it in large numbers.

The third source of downside risk to the Japanese economic outlook comes from the international front. Even though the current situation in Japan is largely caused by domestic factors and policy choices, it has significant effects on the economies in its region and the rest of the world. Moreover, these effects can feed back directly into the functioning of the Japanese economy itself. The most obvious and direct sources of feedback are from the collapse of demand in its Asian neighbors and the rising pressures for trade protectionism in the United States and other countries that have seen their current account deficits rise with the Asian crisis (and Japanese net exports). Still more dangerous, however, is the possibility that these events, or the risks to consumer confidence and Japanese banks in combination with them, would prompt large-scale capital flight from Japan. As will be discussed below, this is a far from unlikely scenario, and its implications would be far-reaching. Japan could find itself simultaneously facing a rapidly depreciating yen and a domestic financial crisis. The measures necessary to stabilize the yen could work contrary to those necessary to stabilize the financial system; if the need to inject liquidity into the financial system were emphasized, such policy could accelerate the yen's decline. In such a dilemma, little could be done to prevent some major further decline in Japanese and world economic growth.

These compounding risks are the reason that stabilization—of consumer confidence, of the financial system, and of the yen's purchasing power—should be the main concern of Japanese economic policy. Each of these can be stabilized, through a combination of fiscal, monetary, and financial measures, so long as the effort is begun before the risks begin to realize and then reinforce one another. It is in this regard that monetary policy and financial reform become almost as important as fiscal expansion in determining the performance of the Japanese economy. As a result, I take into account two significant implications for economic policy in chapter 5, which offers a program for Japanese economic recovery: measures to raise and anchor expectations regarding purchasing power take precedence over efforts at monetary expansion (such as yen depreciation) that might be destabilizing; financial reform must focus on giving the Japanese savers and international capital markets incentives to keep their money in, or return their money to, the private banking system. Japanese economic reforms to date, including the so-called "bridge bank" of uncertain purpose, aid only indirectly, at best, in restoring these incentives, and so risk too much in their effort to keep credit flowing.

What might seem prudent policy restraint or laissez-faire for the Japanese economic situation as it is in 1998 becomes imprudent when the risks to the Japanese economy are properly assessed. Prudence in the manner of policymaking is no substitute for risk minimization in practice. Sometimes, very active policy is the most responsible course open to policy makers if the downside risks are sufficiently great.

Confidence Is the Key

Most people's as well as most economists' intuition tells them that economic growth has something of a self-fulfilling quality to it. If I believe that the economy will grow, whether I am an individual or a business CEO, I will be more likely to invest and to spend, so long as I believe that my belief is shared by others. The opposite holds if I believe that others are unlikely to spend and invest (this is the more general statement of what drives the "paradox of thrift" discussed in chapter 3). Investment would appear particularly susceptible to such "animal spirits" because it involves planning for the future based on profit expectations. A project that might prove profitable when demand is rising might fail to be so when stagnation sets in, even if the project itself is unchanged.

This intuition underlies a great number of the analyses of economic development—economies that make the leap to growth usually do so when a sufficient number of businesses and households in the economy make the jump together. Without trust or a critical mass of mutually reinforcing contracts and expectations, no one individual or firm can afford to make the move. Self-fulfilling shifts in economic confidence also underlie the idea of market panics, that is, macroeconomic situations that on some reasonable set of underlying factors ("fundamentals") are viable, but are far from viable when capital is broadly withdrawn and everyone else needs to withdraw capital or lose their stake.[1] If panic is the driving cause of switches between good and bad economic states, the restoration of confidence becomes all important; if confidence is lost, it takes a great deal of visible economic success to bring the economy out of its perception-driven decline.

These intuitions are very much the stuff of reality. Historically, the worst macroeconomic collapses have occurred in the aftermath of financial crises, especially the withdrawal of funds from banks.[2] Given the role of financial intermediaries, particularly banks, in bringing expectations to fruition (e.g., extending loans for investment, safekeeping deposits, providing credit in times of temporary distress), this pattern is broadly consistent with the importance of confidence in determining macroeconomic fluctuations.[3] Hamilton (1989, 1990) and other researchers following his work have documented that time-series data on the United States support the picture that the economy fluctuates between states of low and high growth (rather than growth that smoothly varies over time). Economic theory has caught up with this historical pattern and deep-seated intuition in recent years and spelled out the financial mechanisms through which such switches between good and bad states of the economy arise. Bernanke and Gertler (1989) and Kiyotaki and Moore (1997) provide models where realistic imperfections in credit markets can strongly reinforce and transmit asset-price movements (which are presumed to be driven by expectations).

Azariadis and Smith (1998) develop a particularly persuasive model wherein the sound assumptions that (1) capital investments require intermediated financing[4] and (2) adverse selection exists[5] are sufficient to generate an economy characterized by switches between high and low levels of growth. In their model, if people expect too low a return on investment, savers transfer money out of the banking system and into lower-yielding assets such as cash (note here the shades of the liquidity trap described in chapter 3, which provokes credit rationing and a drop in investment

---

1. See Sachs (1997) and Stiglitz (1998) for characterizations of the Asian financial crisis (outside of Japan) in just these terms.

2. See Friedman and Schwartz (1963) for a history explaining most of the pre-Second World War economic fluctuations in the United States in terms of such financial breakdowns. Mishkin (1994) gives additional examples.

3. Of course, financial firms have effects on the economy directly as well as through confidence, and their disruption has other effects, which I discuss in the following section.

4. That is, bank loans rather than the issuance of securities, which is true for most investment even in the United States, let alone in Japan, where banks play a much larger role (see Jenkinson and Mayer 1992).

5. Which means that because lenders cannot always tell who the good borrowers are, movements in interest rates can attract too many of the poor risks, so lenders sometimes lend less than they could given outstanding demand.

and aggregate demand. Alternatively, if enough savers are convinced that the future returns on investments in the economy are high, a rise in interest rates can be self-fulfilling and bring higher growth. Evans, Hankapohia, and Romer (1998) produce a similar model of an economy with inherent fluctuations between high and low growth states that coincide with swings in growth expectations. They work from the equally realistic assumptions of imperfect competition (due to start-up costs for firms) and complementary demand for capital goods (e.g., computers increase demand for printers and telephone networks).

From a policymaker's perspective, the combination of historical and theoretical results means that household confidence has to be taken seriously. It is not simply a random variable, switching with whim and fad and without regard to the economic environment. The rational-expectation foundations of the models discussed here and the consistent historical pattern of factors that tend to lead to financial panics and bank runs (discussed below) strongly suggest that most declines in confidence are driven by actual economic events, even if random shifts in confidence cannot be ruled out. Furthermore, such shifts in confidence are not just matters of opinion or politics that can be ignored while economic policy concerns itself with the "long-run fundamentals"—economic confidence is itself a fundamental that can become self-fulfilling. Policymakers who allow slow growth to persist (as, I argue, Japanese policymakers have done in 1994-98) might find that the economy gets locked into that stagnant or declining state. There may not always be a continuum of choices about economic performance—instead, there may sometimes be a choice between keeping the economy in a high-growth or a low-growth equilibrium. The perception of there being smooth trade-offs and gradual variations in macroeconomic performance assumes that local, linear deviations around a steady state can occur without dislodging the economy from that state. This is a useful assumption for both modeling and policymaking in normal times, but the assumption need not always hold.[6]

In 1997-98, the Japanese economy appears to be making just such a switch from downturn in a high-growth state to an ongoing low-growth state. The key was the decline in confidence among Japanese citizens and businesses. As seen in table 2.6, after 1996, economic forecasts had caught up with the slow-growth reality rather than being surprised by it. The combination of strong growth in 1996 because of the 1995 fiscal-stimulus package and the sharp reversal that succeeded it because of the

---

6. As Dornbusch (1991) put it when discussing a related gap between historical instances where economic shocks transmitted widely across borders and our usual small estimates of cross-border economic linkages, "A highly synchronized decline in world demand is not studied with macroeconomic models because we only feed them small sympathetic shocks; we do not feed them crisis scenarios in which everybody says, 'Oh, no, the world is going down, bad idea to invest today'."

Figure 4.1   Consumer Sentiment Index, 1984-98

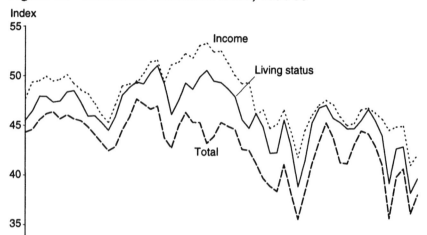

Note: Total index is seasonally adjusted, others are not seasonally adjusted.
Source: Consumer Sentiment Index, Economic Planning Agency.

contractionary fiscal policy of 1996 and 1997 (see chapter 2) seems to have
brought about the reassessment. Figure 4.1 shows the Japanese Consumer
Sentiment Index, which remained at levels comparable to the mid-1980s
(a time of normal, near-potential growth) through 1992-1993, and which
almost returned to those levels in late 1995 and 1996. With the 1997
contraction, confidence has plummeted and seems to be varying around
a new level that is lower than that held throughout the previous 15 years.[7]

Figure 4.2 plots the ratio of job openings and new jobs offered to the
number of applicants, and again the 1997-1998 figures are beginning to
drop for the first time below those of the early 1980s. While job openings
is an actual measured number, not directly a question of consumers'
expectations, an increased likelihood that you, your child, or someone
you know will be unable to find a job should they enter the labor force
or be laid off is one of the most visceral indicators for average citizens
of the state of the economy. Figure 4.3 plots the annual and then monthly
unemployment levels for new graduates. The number of unemployed
new graduates soared as the economy sank in 1998. Here, the effect is
on the long-term expectations of young people—if they have trouble

---

7. There is insufficient data (because of the length of time involved) to verify this claim
with econometric methods.

Figure 4.2　Job openings ratio, 1984–98

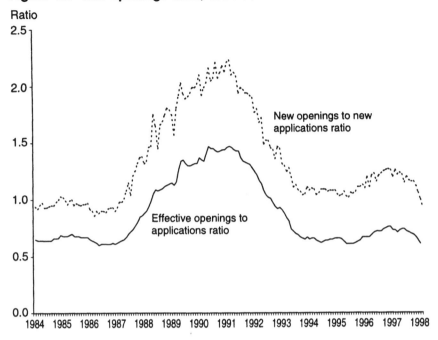

Source: Ministry of Labor, Job Offers and Applicants.

Figure 4.3　Unemployment of new graduates

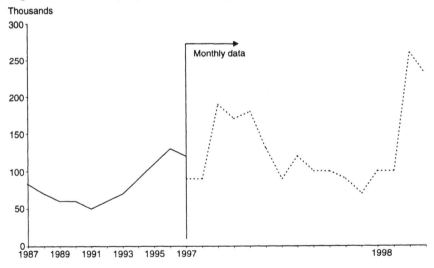

Source: Management and Coordination Agency, Labor Force Statistics.

getting a first job, or they know people who did not get to enter the labor force, they must face the realistic possibility of being shut out of work completely for long periods.[8] This growing sense of insecurity is based on low expectations for their own and the Japanese economy's income growth, which, in turn, is based on the extended stagnation of the Japanese economy. This insecurity, consistent with the rise in precautionary saving documented in figures 3.4 and 3.5, has potentially disastrous interactions with the financial system, to which I now turn.

The Risk of Financial Crisis

The purpose of financial markets is to accumulate and evaluate information about investment opportunities. Is a proposed investment a worthwhile project? Does that investment continue to pay as expected when implemented under changing conditions? How do the changing fortunes of that investment relate to changes in other investments? Only when these questions are properly answered will capital (a society's accumulated savings) be efficiently allocated to the best projects. The job of a financial intermediary is to answer these questions, that is, to evaluate, to monitor, and to assess risk. These are not easy tasks. Information is imperfect. That is the economist's way of saying that not all information available is equally credible and free of bias and that not all information can be utilized at no cost or without judgment. In particular, information is asymmetric, meaning that the prospective borrower inherently has far better information about the project he or she proposes than the lender has when deciding whether or not to invest. This asymmetry causes two general problems to arise in capital markets: adverse selection and moral hazard. To cope with (but not remove) these problems, most financial transactions are conducted through financial intermediaries, because these firms are expert at screening and monitoring risks. Capital is usually invested by financial intermediaries in the form of (bank) loans because only such loans allow lenders to take collateral, maintain an ongoing relationship with the borrower to monitor performance, and threaten to cut off credit for nonperformance.[9]

A financial crisis occurs when there is a major disruption in the provision of these financial intermediary services to an economy, either because

---

8. These periods could perhaps be until an economy runs in a sufficiently good high-growth state for long enough to drag those potential workers back into employment, as arguably seen in the United States in the mid-1990s.

9. Another reason for the predominance of lending as the form of corporate financing is the inability of all but the most well established and large firms to issue securities and go to capital markets directly. This also reflects the adverse selection aspects of asymmetric information (see Myers and Majluf 1984).

something has happened to a significant number of the intermediaries or because economic conditions have caused such an increase in the adverse selection and moral hazard problems that the provision of capital to good investment projects declines significantly. A financial crisis matters for macroeconomic performance because there is no readily available or close substitute for these intermediation services, either for a specific borrower who loses access to the lender that knows him or her, or for large parts of the nonfinancial sectors of the economy that, in general, cannot go directly to securities markets.[10] Bernanke (1983) shows that just such a widespread loss of banking services was a primary reason that the stock market crash and downturn of 1929 became the Great Depression in the United States. Small and medium-sized businesses are hit in particular by a loss of intermediation because their flow of liquidity is dependent upon the information they make privately available to their lending bank. To the extent that such businesses are a source of economic innovation and growth, this inefficiency is destructive over the long run beyond the businesses lost.

In the economy as a whole, therefore, a contraction in bank lending lowers both aggregate demand and aggregate supply, the latter because forgone or investment opportunities that are prematurely called in lower productive capacity. Investment demand will drop because it will be more expensive for nonfinancial firms to get credit, as they must either compete to establish a new relationship with the few remaining banks, or they must turn to alternative sources of credit that are not as well suited to their needs. If a flood of passed-up investment projects are submitted to remaining lenders, it becomes more difficult to distinguish the promising from the unduly risky (adverse selection), and remaining lenders will further cut back credit availability. Meanwhile, the decline in lending perpetuates itself, because every loan not rolled over harms a nonfinancial firm, whose leverage rises and collateral falls as the downturn continues.

Once these intermediation services are withdrawn, there is no policy response that can quickly replace them. Simple injection of liquidity by the central bank, while seeking to maintain total lending, is insufficient to restore efficiency and economic growth, because private information and specialized skills have been lost "because of the relationship-specific capital each [lender] has accumulated, reserves at one bank are an imperfect substitute for reserves at another" (Summers 1991, 149). This is why

---

10. It is possible for instances of extreme financial *volatility* to arise that do not occasion such crises or loss of intermediation services (e.g., the 1987 US stock market crash). It is also possible for an economy's capital markets to operate inefficiently for an extended period because of a rise in information problems or institutional failings without that causing a sharp crisis, either, as one could argue was the case in east Asia prior to the summer 1998 crisis (see Goldstein 1998). Mishkin (1994) discusses some of these definitions of financial fragility versus crisis.

government lending programs, or active use of a "bridge bank," are palliatives at best. The intermediation skills and the specific knowledge of these substitute lenders are inferior to those of the original private banks. Such public lending banks also have less incentive to properly monitor risk, because their motive is to maximize lending not make a profit. This in turn engenders risk taking by borrowers beyond an efficient level, given easing credit standards.

The loss of financial intermediation can occur through many channels. An increase in regulatory scrutiny can lead to a contraction in lending either through the closure of banks or through forcing those banks still open to increase their reserves and write off more of their outstanding loans. Even when the supervisory authorities are simply bringing the banks up to actuarial fairness, this can decrease the overall supply of loans. On the whole, as advocated in chapter 5, such fair supervision benefits the public because it insures these banks through deposit insurance; insolvent banks or banks with very low net worth have an incentive to engage in excessive and excessively risky lending, because they have little or nothing to lose but will share fully in the benefits if their gambles pay off. Thus, although tightening supervision also tightens lending conditions in the short run, on net it helps by preventing moral hazard on the part of insolvent banks and by preventing adverse selection whereby only those projects willing to pay high interest rates (something that many of the better projects should not and will not pay) continue to get credit. The message is that a smaller provision of proper intermediation is better than improperly supervised intermediation, although once you have to choose between those two there will be a contraction in credit sooner or later.

Banks can also cut down on lending because of a "capital crunch," that is, a decline in the value of their own equity.[11] In the current environment, where all industrial-country banks are supposed to maintain capital sufficient for the Bank for International Settlements (BIS) Basle Capital Accords (i.e., 8 percent of their outstanding assets), there is a clear standard below which banks are to cut back their lending if they do not have sufficient capital. A stock market decline will usually directly lead to a drop in the value of a bank's equity; in economies such as Japan's, where banks own stock in other nonfinancial firms, the decline in stock prices erodes that component of their capital as well. As equity and, therefore, net worth decline, and all banks suffer this at the same time, it becomes more difficult for banks to raise new capital by issuing equity or other securities, and interbank lending obviously contracts. Efforts to promote consolidation in the banking industry through mergers might prove necessary, but

---

11. Bernanke and Lown (1991) analyze this situation in the United States in 1990-91, arguing that lending did drop significantly with a decline in bank capital at that time.

they will not restore capital ratios if they occur only after the solvent banks see their capital ratios declining. There certainly is little capital left over (and less reason) for such good banks to acquire other insolvent banks, absent direct government injection of funds.

A sharp fall in the supply of loanable funds available to banks, that is, deposits, is the most dangerous channel through which financial intermediation can be withdrawn. In such a situation, banks have to build up their reserves and cut back on their lending immediately, which induces a rise in interest rates because liquidity is sharply decreased. In fact, a trend toward taking money out of the banking system is called disintermediation, because it deprives the financial intermediaries of the supplies that they need to work. In its worst form, disintermediation becomes a bank panic. Bank panics arise for three rational reasons: (1) there is a true advantage to being first in line to get one's money out before the bank runs out of liquid assets (which even in solid banks are only a fraction of the liquid deposit liabilities, because banks are lending long); (2) there is poor information available to the depositors about which banks are solvent and which are not, so runs on one bank can be treated as signals about the health of others; and (3), like confidence with regard to economic growth discussed previously, bank runs can be self-fulfilling.

Ideally, government deposit insurance will prevent bank runs because it removes the advantage of being first in line and makes information on specific banks irrelevant to the depositor.[12] The problem is that the line where deposit insurance guarantees is drawn can never be made completely credible. On the one hand, if enough banks go broke at once, the government is tempted to partially renege on the guarantee and perhaps assess the depositors a charge or refund them only up to less than the announced amount. This is because the government does not expect to have to engage in so widespread a payoff on another occasion (at least not soon), and the faith and credit of the guarantee has already failed to prevent either the run or was undercut by poor supervision, so that the government does not really have a reputation to lose in this area.

On the other hand, if a large share of deposits, such as large corporations' cash accounts or foreigners' holdings, are not covered by deposit insurance, failure to extend deposit insurance to these accounts can result in a breakdown of the payment system, and so people will not believe that these will not be insured in the event of crisis. Meanwhile, the longer the financial system is left in a weakened state, with low net worth or insolvent banks, prior to either cleanup or a run, the more incentive the

---

12. Of course, this is precisely why there must be strict bank supervision where deposit insurance exists, because the depositors themselves have no incentives to monitor the lending standards of the bank, whereas the insurer has the incentive to make sure that it does not incur unnecessary losses. Meanwhile, the bank has an incentive to gamble for high returns with the deposit-protected money because its losses are bounded from below at zero.

banks have to keep adding to the insurance burden by attracting deposits to engage in further high-risk lending (the moral hazard previously discussed). Of course, this would diminish the credibility of the deposit guarantee because the higher the bill due, the more that complete repayment is doubtful.

Now, again, it is necessary to establish the relevance of all this for Japan in the late 1990s. Japan remains a bank-based financial system, compared to, say, the United States or the United Kingdom, so that even more of its corporate financing is intermediated through banks than is financed that way elsewhere. To the extent that Japanese banks are in long-term relationships with their borrowers and have shareholdings in them, it is harder for these borrowers to substitute a new lender or nonbank financing for their specific bank's services; such relationship lending also implies that the net worth of borrowers, their collateral, and their lenders' equity all decrease in tandem, making for a vicious spiral of declining liquidity. After years of "regulatory forbearance" in hopes that Japanese banks would be able to lend and grow their way out of their bad loan problems, the supervision of Japanese banks is correctly—albeit long after the problem worsened—being stepped up, with the expected contractionary effect on lending. The equity of Japanese banks has declined significantly, to a level well below the Basle accord 8 percent, while loans classified as "behind in payments" down to "nonrecoverable" total 77 trillion yen, or 15 percent of GDP (see Ito and Zzamosszegi 1998).[13]

Japanese savers have begun to lose faith in the private banking system, further decreasing the availability of liquid funds. As seen in figure 3.2, even M1 growth has slowed significantly since 1996, and, as shown in figure 3.3, a greater share of that is held in cash, meaning that bank deposits are stagnating at best while total savings are rising. Figure 4.4 plots the relative shares of various types of savings in total savings outstanding. It shows that more of the increase in Japanese savings is going to insurance funds and to the public Postal Savings system, which also contracts credit and raises its cost, because neither is a good substitute lender for borrowers who were dependent on banks. In fact, the share of savings held in the Postal Savings system has been rising steadily since the Japanese market first turned down in 1990, and this trend has been strengthened by the declining differential between the interest rate offered to savers on private-sector bank accounts and that offered by Postal Savings (see figure 4.5).

Since the government directly guarantees Postal Savings and (barring inflation) currency, the substitution away from bank deposits constitutes

---

13. Japanese banks also have unrealized gains on their books from their stock holdings in other firms, which are recorded at historical purchase value. In general, when the Nikkei stock index sinks below 15,000, banks move from unrealized gains to unrealized losses on this set of assets as well.

Figure 4.4   Types of savings as a share of total savings, 1980-98

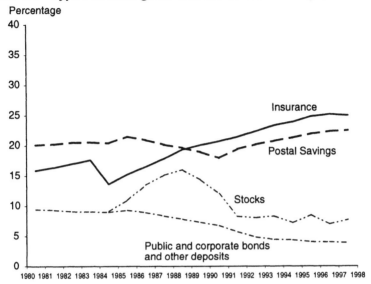

Note: Data on stocks are available from 1984.

Source: Economic Statistics Monthly, Bank of Japan, various issues.

Figure 4.5   Postal Savings interest rate differentials and share of total savings, 1984-97

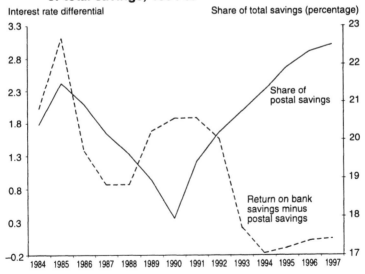

Note: Returns on one-year installment savings are compared.

Source: Economic Statistics Monthly, Bank of Japan, various issues.

a trend toward disintermediation by the Japanese public in the face of government deposit guarantees. The laissez-faire attitude toward accumulating bad loans by the government has logically eroded savers' confidence in the guarantee.[14] In addition, since the government has the ability to set the interest rate for Postal Savings (and control its growth more broadly), the Japanese government is effectively subsidizing this disintermediation (I return to this point in chapter 5). Add to this the rising capital flows abroad and the funds going into foreign banks (which inherently do not have Japanese deposit insurance coverage), and it is clear that savers believe that the risks of holding deposits in the Japanese banking system outweigh the perceived value of the guarantees. Again, these are mostly developments that either have accelerated in the past two years or have become dangerous because they have been allowed to persist for historically unprecedented lengths of time. Either way, they become self-reinforcing if left unchecked.

Even though a true financial crisis complete with a bank panic or sharp drop in banking services has not yet occurred, the availability of credit and the efficiency of financial intermediation in Japan have declined (see table 4.1). Figure 4.6 shows that the willingness of banks to lend to firms, as captured in the widely cited *Tankan* survey conducted by the Bank of Japan, has declined sharply since mid-1997. I argue that it was then that confidence began to turn and disintermediation became a factor[15]; in fact, from when the bubble burst until mid-1997, lending was readily available, according to historical standards on this measure, for those firms that wanted it. The last is a key point—until the 1997 contraction, the decline in investment came largely through an absence of demand for investment because firms had excess capacity and low net worth. The unavailability of credit reported by the *Tankan* survey should be interpreted as the decline in credit *supply* factors finally outpacing the drop in demand, for the reasons given above. This again is consistent with a transition from financial fragility to disintermediation and potential crisis.

Figure 4.7 tracks the issuance of corporate bonds and commercial paper, which should rise when borrowers are forced to substitute for bank loans; here, there is largely stability rather than trend change, which may be indicative of the simple unavailability of these alternatives to Japanese

---

14. When potential bank failures become spread throughout the economy, the value of deposit insurance diminishes inherently because people realize they will have to pay out with one hand what they receive in the other. Insurance is worthwhile when only some of the policyholders fall victim. This is yet another reason why slow response to financial weakness increases the likelihood of outright financial crisis.

15. This question on the business survey asks firms whether they believe lending conditions that they face are tight or not, and the score is the number of yes answers minus the number of no answers. This is done separately for small versus principal enterprises, given that principal (large) enterprises normally have more alternatives to bank loans.

Table 4.1 Private debt and interest burden, 1984-96

	Total debt outstanding (percentages of GDP)				Interest payment flow (percentages of GDP)			
	Private	Nonfinancial companies	Financial institutions	Households	Private	Nonfinancial companies	Financial institutions	Households
1984	488.5	175.9	251.6	61.0	34.0	8.9	21.4	3.7
1985	501.8	175.6	265.2	61.1	33.1	8.7	20.7	3.6
1986	527.9	174.6	290.5	62.8	32.5	8.2	20.8	3.6
1987	571.7	187.6	316.1	68.1	32.3	7.5	21.2	3.6
1988	594.5	191.3	332.2	71.0	33.0	7.4	22.0	3.5
1989	614.1	192.7	347.8	73.6	36.3	7.9	24.7	3.7
1990	625.0	198.9	350.2	75.9	42.1	10.1	27.7	4.3
1991	614.7	197.9	342.1	74.7	40.8	9.9	26.5	4.4
1992	612.0	194.6	344.8	72.6	34.6	8.3	22.3	4.0
1993	624.8	197.4	354.1	73.4	31.2	7.4	20.2	3.5
1994	633.6	198.3	360.2	75.1	28.1	6.5	18.4	3.3
1995	645.7	200.1	368.8	76.8	26.2	5.9	17.5	2.9
1996	638.5	195.9	368.2	74.4	22.7	4.8	15.4	2.5

Note: Private category excludes nonprofit institutions.
Source: Economic Planning Agency of Japan, Annual Report on the National Account.

**Figure 4.6 Business survey (*Tankan*), lending attitude of financial
institutions, 1990-98**

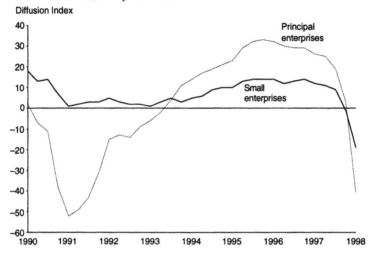

Notes: Principal enterprises include firms with capital greater than 1 billion yen. Negative
indicates "tight" credit conditions.

Source: Economic Statistics Monthly, various issues, Bank of Japan; BOJ web page,
http://www.boj.or.jp.

**Figure 4.7 Corporate bond and commercial paper issuance,
1984-97**

Source: Bank of Japan, *Economic Statistics Monthly* (various issues).

Figure 4.8 Risk spread, 1985-97

Percentages

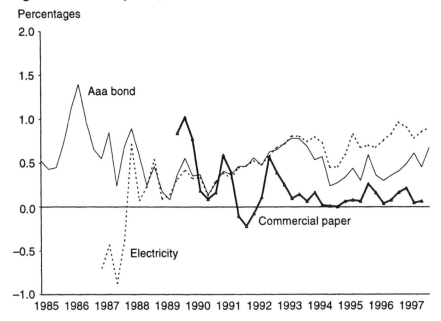

Note: Risk premium is defined as (corporate bond-rated)) Aaa yield (12-year) or electricity corporate bond yield (longest) minus JGB yield (10-year), and commercial paper yield (3-month) minus JGB yield (3-month).

Source: Bank of Japan, *Economic Statistics Monthly*, various issues.

firms, even when desired.[16] The movement of bond risk spreads between private and government borrowers, graphed in figure 4.8, supports such a reconciliation of figures 4.6 and 4.7. In a time of credit contraction, the interest rate spread should widen between low- and high-quality borrowers, because lenders will be more suspicious of those who want to borrow at high interest rates. We can see occasionally interrupted but ongoing rises in both the Aaa-Japanese government bond and the electricity-Japanese government bond spreads since 1994-95; the commercial paper spread has varied a great deal less in the 1990s and remained negligible, which is consistent with the interpretation that only the very best borrowers can access commercial paper in Japan and that it has not become a major alternative source of capital.[17]

---

16. More anecdotal recent data, however, do indicate a sharp rise in commercial paper issuance as those nonfinancial firms that can go directly to credit markets do so.

17. Bond-rate data on lower-quality Japanese borrowers are difficult to come by because so few firms get access to Japanese credit markets without bank intermediation—which again stresses the importance of this channel. Friedman and Kuttner (1993, 1994) discuss

Figure 4.9 Business survey (*Tankan*), financial position, 1983-97

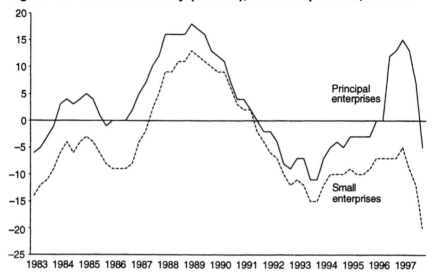

Note: Negative indicates financially difficult conditions.

Source: Economic Statistics Monthly, various issues, Bank of Japan.

This recent credit crunch has been associated with real macroeconomic effects. Unsurprisingly, the financial position of businesses has declined sharply since the fiscal contraction of 1997 (according to the *Tankan* survey; see figure 4.9). More tellingly, small enterprises, which are more dependent on bank-intermediated lending, remained in the negative "financially difficult" position during the upswing of 1995-96, while large principal enterprises with access to other forms of credit were able to take financial advantage of the situation.[18] The gap between principal and small enterprises' financial positions widened at this time, and even as principal enterprises' positions have declined, the gap has remained wide, again consistent with a credit crunch (as opposed to the narrower gap seen through the 1990s up until mid-1996). Figure 4.10 plots the liquidity ratio of firms in the same survey and shows less difference. For both large and small firms, however, liquidity was actually rising through mid-1994, which could go with a voluntary cutback in investment. The decline in liquidity has been strong since then. Finally, figure 4.11 displays the total

---

risk spreads and the reasons for their predictive powers in general terms, with particular attention to the commercial paper spread.

18. This may also be attributable, in part, to the fact that net exports were strong in 1996-97, and fewer small firms tend to be export oriented. This survey question, however, measures financial difficulty, a function of liquidity, which is correlated positively but imperfectly with sales.

Figure 4.10 Business survey (*Tankan*), liquidity ratio in manufacturing, 1984-97

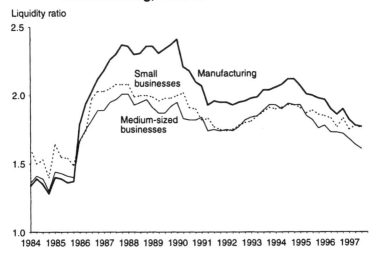

Note: Liquidity ratio = (quarter-end balance of cash and deposits + quarter-end balance of securities) / monthly average sales during the fiscal year to which the quarter-end figures belong. Sales is the annual projection when the quarter-end figures were finalized.

Source: Bank of Japan, *Economic Statistics Annual*, various issues.

Figure 4.11 The number of bankruptcies, 1984-98

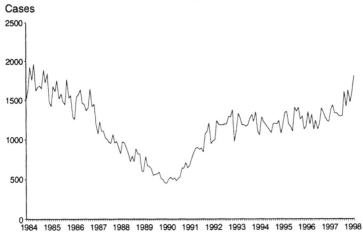

Source: Tokyo Shoko Research.

number of bankruptcies in Japan per month, a number that had remained within historical norms until mid-1996 despite press attention suggesting otherwise. This again should be associated with the financial fragility that is giving way to a more serious credit contraction, because the Japanese relationship banking system is meant traditionally to help distressed firms work through temporary illiquidity and avoid bankruptcy, so the rise in bankruptcy must stem from a decline in this kind of traditional bridge lending.[19]

In summary, the nature of the financial problem in Japan has changed in the past year, from one of financial fragility, where investment demand was low and banks were engaged in risky lending, to one of credit contraction, where banks are ceasing to lend in response to declining equity, tougher regulatory supervision, and decreased availability of loanable funds.[20] The effect of this has been to increase the inefficiencies of credit allocation, which has particularly harmed small borrowers, and to increase the amount of macroeconomic contraction attributable to financial rather than broader aggregate demand or fiscal factors. The risk to the Japanese economy is that this could turn into outright financial crisis if the trend toward disintermediation were to lead to a rapid removal of deposits from the private banking system. That would lead to a contraction in bank lending much greater than seen so far and to a large decline in investment and aggregate demand as a result. This development would interact with and reinforce the risks from a collapse of economic confidence, a risk that was already rising in the aftermath of the fiscal policy and growth reversal of 1996.

How likely is a true financial crisis? One would hope that it need not be all that likely for the Japanese government to want to take preemptive steps. Some of these are outlined in chapter 5, but the emphasis should be on changing the incentives for savers to put money back into the private banking sector and for that banking system to be *quickly* reconstituted. The emphasis of policy should not be on maintaining the flow of credit to borrowers, despite the real short-run macroeconomic costs of further lending declines, because that could lengthen the financial reform process and do nothing to stem disintermediation and will at best be an inferior substitute to private-bank lending. If the disintermediation can be reversed, however, the worst of the credit contraction will be reversed as well, and the longer-term stability assured.

In addition, it is mistaken to believe that monetary policy can easily reverse the effects of a financial crisis, particularly a bank panic, once it

---

19. See Hoshi, Kashyap, and Scharfstein (1993) for a discussion of Japanese banks' relation to those borrowers in financial distress, both in theory and prior to the present period.

20. Working with data through 1995, Bordo, Ito, and Iwaisako (1997) decided that there was no financial crisis in Japan to that point precisely because there were no signs of a significant rise in the currency/deposit ratio or a flight to currency. As documented in this and the previous chapter, however, that situation has since changed for the worse.

has occurred. Meanwhile, monetary-policy efforts by the central bank to inject liquidity will not only be just a partial substitute for bank lending, as discussed above, but their stance and effectiveness will be difficult to assess. In a contraction of the money supply such as a bank run, if the central bank makes M1 grow, then M2 will likely decline and interest rates will vary, yet credit will remain scarce. There will be huge velocity shocks to the normal money multiplier relationships (see Volcker 1991, 176; Bernanke and Lown 1991, 237). In addition, if there is price stickiness in wage and product contracts near zero inflation, as discussed in chapter 1, then when the money supply shrinks the price level will remain stable, which means that real interest rates will skyrocket. There is good reason for the Japanese government to get out ahead of these dangerous trends, by restoring confidence through a combination of fiscal stimulus and financial reform. As I discuss in the next section, monetary expansion to respond to a financial crisis can have devastating side effects as well, especially if it must be large, imprecisely controlled, and, therefore, some-what destabilize expectations for the reasons discussed here.

Meanwhile, any explicit statements about the extent of deposit insur-ance made *after* the run has begun will be interpreted as a partial renege on the guarantee, because the current extent of protection is uncertain in people's minds and lack of quick response will be interpreted as a failure to stand by the complete guarantee.

The Risks of International Feedback

So far, I have only spoken of the risks to Japan from internal problems of confidence and financial fragility, but the Japanese economy finds itself in a fragile international context as well in 1998. The risks to Japan from abroad include diminished trade with and demand from its neighbors should the East Asian economies decline further in their crisis' aftermath. There are additional, more pressing, risks to the Japanese economy from abroad, however, that can directly amplify the effects of a financial crisis or a collapse of confidence at home. Most critically, there are dangers of capital flight from domestic Japanese sources that could send the yen hurtling downward and exacerbate the risk of a collapse in consumer confidence and of financial crisis. In addition, there is the serious prospect that a further rapid yen decline and capital outflow, leading inevitably to a rise in Japan's balance of payments surplus, could provoke a protec-tionist response, given the current political and economic climate in the United States, East Asia, and perhaps the European Union.

Neither of these risks are unlikely at present, and as the Japanese domestic situation worsens, absent policy action, their likelihood increases. If the yen falls rapidly in combination with a financial crisis in Japan—where each one is likely to provoke and then reinforce the other—Japan will perhaps be unable to stabilize the situation using its policy instruments alone. The monetary and fiscal policies most appropriate to restore confidence in the yen would be opposite to those needed to restore the Japanese financial system. Then, Japanese recovery would require coordinated macroeconomic policies in the G-7. Such coordination is a difficult and uncertain process, and one likely to wait until after the crisis was strongly felt abroad. That is why monetary stabilization and stimulation of growth should be undertaken by Japanese policymakers before such a crisis occurs.

Japan could see the exact opposite of the spiral that preceded the Asian financial crisis in 1997. A persistent current account surplus and domestic lack of liquidity could produce an investment bust: higher interest rates (nominal and real) abroad than at home attract capital away from domestic uses. The outflow of capital draws down asset prices in Japan, further weakening companies' net worth and collateral and increasing the number of bad loans. More bad loans make the banks less willing to lend, decreasing liquidity.

Precautionary savings rise and increase the trade surplus. This flight-driven credit contraction cycle—even in the absence of the factors discussed in the previous section—would be sufficient to erode confidence and financial stability and repeat itself indefinitely. With the fragile state of the Japanese financial system and investor confidence, it could accelerate rapidly, being amplified either at the capital flight or the credit contraction stage of the process.

The effects of such a cycle would not only be financial, but would have significant effects on trade and trade politics. The Japanese market absorbs 19 percent or more of the exports of China, South Korea, Indonesia, Thailand, and the Philippines, as well as 13 percent of Taiwan's, and Malaysia's (see Noland, Liu, Robinson, and Wang 1998). Japan's depreciation would limit imports from those countries that must export to restore their living standards, even though Japan does not compete with them directly for export markets. As the Japanese current account surplus widens, trade frictions with the United States and other Japanese trading partners would increase, especially in the current context where the United States, the "consumer of last resort," is already taking in what Congress perceives to be more than its fair share from these other Asian economies.[21] With a lag of two years, every 1 percent decline in the trade-weighted yen

---

21. And the Congress is generally opposed to global efforts, having voted down fast track and slowed IMF funding in 1997-98.

Figure 4.12 Trade balance, 1984-98

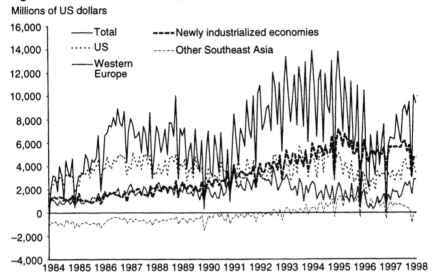

Millions of US dollars

Note: The numbers from March 1996 are calculated from yen using the yen/dollar spot exchange rate of the Tokyo interbank market (end of month).

Source: Ministry of Finance, *Trade Statistics Monthly.*

exchange rate raises the Japanese current account by $3 billion (and the US trade deficit by $1 billion) (see figure 4.12 for the rising Japanese trade surpluses).[22]

Even if the cycle of trade threat and response does not play out as it historically has, there is no question that economic effects can spread from large countries to small, prompting flights to safety (here, mostly US Treasury bills) from mobile capital everywhere, and, thus, further increasing the bilateral trade imbalances. It also should be remembered that, while flexible exchange rates in theory isolate one economy from another's policy mistakes, that process takes time and is not always smooth. The resort to trade restrictions and quotas can always be opted for instead. As Frenkel stated, "I think it is important that we include protectionism as one of the known dangers [of internationally transmitted

---

22. Noland, Robinson, and Wang (1998) argue that under plausible disaggregation of sectoral effects, the response of the US trade balance could be much larger. The yen historically shows a need to eventually return to fundamental values. This would lead to a subsequent sharp rise against the dollar, prompting a new round of adjustments (see Bergsten 1998 and Bergsten and Noland 1993 for examples of such "currency and trade" cycles).

Figure 4.13 Foreign direct investment, 1984-98

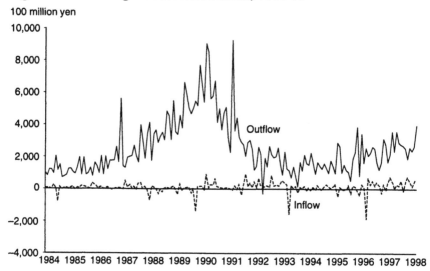

100 million yen

Note: The numbers from 1984 to 1995 are calculated from the dollar using the yen/dollar spot exchange rate of Tokyo interbank market (end of month).

Source: Bank of Japan, *Balance of Payment.*

crises] because extended protectionism has implications beyond just trade flows. It makes the difference between an inward and an outward orientation, and between open and closed markets" (Frenkel 1991, 124).

This type of protectionist cycle can arise out of sheer neglect by the Japanese government, even in the absence of conscious efforts to depreciate the yen, because capital outflows are driven by domestic factors. While we may be unaccustomed to hearing about capital flight from wealthy, politically stable countries, it can happen (and there is anecdotal evidence in Japan that it has begun). The decisions of where to invest are made at the margin based on the likely returns for that investment. If everything in Japan—lack of confidence, low liquidity, low interest rates—disadvantages those investments, the capital will go elsewhere (figure 4.13 shows the rising outflow of even long-term foreign direct investment). The fact that Japan has very little debt held abroad and no foreign-denominated government debt means that more has to go wrong in the Japanese economy before flight would begin in earnest, but it by no means precludes such flight.[23] The target-zone literature tells us that even under flexible

23. Poole (1991, 174) came to the same conclusion discussing the opposite situation of the United States, then and now the world's largest debtor: "The argument that we will have to pay increasing attention to the exchange market as the amount of foreign-owned capital in the United States rises does not make good sense to me. U.S.-owned capital is just as mobile as foreign-owned capital. Capital flows respond to relative risks and returns; policy

exchange rates, small fluctuations (or perceived nonresponses) by the central bank can produce sharp jumps in the exchange rate.[24]

With the United States and Japan having defended the yen at 140 to the dollar in mid-June 1998, they could well have created a scenario for such a jump if the countries were seen as not defending that rate once it were seriously challenged again after the Japanese upper-house election. If the Japanese financial system is sufficiently fragile that foreign counterparties are withdrawing their funds from it or proving less willing to roll over loans in the interbank market (as can be seen in the "Japan premium" that even large Japanese banks were paying in the late 1990s), then an exchange rate attack and a financial withdrawal would reinforce each other. These will, of course, fuel further capital flight in turn.

Such a rapid fall in the yen would not only occasion trade frictions, it would also be likely to bring about a rapid rise in Japanese inflation.[25] While there are factors that would limit the inflation rise, such as the underutilized capacity in the Japanese economy and favorable shocks to commodity prices from which the entire OECD has benefited, these cannot completely shield an open economy that must pay world prices for a number of inputs and consumer goods. Moreover, even to the extent that yen depreciation contributes to growth by increasing net exports, it does so in a selective way: on the first pass, it harms everyone but stakeholders of equity in the traded-goods sector. Japanese consumers, feeling their purchasing power erode, would likely withdraw more money from the economy, both in hoarding of savings and in capital flight. It would also not be seen as a sustainable restoration of profits and, therefore, of investment expectations, given the political and fundamental reasons for an eventual reversal of the yen's course. Finally, it would do nothing to stabilize the financial system or to increase deposits to it, because Japan is far from an exporter of financial services.

Most pressing, however, is the conflict between external and internal stabilization that would be engendered by capital flight and yen depreciation. To restore liquidity to the financial system, which is likely to be harmed by disintermediation to abroad and certainly by having ever more bad loans to bear with ever lower equity, the Bank of Japan would have to lower interest rates or increase the money supply. To restore the confidence in the stability of the yen, the Bank of Japan would have to raise interest rates to halt depreciation and close the gap in returns with dollar- and other foreign-denominated assets. The Bank of Japan's duties as

---

constraints [on the United States] have changed little over the last decade [as foreign holdings of treasuries rose]."

24. See Krugman (1991) for a brief summary of these results.

25. The advantages of a *limited and expected* rise in Japanese inflation are discussed in chapter 5.

lender of last resort would be in direct conflict with its commitment to price stability, and it would have only one policy instrument with which to address this dilemma.[26] Clearly, a small inflation is strongly preferred to deflation, especially under conditions of financial fragility, but, as I discuss in detail in chapter 5, it is dangerous to attempt to engineer such price stability (or slight inflation) through exchange rates, which tend to overshoot without a nominal anchor. Moreover, capital that leaves tends to be reluctant to come back unless returns are front-loaded via high interest rates, which adds to the conflict facing the central bank (see Dornbusch 1991).

So, to summarize the downside risks to the Japanese economy, consider the following scenario:[27] The US government makes clear that it will not defend the dollar/yen exchange rate any further without a change in Japanese macroeconomic policy.[28] Before the Japanese government can affect the situation, the credibility of this threat, given the obvious pressures for trade protection, prompts capital flight from Japanese assets. The Nikkei stock index plummets, putting some securities firms that had taken too many risks out of business. Rumors of nonpayment by these collapsed firms lead counterparties of banks associated with those firms to withhold payments from those banks (as collateral in case of payments failure). Even though these were securities firms, lines of depositors begin to form at Japanese banks, visible for all to see, to withdraw their deposits and put them into Postal Savings or dollar-denominated assets abroad. Foreign holders of credits to Japanese banks fear further declines in the yen as a result of the impending capital flight and refuse to roll over loans.

The Japanese government announces the extension of the deposit guarantee of 10 million yen per account to all customers at securities firms, but the announcement (in line with the discussion above) is interpreted more for who it appears to say will *not* be protected. So when the Bank of Japan follows the announcement by making guarantees of liquidity to any major bank, large (nonindividual) account holders such as corporations and anyone doing business with small banks join in the panic. The government's infusion of liquidity is more than offset by the decline in money supply as the deposits go abroad or under the mattress. Under deflation, while most labor and debt contracts remain in fixed nominal

---

26. Volcker (1991, 175) states, "[I]n the stabilization crisis, there are no 'right' answers, because the general tools that one uses to deal with the crisis, particularly easing the money supply, may undermine confidence. Further, the international financial repercussions can lead to a depreciation of the [currency] which feeds back to internal inflation."

27. This scenario was inspired by that of Summers (1991) about the hypothetical possibility of an international crisis beginning in the United States through policy mistakes.

28. In the last section of chapter 5, I suggest why such a threatening strategy on the part of the United States is likely to backfire.

terms, this results in a substantial short-run spike in Japanese real interest rates.

Japanese banks left standing pull in their lines of credit. Any liquidity given to them by the Bank of Japan or the Japanese government is invested in Japanese Government Bonds or US Treasuries, given the extreme adverse selection of who is willing to borrow at the prevailing interest rate. Nominal interest rates then rapidly drop, and Japanese financial markets go into wholesale decline. Aggressive lender-of-last-resort action to increase liquidity further decreases the return on deposits, capital flight continues, and expectations for further yen depreciation become entrenched. Government deficits, meanwhile, rise sharply when the downturn becomes severe, unemployment exceeds its historical highs, and there is a collapse in tax revenues. The Japanese government, under the guidance of the Ministry of Finance, calls for extreme fiscal austerity to restore confidence in the Japanese economy and to pay for the various financial infusions. As in 1996 and 1997, fiscal consolidation is anything but expansionary in Japan and, following the pattern presented in chapters 2 and 3, provokes further panic by increasing precautionary saving and lowering confidence in the economic future (as much by government justifications given for the contraction as by the direct impact on growth).

There is, thus, a complete conflict between responding to the liquidity crisis and the currency crisis, between restoring faith in the financial system and restoring faith in the yen. The size of these capital flows and the uncertainties they cause provoke renewed crisis (an understatement) in the rest of east Asia, with capital exiting there even faster than in Japan. World economic growth and stability are imperiled. The only way out of the dilemma would be for foreign central banks, primarily the United States Federal Reserve and the new European Central Bank, to lower their interest rates to encourage capital to flow back into Japan. Stabilization of the currency would allow Japanese monetary and fiscal policy to dedicate themselves to their domestic financial requirements. Whether these independent central banks would be willing to engage in such a coordinated loosening is in doubt, especially because their stock markets had already been rising before being pumped up further by the inflow of funds from the Pacific and because their economies were growing at rates that (at least historically) presaged inflation.

Perhaps this sounds exaggerated, but it is difficult to point to any step in the scenario that is particularly unlikely. The main point, however, is to illustrate the mutually reinforcing nature of the downside risks—confidence, financial, and international—that Japan faces in mid-1998, and to show how preemptive policies today are required because policies in reaction to crisis once it hits may be ineffective or have perverse effects. I offer such a program for sustainable Japanese economic recovery in chapter 5. The potential need for international coordination, should the crisis get out of hand, should not obscure the reality that such coordination cannot substitute for appropriate changes in Japanese domestic policy. For both Japan and the United States, the discussion should not simply be about what Japan could and should do to return its economy to its potential rate of growth, but why it must do so as soon as possible. Ignoring the downside risks enumerated in this chapter for gradual, supposedly long-term policies or for laissez-faire will be dangerous indeed.

5

A Program for Japanese Economic Recovery

The appropriate policy response to Japanese stagnation is one, first and foremost, of expansionary macroeconomic policy. As argued in chapter 1, strong potential growth is being forgone because of a lack of aggregate demand, so stimulus is called for. As documented in chapter 2, fiscal policy was successful in raising the Japanese growth rate in 1995, the one time it was tried. As demonstrated in chapter 3, the current conditions of the Japanese economy, if anything, increase the likely effectiveness of fiscal policy, and the aging of Japanese society has little to do with such a policy's benefits. Finally, as discussed in chapter 4, the mounting financial distrust at home and the apparent recurrence of economic crisis abroad mean that a rapid response to restore the confidence of Japanese citizens in the stability of their purchasing power and their financial system is required. So long as the economic turmoil of Japan in summer 1998 does not generate wholesale capital flight, this program can still be effective. It is within the power of Japanese policymakers to bring about lasting economic recovery in Japan without unnecessary pain or complete overhaul of the Japanese system. Delay in undertaking the required efforts costs the Japanese people more wealth forgone and risks a crisis that policy cannot easily repair.

In summary, Japanese macroeconomic policy should begin with the passage of a true fiscal-stimulus package. This package should be of sufficient size to raise growth above the Japanese potential growth rate of 2 to 2.5 percent, that is, 20 trillion yen, or 4 percent of GDP based on current data.[1] Unlike the package of the Hashimoto government of April 1998, discussed in chapter 2, the amount spent should equal the headline total, it should be implemented completely before calendar year's end, and it should consist primarily of permanent income tax cuts. This fiscal policy should be accompanied by a monetary policy that is committed to reversing deflation and minimizing uncertainty about the future price level—a goal best served by the announcement of a small positive inflation target of 3 percent and not by the conscious depreciation of the yen. The idea is to encourage stabilization and long-run planning, not simply to inflate in an unanchored manner. Cleanup of the Japanese financial system is needed to make the recovery sustainable. The restoration of incentives for Japanese savers to keep their money in identifiably solvent private-sector banks should be the fundamental goal of financial reform. This requires steps to close banks, shore up the credibility of deposit insurance, and encourage the shift of savings from the public to the private sector. The details of how to implement these policy measures, and the reasoning behind them, are given in the course of this chapter.

There is no shortage of policy advice available to the Japanese government, from Japanese, American, and other sources. Some of the components of the program I offer here have been advocated and opposed, singly and in various combinations, by numerous observers. My hope is that, by having brought the reader to this program through a systematic analysis of the Japanese economic situation, these recommendations will follow logically from that analysis and, therefore, be both more persuasive and form more of a consistent whole than they would if such a program were simply listed. Although the current Japanese situation is indeed dire, and without decisive policy action subject to the possibility of rapid decline, this program for recovery is not a complicated "all or nothing" shock-therapy plan. No wrenching transformation or overhaul of the Japanese model beyond banking reform is required.

That being said, the components of the complete program do reinforce one another in bringing Japan out of its current economic stagnation. The combination of fiscal stimulus and expansionary but anchored monetary policy should raise return on investment and stabilize price expectations and the yen. In turn, this should encourage reinvestment and spending in the Japanese economy, which should improve the balance sheets of banks and households. The proper sorting of viable from insolvent banks should make sure that this capital inflow is not wasted on further risky loans. The issuance of short-term government debt to fund the fiscal stimulus, the conscious contraction of the Postal Savings system, and the refinement of deposit insurance should reinforce incentives for Japanese

---

1. This assumes a contraction of the Japanese economy of 1 percent in 1998, much less than the −5.2 percent annualized rate announced for the first quarter of 1998, but still the decline that would occur without fiscal action.

savers to reinvest in their private economy. Together, these measures will restore financial confidence sufficient to promote the maximum lasting effect of the tax cuts.

Moreover, even taken as a whole, this program is not one that should lead to policy overload, either political or financial. In expenditure, it consists almost entirely of the fiscal expansion effort, which, as discussed in chapters 2 and 3, should be seen as money well spent and not out of line with international standards for fiscal expansion. The monetary and financial recommendations consist of changes in the conduct of policy rather than new spending. In political terms, because these are for the most part macroeconomic policy suggestions, they can be accomplished with minimum exposure to special-interest or even legislative interference, especially because they do not directly reallocate benefits among groups (except, perhaps, the power of the Ministry of Finance). Only the financial reform aspects of the program would require some real political leadership in facing up to the ties between bureaucracy and business, as the stasis to date on this front has demonstrated, but none greater than that required in the US savings and loan crisis, for example. Programs that instead call for the total and drastic structural reform of the Japanese economy risk bringing inertia at best and open resistance at worst, and ultimately, they are unnecessary. Most "reform" beyond the immediate amount required for the cleanup of the bad loan problem, even if salutary in the long run, presents opportunities for future growth that can wait until macroeconomic policy has taken effect.

Thus, this program and its salutary impact on the Japanese economy are well within the realm of the attainable. My program's benefits would be sizable, both for Japan and for the world economy. First and foremost, true fiscal stimulus in combination with stabilization of inflation expectations should at least be attempted, before resorting to aggressively inflationary policies or accepting current growth rates. This course seems obvious, especially because fiscal policy was effective in stimulating growth in 1995 and in mistakenly contracting the economy in other years, while monetary ease and the yen's decline have already proven ineffective in bringing growth to Japan. In comparison to the calls made by some for the acceptance of continued stagnation either under the heading of "creative destruction" or as the only real spur to break deadlock or both, it offers more solid ground for sustained growth. Compared to the combinations of forced structural change and outright economic suffering being borne at present by most of Japan's neighboring nations, its requirements are meager. This stands to reason because Japan is far more a transparent market economy and far less subject to uncompetitiveness and foreign indebtedness than any of the Asian-crisis economies, rhetorical comparisons aside.

To close this chapter, I address the question of whether the United States has a role to play in Japanese economic recovery. Change in Japanese economic policy must come through a recognition of Japan's own self-interest in making that change, and this book is premised in part on contributing to such a recognition. It is possible that American diplomacy and economic policy could contribute to the likelihood of such a change. Furthermore, to the extent that the international environment in general, and the yen/dollar exchange rate and the US-Japan bilateral trade relationship in particular, affect Japanese economic prospects, American policy can influence the course of events. My primary recommendation is that the United States should end the intermittent jawboning of Japanese policymakers and most forms of diplomatic pressure based on low-level intergovernment communication. Instead, if the United States is to do anything, it should offer the Japanese government a *positive* opportunity for cooperation in a centralized, explicit manner (e.g., concerted foreign-exchange intervention) in return for an explicit timetable of fiscal expansion and financial cleanup in Japan. The key is to offer benefits that Japan cannot attain through unilateral action and that can be withheld until Japanese policymakers act. The United States has no punishment strategy to use upon Japanese policymakers that will not impose unacceptable risk of some harm to the rest of East Asia and the United States as well, which is why the positive should be emphasized.

Fiscal Policy Measures

True Fiscal Stimulus of 4 Percent of GDP

Fiscal stimulus will work to raise the Japanese economic growth rate. As discussed in chapters 2 and 3, a stimulus package must consist of actual government return of funds to the private sector, that is, an increase in the deficit, to be effective. In size, fiscal stimulus must at a minimum be large enough that its effects can be seen and felt by all citizens. The best way to assure this response is to promote growth *above potential*. Only above-potential growth would start to take up the ample excess capacity and reemploy the unemployed in Japan, both of which are necessary to raising growth expectations and decreasing uncertainty in the Japanese economy. As analyzed in chapter 1, Japanese potential real GDP growth is likely between 2.0 and 2.5 percent annually. Fiscal policy that merely keeps growth nonnegative, but below potential, will allow excess capacity and unemployment to continue to rise, likely further damaging confidence. Such limited spending will therefore be transitory and a waste of money in a way that a sufficiently large program would not. For these reasons, the impact of fiscal policy will be felt only with a stimulus of at least 4 percent of GDP, or 20 trillion yen, given current forecasts for Japanese economic contraction of 1 percent or more in 1998 and potential growth in excess of 2 percent.

This recommendation assumes a multiplier on fiscal policy of at least one. Given that the combined 1.6 percent of GDP spending and 1.3 percent of GDP consumption-tax shift[2] of 1995-96 resulted in GDP growth of 3.6 percent in 1996, when there were no other positive developments (as discussed in chapter 2), this multiplier seems reasonable once the potential growth minimum is exceeded. That such a sizable fiscal stimulus will feed into a sustained upswing in growth, of course, cannot be completely guaranteed. Even in the unlikely event that such a stimulus were to be mostly saved or were to simply increase this year's growth at the expense of next year's—neither of which is likely to occur, as argued in chapter 3—this stimulus would still have been useful by staving off a collapse of financial confidence in Japan until the world economy would be better prepared to handle it and by aiding both Japanese banks' and consumers' balance sheets. As argued in chapter 3, there is every reason to expect that appropriately strong fiscal policy will accomplish a great deal more than that in the current Japanese situation.

The Japanese government should, in fact, complete its U-turn in a decisive manner and repeal the law that requires a limit of deficits by the year 2005. The law has already been revised to push back the target date from 2003 and to include an escape clause for severe economic downturns. Such explicit budget rules are never credible or effective—the Maastricht deficit and debt criteria failed to be met even less than strictly by most of the participants in the European Monetary Union; the Gramm-Rudman-Hollings and other balanced-budget rules were ignored in the United States in the 1980s and 1990s. Furthermore, the premise of an exact deficit target is misleading because there are limits to what economic effects deficits capture, and it is the trend of net debt that matters. Keeping the budget austerity law on the books just undercuts the government's credibility that it is doing right by stimulating. The Japanese government should accompany this package with accurate statements to the effect that the 1995 fiscal package was a success, that other previous packages do not constitute evidence that fiscal stimulus does not work (in part because there was also contractionary fiscal policy undertaken), that other countries have engaged in fiscal policy of this magnitude when required, and that there really is as much in this package as claimed. In essence, an exercise in honest confidence building would increase the likelihood of success.

Make the Stimulus Consist of Permanent Tax Cuts

The 4 percent of GDP stimulus could conceivably be reached through public works spending, corporate tax cuts, temporary tax rebates, or

2. A 2 percent cut in taxes times the 0.65 share of consumption in GDP.

some combination thereof. Best structured, however, the stimulus package would consist of permanent cuts in taxes. As is well known, permanent tax cuts will have larger effects than will temporary ones because consumers will treat them as an ongoing rise in income rather than a one-time windfall to be spread out over several years. Because there is no good evidence that Japanese citizens (or anyone else) are fully Ricardian, they are therefore unlikely to treat much of a current tax cut as a future tax rise that is relevant to them (see chapter 3). If anything, the return to their control of a greater share of their own current income should decrease their income uncertainty, whatever their long-run expectations, and work to diminish precautionary saving. Another reason that permanent tax cuts will have larger effects than will other forms of stimulus is that for Japanese households their effects are immediate and tangible, whether on consumer purchases or on take-home pay.

There are several other reasons why permanent income tax cuts are to be preferred to the public works spending that has been the mainstay of Japanese economic proposals to date. First, reducing direct taxes lowers distortion of pricing in the economy, thereby increasing economic efficiency, while the creation of targeted public works projects adds to distortions by supporting sectors (e.g., construction) and projects (e.g., large bridges that carry no traffic) that the market would not. Of course, these effects are second order compared to the ultimate need for fiscal stimulus, but, given the choice of composition of that stimulus, tax cuts yield benefits greater than their listed size, while many forms of government spending yield less. In addition, public works can impose future carrying costs, such as bridges that require maintenance, which further distort allocation. Reduction of income taxes can, at the margin, increase the supply of labor and investor effort in the economy by increasing the incentive to pursue earning opportunities.[3] In general, economic performance is improved by moving resources from the public to the private sector.

Second, permanent tax cuts now are likely to force permanent cuts in public-sector spending in the next several years, much as Reaganomics did in the United States.[4] It has recently been established that fiscal consolidations that rely on cuts in government expenditure are much more likely to be successful (in the sense of the improvement in fiscal situation being sustained) than consolidation efforts that rely on tax increases.[5] Spending

---

3. This last possibility should not be oversold. Even strong supporters of Reaganomics are unable to demonstrate large benefits on this front in the United States as a result of the 1980s tax cuts. Lindsey (1990), a Bush administration official, puts the total benefit of Reagan-era tax changes at less than 1 percent of GDP, while others put it much lower.

4. Some would argue that this was, in fact, the underlying intent of the Reagan fiscal policies (see Stockman 1987).

5. See Alesina and Perotti (1995, 1996) and the discussion in IMF (1996).

increases have the opposite dynamic, tending to become entrenched. Moreover, a tax cut establishes a usefully transparent "line in the sand" for Japanese policymakers, who are subject to the sort of pressure for stealth austerity discussed in chapter 2—they would have to expose any efforts to undercut the stimulus package before it runs its course, by either raising taxes or visibly cutting main-budget spending. A stimulus based on public works would run the wrong way in both the long and the short term by adding to the fiscal burden in a manner that is far more difficult to reverse while allowing cuts in the stimulative program to be hidden (as they were in the consistently large gap between stated and actual spending in all prior Japanese fiscal packages).

Third, permanent tax cuts are more restorative than are public works for an economy hindered by a lack of confidence and by overcapacity. For one thing, they are widespread rather than targeted to particular regions or sectors, and they are, if anything, progressive so that those with the most to fear from continuing stagnation (e.g., the potentially unemployed) benefit the most. For another, they would be likely to produce visible effects quickly. This is not only because of tax cuts' lack of implementation lag, but because the efficiency of the mostly tradable-goods sectors in the Japanese economy, from which consumption and durable goods would be purchased (e.g., cars and electronics), is much higher than that of the sectors usually targeted for public investment. These efficient sectors would be expected to respond quickly with production as they head back toward their efficient scale of operation, which is likely to further increase demand. Public works spending is self-limiting as well as oriented toward the less efficient areas of the economy—people know exactly where the money is going (not to them) and when the flow will end. This is why even Japanese government estimates of the multipliers on tax cuts, which play down their immediate effects, are greater over multiyear periods than are estimates of the multiplier for public works, which drop off after the first year.[6]

Finally, the decision to make the fiscal-stimulus package consist mostly of tax cuts would be seen as a clear confidence-restoring break with past policies by Japanese elected officials. The LDP's relationship with local construction and agricultural firms, and the role of public works spending disbursement in that relationship, reflects the overweighting of rural votes in the Japanese electoral system. This reality is well known to the Japanese public. Efforts to pursue national goals without obvious side payments would be a refreshing break from "business as usual," a break likely to be welcomed in an atmosphere of general concern about corruption scandals that involve Diet members and bureaucrats.

---

6. See, for example, Kawasaki (1996). The difference in multiplier estimates between tax cuts and public works would be higher if they were permanent rather than assumed to be temporary as in most Japanese government analyses.

Of course, it is naive to pretend that this pork-barrel setup is not precisely the reason that past Japanese fiscal-stimulus efforts have largely consisted of public works spending. There are reasons to think that this might be subject to change, however, in addition to the one based on the present popular desire for clean government in Japan. One is that the wasteful nature of this process was less noticed and remarked upon while times were good, while in today's stagnant economic times the Japanese public is far more aware of the costs. Another is that Japanese politicians are becoming more aware of the limited relevance of such spending to their reelection prospects. As summarized in Cargill, Hutchison, and Ito (1997, chapter 7), the only solid evidence of a political business cycle in Japan indicates that there were attempts to time the calling of elections to coincide with good economic performance. This is hardly an option in the current situation. Furthermore, their research does not support the idea that public spending buys votes.[7] The results of the 12 July 1998 elections for the Upper House of the Diet appear to confirm that generalization. A third reason to believe that it is politically feasible to pursue tax cuts rather than public spending is that Japanese business lobbies have come to see their interests as closely tied to the restoration of Japanese economic confidence and efficiency, rather than to the continuation of the subsidization of the LDP's local construction and agricultural support network (as with the public in general, more difficult economic times diminish tolerance).

There is a choice between cuts in income and consumption taxes. While consumption tax cuts might provide a greater initial bang for the buck, as seen in the 1996 response to the change in the consumption tax rate, there are long-term reasons why income tax cuts are to be preferred. In general, indirect taxes (such as sales taxes) distort private economic decisions much less than do direct taxes (such as consumption taxes). In a time of heightened concern about structural inefficiencies in the Japanese economy, it makes little sense to increase the proportion of taxes raised by distortionary means. A consumption tax cut would also be a less credible permanent commitment because of the long-run need for Japan to move toward greater reliance on indirect taxes as the population ages (and fewer citizens are wage earners). Internationally, most countries in the OECD and outside it are shifting the tax burden in this way. These pressures would explain the widespread presumption that political resistance, especially from the Ministry of Finance, would be stronger against consumption than income tax cuts.

---

7. This is not to suggest that Japanese LDP members plan their party's strategy on the basis of reading academics' books. This is rather to point out that such political disbursement of goodies has not played a systematic role in previous Japanese elections and, therefore, should be seen as a luxury that helps members to enjoy their careers but not a necessity to keeping those careers.

Cutting income taxes would in fact be a tax *reform* in and of itself because of the current inequities of the Japanese tax system. Half of Japanese households pay no income taxes, with those who are too wealthy to receive income from salary or who manage to classify themselves as farmers or business proprietors, as well as the poor, avoiding the burden. Wage earners' disproportionate burden should be eased. By cutting withholding taxes, the very salarymen who have the greatest combination of a motive for precautionary savings (because they have a job to lose) and discretionary income (because they are above the income minimum for taxation) get the benefit of the stimulus. Ultimately, the total size and timing of fiscal stimulus and the concentration of it in permanent tax cuts rather than public works spending are more important than the allocation of tax cuts between consumption and income taxes. Given the choice, however, income tax cuts should be emphasized.

Issue Short-Term Debt to Fund the Stimulus

Part of what afflicts the Japanese economy at present is excess demand for liquidity, as discussed in chapter 3. Although expansionary monetary policy is currently unable to satisfy households' desire for cash, fiscal stimulus drives up the return on investment and increases the absorption of savings. Proper debt-management policy, that is, the conscious structuring of the maturities of the government's portfolio of outstanding debt, can aid in this regard as well. Short-term government bonds (with a maturity of three years or less) are distinct both from currency and from long-term government bonds in their characteristics and in their perception by investors.[8] When the recommended fiscal-stimulus package of permanent tax cuts requires the Japanese government to issue 20 trillion yen in new debt (as well as the inevitable increase in the debt because of the ongoing recession), the government should take advantage of this fact and issue the debt with short maturities. If this infusion of short-term government-guaranteed obligations into the market provides securities with a mix of safety and liquidity that some hoarders of cash are willing to accept, it will relieve the demand for liquidity and increase the effectiveness of future open-market operations.[9] If the relative supply of long-term Japanese government bonds decreases, there should be some "crowding-in" of longer-term corporate investment, because at the margin some bondholders will prefer corporate assets to short-term government

---

8. See Friedman (1978) for a discussion of how the imperfect substitutability of different government obligations leads to financial effects of debt management.

9. As Ueda (1990) notes, the relative unavailability of short-term Japanese government obligations has been a continuing source of illiquidity in Japanese bond and broader markets. Thus, this issuance of short-term debt would have an additional long-term benefit.

debt when forced to choose between various imperfect substitutes for the long bonds.

Issuing short-term obligations to cover the deficit will also minimize the interest burden of the fiscal stimulus package by taking advantage of current low Japanese interest rates and of the usual spread between long- and short-term rates. Increasing the depth and liquidity of the short-end of the Japanese government bond market will support the long-run development of the yen as a reserve currency. Finally, funding the additional deficit with short-term debt will provide another impetus to eventual government spending cuts, which would complement the tax-cut pressure cited above, by forcing the Japanese government to quickly and visibly confront the decision of whether to roll over or pay off some of the debt.

Monetary Policy Measures

Announce an Inflation Target of 3 Percent for 2000

The primary contribution that monetary policy can make in today's Japan is to stabilize inflationary (and deflationary) expectations. Uncertainty about future price levels, and deflationary expectations in particular, can have disastrous effects on the real economy. The current deflation in Japan increases the real burden of outstanding nominal long-term debt, discourages consumption if people wait for prices to drop before making durable-goods purchases, and raises the rewards of holding cash. There is no question that the Bank of Japan can prevent a full-fledged deflationary spiral—even when a central bank cannot affect interest rates or investment as usual, it can still affect nominal quantities such as the price level, simply by changing the rate at which it prints money. There is little question that the Bank of Japan is already attempting to do so through money creation. This is insufficient, however, because there remains great uncertainty about whether prices will stabilize or whether the yen's decline and government debt will ultimately lead to inflation. Any sort of long-term planning is severely hindered by such uncertainty and, as discussed in chapters 3 and 4, investor and consumer uncertainty is the true source of danger to the Japanese economy. Moreover, if the Bank of Japan inflates without a target, it gains little credibility from any success it has stopping deflation, because it does not offer a goal or standard against which its progress can be measured.

What is needed is a nominal anchor, that is, some visible commitment by the monetary authority, the Bank of Japan, to a specific path for the price level. Such an anchor, with which Japanese markets and individuals can monitor the maintenance of this path by monetary policy, will pin down price expectations. The Bank of Japan's best option for removing price uncertainty is to announce an inflation target.[10] An inflation target is a publicly announced, numerical goal for a specified measure of the inflation rate over a set time horizon. While it is usually seen as a way to cap inflation expectations, an inflation target is actually a *floor* as well as a ceiling for the rate of price increase; the central bank can create inflation with reference to the target without fear of igniting inflationary expectations or having its policy moves misunderstood. To cite two examples, Canada in the early 1990s and Sweden during the Great Depression used announced inflation targets in just this manner, first to anchor long-run price expectations, and then to create sufficient inflation to offset deflation in the short run.[11] In Japan today, such a target would lead to a firming not only of consumer prices but of asset values, because it would limit how much the yen could fall (assuming that there are Japanese and foreign investors "bottom fishing," that is, waiting to put their money back into Japanese corporations in hopes of finding bargains, as indeed seems to be the case).

Visible increases in inflation without an explicit commitment to its future level, however, will just add to uncertainty and harm investor confidence. That is why a public and positive but specific and finite inflation target is preferred to an unanchored monetary policy based on just "turning on the printing presses," as has been advocated for Japan by Milton Friedman, John Makin, Paul Krugman, and others. While both policies would be effective in stopping deflation, aggressive monetary expansion without reference to a specific finite target will on net increase rather than decrease uncertainty. The question of when the Bank of Japan would slow the printing presses would arise, as would concern that the Japanese government wished to inflate away its and the banking system's nominal debt. Together, these would encourage further withdrawal of capital from the Japanese economy. Investors waiting to put money into Japanese assets would only see their estimates of currency and default risk rise, likely more than offsetting any purchase incentive arising from the halt of declining prices. Similarly, Japanese consumers that face a rising inflation rate of uncertain duration and without a clear upper bound would have some additional incentive to spend now, before their cash holdings eroded too much in value, but this effect would likely be overwhelmed by greater precautionary panic as they watched their yen-denominated purchasing power, domestic as well as international, further

---

10. Bernanke, Laubach, Mishkin, and Posen (1998) give a comprehensive analysis of this monetary framework in theory and in practice (but make no specific reference to Japanese monetary policy).

11. Bernanke, Laubach, Mishkin, and Posen (1998, chapter 6) discuss the Canadian experience in the 1990s. Jonung (1979) gives a history of Sweden's success in avoiding the worst of the Great Depression through target-based monetary policy.

erode. A 3 percent inflation target should be sufficient to capture many of the gains to be won by engendering belief among consumers and investors that prices will not drop further, without incurring additional costs to purchasing power and confidence.

In addition, inflation and especially inflation uncertainty have costs themselves.[12] Deflation is without doubt much more costly than single-digit inflation, as recent Japanese experience reconfirms, so achieving a positive rate of inflation in today's Japan is a worthwhile endeavor. Rises in inflation expectations tend to be persistent, however, especially when inflationary policy is a clear break from past practice, as would be the case for the Bank of Japan.[13] This would potentially present Japanese policymakers with a dangerous dilemma just a little bit down the road, because they would face whatever inflation level they incurred as part of the monetary ease in addition to inflationary pressures that arise when the Japanese economy does recover sufficiently. They would be left with the terrible choice of disinflating by contractionary policy the moment the economy picks up slack or allowing inflation rates and expectations to rise further as additional inflation is accommodated. By committing to a finite, small, publicly known inflation target, one that anchors expectations over the longer term, the Bank of Japan can avoid this additional cycle of rising inflation and the pressure to reverse it.[14] Thus, on several grounds, if the Bank of Japan engages in money creation, as it should, it should do so through the framework of an inflation target.[15]

In operational terms, the Bank of Japan should announce an inflation target of 3 percent annually for summer 2000. It should also announce that over some appropriate longer term (say by 2003) the rate would be brought down to 2 percent.[16] The 3 percent rate is chosen to be clearly

---

12. See Fischer (1981) and Briault (1995) for excellent summaries of these costs and Sarel (1995) for evidence that the direct costs rise sharply once inflation rates of 8 percent are exceeded.

13. See Ueda (1990) and Cargill, Hutchison, and Ito (1997) for histories of the success of the Bank of Japan in combining low inflation with steady growth through most of the 1970s and 1980s.

14. It is true that in so doing, the Bank of Japan would forgo the reduction of real outstanding debt that rising levels of inflation greater than a steady 3 percent provides, something that often historically has been used to alleviate wide debt burdens. Yet, by giving up this benefit, the central bank would also avoid the rising interest rates with which today's global financial markets punish countries that are perceived to be attempting to inflate away their debt.

15. It should be noted that when the Bank of Japan was given greater legal independence in April 1996, there were indications that the Bank would adopt an inflation-targeting strategy. While this intent has been affirmed at various points, and reports suggest that some members of the bank's new Monetary Committee are in favor of such a move, such a policy has not yet been adopted in the form of a publicly announced target.

16. Mishkin and Posen (1997) discuss in general terms the operational issues involved in the design of inflation targets.

positive. Because biases in the measurement of inflation mean that CPI inflation of 1.5 to 2 percent is probably consistent with true price stability, and anything lower is actually deflation (let alone the negative measured inflation of today), the target should be greater than that bias.[17] The additional amount above the measurement bias in the short-term inflation target of 3 percent is intended to put enough distance between the target and deflation so that it will be clear that inflation expectations should be positive. Otherwise, imperfect control of inflation could lead to continued deflation and deflationary expectations simply by trying to hit a positive target with too little margin for error on the downside. The target is set for two years ahead both because it usually takes that long for monetary policy moves to fully affect inflation and because encouraging Japanese citizens to look to near-term stability beyond the immediate uncertainty is beneficial. The target should be defined as a 3 percent year-over-year rate of *core* inflation, that is, the change in the CPI excluding the influence of energy and food products. The reason for the exclusion is that there can be changes in inflation from commodity price movements (up and down) that will mask general movements in the price level and in expectations, and the latter are ultimately what count.

Do Not Rely on Yen Depreciation as a Policy

To the extent that it is a matter of policy choice, further yen depreciation should not be substituted even for part of the necessary fiscal stimulus and, in fact, should actively be discouraged on its own terms. A depreciation would certainly fit the pattern of some Japanese attempts in the 1990s and earlier to make up for slow growth at home by expanding net exports. Krugman (1998a) sees yen depreciation as a natural and agreeable result of aggressively expansionary monetary policy and Sachs (1998) advocates actively seeking to drive down the yen's value. A depreciation of the yen is, in partial equilibrium, stimulative for the Japanese economy by making Japanese goods cheaper abroad. The ultimate goal of Japanese economic policy, however, is sustainable growth, and a yen decline is at best a very indirect way to increase growth and more likely would actually worsen the Japanese situation.[18] When the yen depreciates, it significantly affects economies throughout East Asia, even ones such as China, with which

---

17. This is true for all countries, because basket-based measures of the cost of living inherently take poor account of quality improvements and changing tastes, even though public discussion of this fact has largely been confined to the United States. See Shapiro and Wilcox (1996) and Advisory Commission to Study the Consumer Price Index (1996).

18. This leaves aside the fact that the export and import elasticity of exchange rate shifts are not the same for large rapid swings as for smaller or slower ones. In other words, even if a 5 percent yen depreciation increases net exports by a given amount, a 20 percent depreciation in the same time span is unlikely to produce 4 times as large a rise in net exports.

Japan is not in direct export competition.[19] This offsets the direct economic boost to Japan from the yen decline in two ways: first, it lowers growth in East Asia and, thus, demand for Japanese goods from, and returns on Japanese investments in, those countries; second, it increases the likelihood of currency depreciation and devaluation in the rest of East Asia.

Even leaving consciously competitive and political pressures for matching devaluations aside, markets recognizing that the real underlying economic conditions of these countries relative to Japan would not be altered by Japan's nominal move will mark down their respective currencies when the yen declines. As a result, any yen depreciation largely shifts the burden of imports from the East Asian economies onto the G-7 (excluding Japan) rather than improving Japanese growth prospects and diminishes the purchasing power of East Asian consumers in the process. In addition, as discussed in chapter 4, the perception that a declining yen is the source of major trade deficits elsewhere could engender a protectionist response (see Bergsten and Noland 1993).

Two additional major disadvantages arise for Japan from any attempt to drive down the yen, and both are analogous to the negative effects of using excessive inflationary finance to stimulate the economy.[20] First is the hit to Japanese citizens' purchasing power and to the attractiveness of yen-denominated assets, both of which result from a sharp fall in the yen; in a time of precautionary-motivated savings, this further shock to people's sense of wealth could have major effects.[21] The second major disadvantage is the ultimate need for the yen exchange rate to return to some fundamental equilibrium value over the horizon of a few years; just as the existence of excessive inflation would prompt an eventual disinflation, further deviation of the currently undervalued yen from its equilibrium rate will simply require an eventual reversal and then giveback of whatever gains were made on the trade front.[22] As seen in 1993-95, and consistent with past experience, such sharp yen volatility in and of itself imposes costly adjustments on Japanese business.

---

19. Noland, Liu, Robinson, and Wang (1998) analyze in a detailed computable general equilibrium framework the macroeconomic and trade effects of devaluations in the region, with special attention to China.

20. This is only logical because a conscious effort to depreciate a currency is essentially an open-market operation where the central bank prints money with which to purchase foreign exchange, rather than to purchase domestic bonds.

21. It is amazing how much ink can be spilled arguing that savers will respond today to a mounting government obligation 30 years down the road that they may never feel, while the reality that they can lose a significant portion of their purchasing power for imported goods and foreign assets in a matter of weeks is assumed not to be of greater immediate concern.

22. Driver and Wren-Lewis (1998) estimate that the fundamental equilibrium exchange rate in 2000 for the yen is 77-95 to the dollar, far from current levels. Other estimates assume a yen at a long-run average of 100-120 per dollar.

In addition, just as sharp or unanchored increases in the inflation rate risk igniting spirals of inflationary expectations that are incommensurate with the intended policy, exchange rates have a well-established tendency to overshoot, and sometimes, when declining, to occasion a run on the currency (see OECD 1988, 18; Bergsten 1998).[23] As discussed in chapter 4, we have already seen the first signs of capital flight from the Japanese economy and yen-denominated assets—further decline of the yen's value could bring about a true crisis, as we had a taste of in June 1998. For this last reason alone, Japanese policymakers should abjure any conscious effort to depreciate the yen. Luckily, the adoption of the main legs of the program outlined in this chapter should stabilize and then appreciate the yen as well as promote growth directly in a way that yen depreciation cannot. There is no reason to adopt a second-best policy of yen depreciation when there are better alternatives that lack such attendant risks.

Financial Reform Measures

Recapitalize Only the Better Banks

There is no issue in the current Japanese economic situation about which there is as much intellectual agreement as the need to recapitalize the viable Japanese banks and close the ones that are not. Current estimates of the outstanding bad loan problem in the Japanese banking system total over 60 trillion yen, up from 48 trillion yen of nonperforming and questionable loans cited in a July 1995 announcement by the Ministry of Finance. It is only logical that the total amount of bad loans would continue to climb without reform, because banks that are already insolvent or close to it have an incentive to continue to take on risky loans in the hope that some will come through. This is an instance of moral hazard in that the shareholders and managers in low or negative net worth banks have incentive to bet what little is left because any further losses will be borne by the taxpayer and the bettors will share fully in any improvement in net worth. Moreover, the continued economic stagnation and deflation make it more difficult for nonfinancial businesses to make their previously set loan payments, also leading to an increase in bad loans. In any event, it would be impossible for the Japanese banking system to recapitalize directly via financial markets today, given the general risk associated with the Japanese banks because the good banks' attributes are not easily separable from the systemic risks and given the sheer size and number of similar securities that would have to be issued at the same time.

---

23. Dornbusch (1976) gives the original theoretical model for exchange rate overshooting.

In theory, the banks could also recapitalize by cutting back their ratio of loans to capital; in practice, only the good (i.e., solvent) banks have an incentive to do so (as discussed), while Japanese regulators have tended to engage in "regulatory forbearance" that encourages weak banks to keep lending rather than take losses. Furthermore, when Japanese banks cut back significantly on lending, as they did in the nascent credit crunch in 1997-98 discussed in chapter 4, economic activity is further sharply contracted.[24] So public injection of trillions of yen into the banking system and public supervision of the disposal of distressed loans, real estate, and other assets are required to restore the Japanese financial system. Government use of the Resolution and Collection Bank to create a liquid market in the disposal of foreclosed real estate, like the activities of the Resolution Trust Corporation in the United States, will be needed. Use of the Resolution and Collection Bank as a "bridge bank" to give loans to small businesses alleviates the immediate concern of a credit crunch for small indebted businesses in Japan, but it is a short-term palliative.[25] The underlying and more dangerous problem is the disintermediation of funds from the Japanese private banking system. That is why the focus must be on the restoration of incentives for Japanese savers to keep money in the solvent private-sector banks; in the long run, reintermediation is the only lasting way to alleviate the credit crunch.

Unfortunately, while there is great intellectual agreement on this need for financial reform, there is great political disagreement. A vocal portion of the Japanese public has conveyed an extreme dislike of the idea of using public funds to "bail out" failed institutions; a less-public constituency of bankers and regulators has shown a more effective resistance to the idea of sorting out which banks should survive and which should not prior to the injection of government funds. Yet, without a decision to put money only into those banks that are currently solvent or can easily be made so, the Japanese government would be encouraging exactly the behavior that has led to much of the current bad loan situation and spending far more than needed to reestablish the nation's financial system.[26] Markets, recog-

---

24. Mishkin (1991) summarizes the asymmetric information view of financial markets in which contractions in credit decrease the efficiency of allocation of investment to productive projects, leading to further decreases in lending and investment, with harmful effects on growth.

25. In an interview with the *Nihon Keizai Shimbun* on 16 June 1998 LDP Policy Chief Taku Yamasaki "envisioned turning the semigovernmental bank into a public bank empowered to extend loans to [nonfinancial] corporations by tapping into the *zaito* [FILP] funds." This statement reveals a continuing misunderstanding of the uses of an entity like the Resolution Trust Corporation in the United States, which is meant to dispose of loans, marked down, to alleviate financial fragility, and *not* to keep nonbank borrowers afloat.

26. Goldstein (1998) discusses the general problems of fixing failed financial systems following a lending boom if supervision has been lax.

nizing this fact, will continue to punish the entire Japanese financial system so long as the uncertainty over particular banks' viability and their potential obligations to other banks are unresolved.

This will lead to a particularly dangerous instance of adverse selection in the lending market for banks—the only banks that will be willing to pay the current "Japan premium" on more than the bare amount necessary to roll over current payments will be those that have the least net worth and the least to lose by gambling with the new capital. Meanwhile the good, or at least better, banks that should be able to borrow at a lower rate absent this general uncertainty will not attempt to raise capital. Financial markets, recognizing the situation facing them, will cut back on the total capital made available to Japanese finance. Thus, the attachment to the past "convoy" or "no failure" policies of the Ministry of Finance hurts exactly those banks that are most viable while continuing the cycle of bad lending by the others. A four-wheel drive vehicle, where each wheel helps the others, can navigate slippery patches where normal cars would skid as one tire slips. The same four-wheel drive vehicle can get thoroughly stuck by going so far off-road to a spot that a normal car would not reach. Spinning all four of the vehicle's wheels at once only sinks it further into the muck.

The Ministry of Finance has made some minor headway in sorting out the viable from the insolvent banks. Starting in December 1994, the Ministry officially announced a departure from strict adherence to its "no failure" policy and threatened some small banks with being declared insolvent if they did not merge with viable institutions. In December 1997, a Financial Emergency Management Account was created in the Deposit Insurance Corporation and funded with a 10 trillion yen new-bond issue to back deposits and to begin disposing of distressed assets. Recently, that 10 trillion yen was supplemented by two loans of 10 trillion yen each from the Bank of Japan to the Deposit Insurance Corporation. Of the now 30 trillion yen total, 17 trillion has been allocated to the replenishment of deposit insurance funds and 13 trillion has gone into the account for recapitalizing banks (Government of Japan 1998a).

So far, however, there is no evidence that in implementation the Ministry of Finance has been selecting the banks for recapitalization on the basis of solvency rather than injecting the money into the entire system. The amount of money now committed may well be sufficient—at 6 percent of GDP, it is four times the amount allocated in the United States in 1991 under the Financial Institution Reform, Recovery, and Enforcement Act of 1989 (FIRREA) to recapitalize the savings and loan industry, and the total bad loan problem in Japan is not much more than 4 to 5 times the size of the savings and loan crisis in the United States—so it is the *conduct* of the recapitalization that is at issue.[27] Giving money to keep insolvent

---

27. Goldstein (1998, 29) criticizes the use of "gimmicks" by Japanese bank regulators—such as postponing implementation of the Basle capital standards or artificially inflating banks' capital stock by allowing the higher of book or market value to be used on equity

banks open, however, will prolong the crisis, add to the accumulation of bad loans, and keep the good banks from getting access to capital. This uncertainty-bred adverse selection will lead to more risk-taking behavior by insolvent banks with Japanese taxpayer's money and *less* rather than more capital available for worthwhile investment. The need to maintain the level of aggregate demand even as credit necessarily contracts during the transition to proper standards is an additional reason for substantial fiscal stimulus to be undertaken simultaneously with financial reform.

The government of Japan should treat the rapid gathering and provision of information regarding bank solvency as a priority matter. The sooner disintermediation can be changed into reallocation among intermediaries and the sooner a tendency toward a harmful run on all banks turns into a beneficial run on bad banks only, the better. Just like mobilization for a natural disaster, the government should be engaged in a crash program of hiring and training new bank inspectors. Over time, Japan's bank supervisory staff (under 300 total) will have to increase in any event, given the size of the banking system, so there is no reason not to accelerate the process. Any young college graduate with a modicum of legal or economics training could be put through a crash course of accounting, finance, and standards in a matter of weeks. Not only would these young people be engaged in public service, they would be reassuring the public that long-time corrupt relationships were not a factor in supervisory decision making. Rather than a standard jobs program, therefore, a "Civilian Financial Conservation Corps" would allow these young no-longer-unemployed to do well by doing good. In the interim, and to conduct their training, private-sector auditors could be hired. The market will try to make these judgments of solvency itself, say, through some savers shifting their money into perceived "too big to fail" private banks and thereby potentially depriving smaller viable banks of loanable funds. Better for the government to provide accurate information.

Protect No One but Depositors

As the process of sorting out the insolvent and the viable banks is completed, some of the insolvent banks will have to be shut down. Deposit insurance exists to prevent systemic risk from arising from this process, that is, to prevent the panic of depositors unable to discern whether their bank is or is not viable causing rushes to their banks to withdraw money and in the process shutting down solvent banks and spreading fear. As noted in chapter 4, even with the existence of freshly replenished deposit insurance, there has been some disintermediation in Japan in the last year

---

holdings—in the previous effort to keep banks open. Mishkin (1994) lists reasons why one would generally expect regulators to prefer not to close banks, although it would be in the public's interest to do so.

(namely, a movement of savings out of Japanese private banks and into Postal Savings and foreign banks and a decreasing deposit-to-currency ratio).[28] Importantly, this process has been going on while shareholders in these banks have been taking their own money out. Calomiris (1998, 3) observes that "[the banks] have chosen to deplete much of their capital via dividend payments. Unbelievably from March 1993 to the present . . . the stockholders of Japan's largest 23 banks managed to remove 1.2 trillion yen from their distressed banks, while those banks recognized cumulative net losses of 2.2 trillion yen." In other words, Japanese bank managers and shareholders are being allowed to increase the likelihood of insolvency and the size of the resultant loss to the Deposit Insurance Corporation while Japanese depositors and taxpayers are suffering from greater fear and putting up more of their money. This is a truly immoral instance of moral hazard.

As stated at the outset of this section, what should be done to clean up fragile financial systems is clear. The Japanese government just must decide to do it. Some delay in recognition and even some pandering to the interests of bank shareholders and managers is only to be expected, given supervisors' strong incentives not to rock the boat. The treatment of savings and loans in the United States in the late 1980s until the passage of FIRREA in 1991 is an example of just such a delayed response, so one need not go too deeply into claims about the nature of the Japanese system to explain the delay so far. What is important is that matters not simply be left to the lowest common regulatory denominator now that years of forbearance have only made matters worse.

The first principle is to make sure that bank shareholders retain no rights or equity when their insolvent banks are forced to merge.[29] The firing, if not criminal prosecution as appropriate, of bank managers would also help. The second principle would be to put uninsured creditors at the back of the line, paying off only the 10 million yen per account that is insured. Until now, even when the Deposit Insurance Corporation has paid, it has indirectly protected all depositors in full, by transferring their accounts to the new bank without losses, and has shielded other financial firms that hold onto the failed banks' paper. The best thing that Japanese

---

28. Deposit insurance in Japan covers up to 10 million yen per account in most depository institutions; some of the smaller banks are covered by a different fund, while postal savings accounts are covered by a direct government guarantee. Cargill, Hutchison, and Ito (1997, chapter 6) give details on the institutional development of the deposit insurance system in Japan.

29. Most of the small bank and credit cooperative mergers so far in Japan in the 1990s have allowed shareholders in the failed institutions to trade for some equity in the new bank. In the 1997 "forced" merger of the insolvent Hokkaido Takushuko Bank with Hokyo Bank, the largest so far, the Deposit Insurance Corporation (DIC) actually bought shares in the failed bank, thereby rewarding those owners who took bad risks.

financial supervisors can do is to close a sizable failed bank soon, and, with great fanfare, directly pay off depositors up to the 10 million yen limit.

It is possible to change these types of regulatory practices quickly—in 1991, for example, the US Federal Deposit Insurance Corporation (FDIC) imposed losses on only 3 percent of the assets of uninsured depositors at failed banks, whereas by 1993, after the passage of reform legislation (the FDIC Improvement Act [FDICIA]), the FDIC imposed losses on 88 percent of the assets of uninsured depositors at banks it closed (Kaufman 1995). This would be an enormous confidence-building measure for a system whose security is clearly doubted by Japanese savers. It would also serve as a warning to managers and shareholders of those banks that are (or should be) in the process of being closed. Again, it would cost no more public funds, but it would require a change in practice.

The Japanese government not only seems to wish to avoid being strict with deposit insurance now, which is perhaps an understandable if ultimately misguided position given the possibility of panic, it also does not seem to grasp the basic concept of moral hazard for investors *in general*. The "Big Bang" financial reforms are slated to significantly liberalize securities markets in Japan in the next two years and break down most of the distinctions between bank and nonbank financial activities. At the same time, the government intends to *extend* rather than contract the safety net, requiring compulsory membership of securities companies in an "Investor Protection Fund," which "will guarantee up to 10 million yen of client assets for nonprofessional investors" (Government of Japan 1998a). A cycle of liberalization combined with deposit guarantees leading to aggressive financial activities by institutions unmonitored by investors is exactly what led to the savings and loan crisis in the United States and contributed to the financial boom and bust in Japan following the last round of deregulation in 1986. In short, even if the Japanese government manages to extricate itself from the current situation, it may well be sowing the seeds of the next financial crisis a few years down the road by repeating its mistakes.

Privatize the Postal Savings System

Given a choice between a savings account with a complete government guarantee offering a high rate of interest on deposits and a similar account with a lower rate of interest and less direct insurance protection, most people would choose the former. As the interest rate differential and the perceived relative credibility of guarantee increase, those people who for whatever reason chose the latter (e.g., free toaster or closer branch location) would begin to switch as well. The Postal Savings system in Japan is just such a "better mousetrap" for depositors. With an explicit government guarantee, it pays no cost in deposit insurance premiums, and can offer better rates of return than can private-sector banks; until recently, this advantage was supplemented by government regulations that allowed the Postal Savings system to offer attractive products that private banks could not.[30] As seen in figures 4.4 and 4.5, the Postal Savings system's share of deposits has been rising since 1990. From a starting point of 30 percent of household deposits (about 30 trillion yen), its total holdings and its share of Japanese deposits have been rising even as total bank deposits in the economy have declined.

This switching of savings institutions in fact constitutes a government-subsidized run on the private banking system. This trend is dangerous because it encourages Japanese savers to deplete the Japanese private financial system of deposits at the same time that those banks need to increase their capital. By emphasizing a safer alternative to even solvent private banks, the Postal Savings system also undercuts any confidence built through correct, prompt action on the part of supervisory authorities. In addition, the existence of such an alternative encourages Japanese savers to believe that a better guarantee than that of the Deposit Insurance Corporation exists and that they should seek investments that are risk free.[31] This is yet another instance of moral hazard, where the existence of insurance diminishes the incentive for the Japanese household to monitor its investments. What is of most concern is that further disintermediation from the Japanese banking system encouraged by the Postal Savings system, out of a combination of both direct movements of deposits into the Postal Savings system and contributions to the general air of distrust of private banks, could provoke a sharp decline in deposits and thereby cut lending to productive investments and cause further contraction in the economy.

Government-supported disintermediation is exactly what the Japanese financial system does not need, either from a view of market efficiency or of confidence building or of easing any credit crunch. Financial intermediation is based on information flows and the proper alignment of incentives for allocating capital. While credit rationing through the withdrawal of banking services (as banks themselves decline in net worth and face lower-quality borrowers) does harm small and bank-dependent companies disproportionately, government lending programs directed at these firms cannot solve the problem. There is good reason on both the information and incentive fronts why public-sector lending is inferior to (properly supervised) private banking. So the combination of Postal Savings with

---

30. Ito (1992, chapter 8) describes the Postal Savings system and its role.

31. Even though the December 1997 package announcing the 10 trillion yen loan from the Bank of Japan to the DIC made explicit that the DIC was now backed by government funds rather than private insurance premiums, switching has continued. This implies that people perceive a benefit to being in Postal Savings and that the guarantees are not truly equivalent.

FILP lending (via the Bridge Bank) is not a substitute for restoration of the banking system and will just perpetuate capital market inefficiencies.[32] So long as Postal Savings takes in new deposits, the Japanese banking system will be weakened.

The Japanese government should therefore declare an immediate moratorium on new accounts in the Postal Savings system and require depositors who hold more than the 10 million yen guarantee limit to either withdraw their excess balances or roll them into short-term Japanese government bonds. As quickly as possible, the entire Postal Savings system should be privatized. Small savers reluctant to return to the private sector should be offered accounts tied directly to the short-term interest rate of Japanese government bonds (backed by the bonds already in the Postal Savings system's portfolio), that is, "narrow banking" should be instituted.[33] Clearly, the privatization of the Postal Savings system would require real political leadership. The Ministry of Post and Telecommunications gains enormous scope for action (as well as size) by having the system under its control; the Ministry of International Trade and Industry as well as the Ministry of Finance gain discretionary control over some sectoral allocation of credit in the Japanese economy through the use of Postal Savings funds in *zaito* (FILP) lending;[34] the saving public with accounts at Postal Savings benefits, of course, from the distortion of credit markets in their favor, although they certainly underestimate, as well, the negative effect on them through Postal Savings' harm to the economy.[35]

Still, any short-run constriction of access to Postal Savings accounts would force Japanese savers to find substitutes for those Postal Savings assets in their portfolio; the primary beneficiaries would be private savings accounts and short-term government bonds (created by this program), because at the margin these would offer the closest substitutes. Movements into either would markedly improve matters by shoring up private bank capital and/or by enhancing the effectiveness of monetary policy on investment. Many OECD economies, including most major European economies, have something analogous to the Japanese Postal Savings system (e.g., the French *Livret*, the German *Postbank*). Though none are

---

32. For a statement of the limitations of and long-run need to replace FILP in the Japanese fiscal and financial framework, see Sakakibara (1998).

33. Kubarych (1998) advocates a wider shift of Japanese savings into mutual funds from banks, which would raise returns (and risks) for the long run.

34. Forty percent of FILP funds come directly from Postal Savings, while close to another 40 percent come from recycling of previous loans (originally funded by Postal Savings as well). This constitutes a leg of Japanese fiscal policy on a par with the Supplementary Budgets (see Schick 1996 and Balassa and Noland 1988).

35. See Dobson and Jacquet (1998) for a discussion of potential gains from international liberalization of financial services.

quite as sizable as the Japanese system, they carry many of the same political protections and costs. All of these are moving toward privatization nonetheless. Of course, the Postal Savings system would have to be broken into chunks rather than allowing one new predominant player.

If the privatization is combined with the prior steps in this chapter's program, that is, with fiscal and monetary policy working to stabilize the yen and raise investment demand and with improved supervisory conduct restoring faith in the right parts of the Japanese private banking sector, the financial system will gain strength through voluntary reallocations. A plan to privatize Postal Savings, perhaps as part of an international agreement on financial liberalization, will strengthen this reallocation trend.[36] The government promotion of private disintermediation through favoring of Postal Savings must be reversed to the full extent politically feasible to reduce the risk of outright financial crisis and panic.

Is There a Role for the United States?

Clearly, the United States has an enormous interest in the recovery of the Japanese economy. In the current East Asian economic environment, a consistently growing Japan is the most important source of stability for the region; a contracting Japan withdraws capital, diverts exports, puts pressure on currencies, and increases uncertainty throughout East Asia. In addition, an economically weakened Japan is incapable of active partnership with the United States, either directly or through the multilateral institutions, in supporting an open world trading system and stable integrated capital markets, let alone undertaking any necessary reforms therein. Finally, an economically stagnant Japan that runs historically high bilateral trade deficits with the United States while the rest of East Asia has to export to the West to extricate itself from severe recession erodes domestic support in the United States for openness at a critical time.

A clear national interest and the ability to pursue that interest are not necessarily coincident, however. Even after seven years of relative economic decline, Japan remains the world's second largest economy and largest creditor nation. Accordingly, it is not only legally sovereign but in many ways resistant to international economic pressure. Unlike a nation whose mistaken policies lead to a balance of payments crisis that makes it subject to the demands of international creditors and even IMF conditionality, Japan's misguided austerity course causes harm without creating obvious leverage points. Until the threat of outright crisis of the sort described in chapter 4 becomes apparent, as in the sharp decline of the

---

36. If the move to shrink Postal Savings also contracts the availability of FILP to achieve public objectives, it will improve transparency and accountability of fiscal policy—an added benefit.

yen in early June 1998, the interdependence of the Japanese economy with the rest of the world does not seem to motivate action by the Japanese government. The United States' appeals to Japan to take on a leadership role and efforts at ongoing political pressure have not significantly influenced Japanese policy so far. Yet it is action to preempt an acute new crisis in Japan and East Asia, if not positive efforts from Japan to help to work out the effects of the preceding turmoil, that the United States and the world need from Japan.

What is striking about the limited ability of the United States to date to contribute to a change in Japanese policy is that the specific policies desired are in Japan's self-interest, that is, they would increase domestic Japanese economic growth. While this would shift the pattern of trade balances in the world economy, it would overall be a win-win move, good for both countries (as well as the global economy). Usually, the difficulty in international economic coordination comes in getting agreement on who should bear the burden of difficult adjustments that require budget cuts or interest rate rises, not in getting volunteers to expand their economies. This odd reality underscores one of the basic contentions of this book: Japanese macroeconomic policy is driven by a misunderstanding of the country's economic possibilities and of the gains to Japan from changing policy. The frustration of the United States to date also illustrates a basic gap in the international economic system. No matter how greatly the macroeconomic policies of a major economy may affect the world at large, there is no multilateral institution or system of rules (as exists for international trade) to steer that policy back on course. Instead, leadership and active efforts at international coordination are required.[37]

So, what can and should the United States do to encourage Japanese economic recovery? There are essentially three options open to it: diplomatic pressure, economic brinkmanship, and active cooperation. Diplomatic pressure is the least costly option for the United States. It can range from public statements by US officials calling for Japan to exercise its "leadership role," to behind-the-scenes attempts to bargain over specific policies, to linkages of Japanese economic policy shifts with a broad range of diplomatic relations between the countries. Edward Lincoln (1998), a former US embassy official in Tokyo, has advocated a particularly strong "tough love" version of this strategy. In response to the US frustration, Lincoln suggests that the United States shut out Japan from consultation on a wide range of standing issues, playing on both Japanese fears of "Japan passing" and cultural proclivities to view exclusion as social sanction as well as imposing direct costs on Japan by its loss of voice. Until recently, a weaker version of criticism without exclusion has been the de facto US strategy toward Japan.

---

37. Bergsten and Henning (1996) discuss the potential role of the G-7 in this regard and its failure to take action in recent years.

There are three major disadvantages to any such approach based on diplomatic pressure. The first is that what is being sought from Japanese policy is a shift in national macroeconomic and financial practices, not a sectoral or other subnational issue. Such a national issue is something that does not respond well to low-level international bargaining. It is a well-established regularity in international relations, both theoretical and empirical, that external pressure can help to effect a policy change when a government wishes to dislodge a domestic special interest and then blame the shift on the international requirements.[38] For national policies, however, such an act can be seen as pure capitulation without obvious repayment by the government and so is not viable domestically. This also explains why the *gaiatsu* (foreign pressure) following the currency intervention of 17 June 1998 seemed to produce the most commitment to progress on financial reform to date (of what commitment there was), because this was a micro issue that could be usefully blamed on outside demands. As discussed above, such reform, while helpful, would be insufficient. In the situation with Japan today, it is not self-evident what change in US macroeconomic policy would be swapped for a Japanese expansion, unlike the instances of successful policy coordination in the 1980s when there were clear steps to be taken by both sides. As a result, the political cost in Japan of seemingly unilateral adjustment may be too great and could even work against Japan's self-interest in such change.

A second, related disadvantage is that macroeconomic policies (such as budget levels and interest rates) are widely viewed as matters of national sovereignty. Especially for a weakly supported government, such as the current LDP majority in Japan, the attraction of scoring domestic political points by standing up to "outside" pressure and defending *amour-propre* may be irresistible. Moreover, in the current East Asian context, most of Japan's neighboring nations are perceived as being forced to accede to foreign, particularly US, demands for shifts in economic policies; Japan has a particular interest as the putative regional model and leader to not be seen in the same light. IMF conditionality, for all the criticism leveled at it, at least comes from a multilateral institution, which gives a softer political blow to the economy required to change than does the embarrassment of a demand from another country.

A third disadvantage is the absence of an identifiable audience for such diplomatic pressure. The actions of Japanese policymakers since 1992 and their refusal to actively expand Japan's economy and stabilize the yen, even during the Asian financial crisis, just emphasize how domestically preoccupied current Japanese policymakers are. The bureaucracy of the Ministry of Finance, the standard counterpart to the United States in

---

38. See the edited volumes of Cooper et al. (1989) and Evans, Jacobson, and Putnam (1993) on two-level games in international relations.

such bilateral relations, especially when the US Treasury is the active US representative as it is today, has both ideological and self-interested reasons for opposing change in policy. It can only help the ministry's internal political standing to be able to characterize pressures for changes in policy as assaults on Japanese autonomy and instances of the United States treating Japan like South Korea and the rest. As discussed in chapter 2, bureaucrats in the Ministry of Finance believe that it is the ministry's job to be guardian of Japanese fiscal probity, if not austerity. Thus, it is no surprise that several years of varying degrees of generalized diplomatic pressure and critical discussion have had little effect on Japanese macroeconomic policies in the 1990s.[39]

The second strategy open to the United States is one of economic brinkmanship. Brinkmanship means making a threat to induce a change in a bargaining partner's behavior, where the threat is made credible by deliberately creating the possibility of a shared punishment not entirely under one's control.[40] This is especially useful if the threatening party might renege on its threats when confronted by a small deviation by its opponent. The classic example was the US commitment to protect western Europe from the Soviets during the Cold War. While the United States could not credibly commit to starting nuclear war with the USSR if just Berlin was taken or if there were incremental incursions, it could credibly threaten that a small risk of nuclear war was always present (especially given the presence of US troops), even if the United States would be trying to prevent war. The United States had to incur a small risk of nuclear war to better deter aggression. Dixit and Nalebuff (1991) illustrate the act of making strategies credible through brinkmanship with an example from *The Maltese Falcon*, a book by Dashiell Hammett: near the end, Gutman and associates have Sam Spade captive in his own apartment. Gutman demands to know where the falcon is, and Spade argues that he does not have to tell Gutman, because only the threat of death would make him talk, but Gutman might not risk killing Spade for then he might lose the falcon forever. The key to the strategy's success is whether Gutman can expose Spade to a level of risk that is unacceptable to Spade without it being a level of risk that is unacceptable to Gutman.

In stylized terms, in the US-Japanese economic relationship right now, the United States can get Japanese economic growth and aid in East Asian stability only if the Japanese give the United States the necessary policy changes of the type discussed here. If the United States directly punishes

---

39. It should be noted that Lincoln (1998, 65-66) makes his suggestion out of frustration, not out of high expectations for the success of the strategy: "Tokyo's response to the Treasury Department's complaints during the past year gives little reason for optimism. Nevertheless, this pressure should continue. American economic policy should also assume that Japan's economy and financial system will perform poorly for years to come. . . ."

40. The classic exposition is given in Schelling (1960, chapters 7 and 8, 1966, chapter 3).

Japan for its unchanging policies, say, through trade barriers, it may bring about exactly what it would like to prevent, that is, further economic contraction in Japan or currency-driven instability in East Asia. The question is whether the United States can create enough risk to compel Japanese change without incurring too much risk itself and, thus, substitute the threat for the action.

There are two major avenues of economic pressure on Japan open to the US government. The first is trade protection: implicitly or explicitly, the Japanese government is reminded that if it continues to run a large bilateral trade surplus with the United States, Congress might enact protectionist measures. The threat is credible because the US executive branch, which does the bargaining, does not control Congress' actions (far from it), and so even if it seems that the US government might cave in on its demands rather than resort to trade barriers, it cannot guarantee that it will not. The second avenue is yen depreciation: as Deputy Treasury Secretary Lawrence Summers set out the scenario in his Senate testimony of 24 June 1998, Japan's repeated refusal to take advantage of the window of opportunity for action bought by the coordinated exchange-rate intervention of a week earlier risked the rapid further decline of the yen. As with Congress, the US government does not perfectly control the foreign markets (far from it), and so even if it might seem that the United States would intervene even if its policy demands were not met, rather than let the yen go into a free fall, it cannot guarantee that such intervention would be successful. Both could be used as the basis for brinkmanship strategies insofar as the United States explicitly brings these to the bargaining table with Japan.

The dangers of economic brinkmanship in the current situation are twofold. First, there is the balancing of risks. Is the amount of increase in the risk either of congressional protectionism or of the yen's rapid fall required to convince Japan that the US threat is credible more than the United States is willing to bear? It would certainly appear that the balance of risks is not clearly in the United States' favor on either issue, because it is the US interest in East Asian stability and the Japanese government's willingness to ignore its region that prompt the issue in the first place. The (risk-weighted) direct cost to the US economy of either protectionism or yen depreciation possibly spinning well beyond the US-Japan bilateral relationship, as well as the likely effect on Japanese growth, which is of course the goal of the exercise, make such a strategy one for those with very strong nerves. As Gutman said to Spade, such matters require "the most delicate judgment on both sides, because as you know, sir, men are likely to forget in the heat of the action where their best interest lies and let their emotions carry them away." It would be irresponsible for the United States to undertake such a gamble in the current situation.

It is the second danger that rules out economic brinkmanship as too dangerous a strategy for the United States to pursue in relationship with

Japan. That danger is the inability of the US government to sufficiently reduce the risk to Japan (and its own interests) should Japan comply. It is one thing to put in place a heightened risk of congressional protectionism or of speculative attack on the yen for bargaining purposes—it is another thing to be unable to get back off the brink after bargaining. Brinkmanship can serve as a strategy only when the threatened party can reduce its risk sufficiently by agreeing. "Otherwise you are damned if you do and damned if you don't, and there is no incentive to comply" (Dixit and Nalebuff 1991, 173).

Additionally, in the international economic environment of today, any decline in the yen or rise in US trade barriers not only puts Japanese economic growth at risk, it also raises the disastrous possibility of a cycle of competitive devaluations and trade war in East Asia and beyond. The United States can and should work to prevent such an occurrence whether or not the Japanese economy collapses, because there is far more at stake and there exist other avenues to diminish those risks. Even though a switch to expansionary policy in Japan of the sort advocated earlier in this chapter would be the best way for such risks to be minimized, there are alternative ways to decrease these risks, albeit inferior ones. Thus, US government action to increase the possibility of congressional or speculative pressure might raise US risks without being a useful threat to Japan. Economic brinkmanship with Japan would be misguided, and probably unsuccessful, because decreasing not increasing these risks is the only credible strategy of the United States.

The third strategy open to the United States at this time is active cooperation. Instead of risking costs too great to bear or making ineffectual diplomatic overtures, the United States should seek to create a *positive* bargain with the Japanese government for the two countries to take on a policy initiative together. In more formal bargaining terms, even if increasing the growth rate in Japan is a win-win or positive sum game, Japan has a rational interest in extracting in the form of additional benefits from the United States much of the United States's own profit from the bargain, so long as Japan is willing to risk forgoing the initial gain if the bargain falls through. To the more realistic extent that the Japanese government is torn over or less than convinced of the net benefits of macroeconomic expansion, anything that the United States can do to offer additional benefits contingent upon Japanese expansion makes the move more attractive. These benefits need not solely be economic, and in fact they might be more effective if they were combined with things—such as security relations or international recognition—that Japan cannot attain on its own and that cannot be dismissed by mistaken austerity mind-sets. Some might characterize this as rewarding bad behavior, but the United States' primary interest right now is the contribution of Japanese economic growth to the world economy. Furthermore, the idea of a reputational problem arising out of this precedent becomes irrelevant because no other country would ever need to be rewarded to pull itself out of a recession (at least since the Great Depression made countries aware of counter-cyclical policy, most countries have been all too happy to expand their economies for their own sakes).

Efforts to establish active cooperation complement the effects of the above program for Japanese economic recovery, though any unilateral US policy move could not substitute for it. To the extent that any US policy contingent on Japanese changes (e.g., coordinated exchange rate intervention) stimulates capital flow back to Japan and East Asia and stabilizes or appreciates those currencies, it will naturally reduce Japanese and East Asian trade surpluses, the dual of the capital account. Neverthe-less, a Japanese shift to growth led by domestic demand, to cite an oft-turned phrase, should be sufficiently sustainable and confidence restoring so as to compensate for forsaking continued attempts to rely on net export growth. Remember, any positive US policy would be *conditional* on the implementation of fiscal expansion, monetary stabilization, and financial reform in Japan, so added capital inflow buying assets, supporting pur-chasing power, and strengthening banks should only amplify the recovery program's effectiveness.

Short of an interest rate drop in the United States, which would be ruled out as contrary to domestic indicators unless crisis were imminent, there is likely little the American government can offer that would serve as a large inducement. Still, the main problem in promoting recovery from previous international financial crises, from Europe in the 1920s to Latin America in the 1980s, was the difficulties in *recycling capital* back to the debtor countries—having them repeatedly export was only a short-run remedy at best. This applies to Japan because, although it is the largely domestic fears that the returns on yen-denominated assets are not worth the risks of investing that underlie the country's stagnation, the result is unmet demand for liquidity there as well. Thus, should crisis levels of capital flight begin to occur, some interest rate flexibility from the United States may in the end be required.

The role of the US in Japanese recovery, however, is ultimately only a supporting role, so long as it avoids the dangers of economic brinkman-ship. The United States-Japan exchange rate intervention of 17 June 1998, combined with explicit G-7 warnings that the markets should not expect too much from Japan too soon and that Japan's time to act is limited, however, seem more likely consistent with a continuation of diplomatic pressure and/or a shift to a yen-depreciation brinkmanship.[41] Expansion-

---

41. Some commentators have suggested that joint intervention to stabilize the yen was actually a result of direct White House and State Department tactical decisions to ensure a more stable yen/dollar rate during President Clinton's trip to China, perhaps over Treasury Department desires. That would be an interpretation even less suggestive that preparations for high-level coordination between the United States and Japan were in the works.

ary Japanese economic policy in line with the program offered in this chapter will be sufficient to restore Japanese growth without US action. Nothing the United States can do unilaterally can substitute for that shift. It is possible, however, that a strong high-level positive initiative by the United States to coordinate policy with Japan could increase the likelihood of such a shift and of its effectiveness. If Japan fails to cooperate, the United States's efforts should be concentrated on keeping the world trading system open and exchange rate changes constructive rather than competitive, so as to limit the damage of Japan's decline.

6

Recognizing a Mistake, Not Blaming a Model

Imagine that you have a next-door neighbor with whom you used to work on projects and play sports (at which he would sometimes beat you). This summer, leaning over the fence, you notice that he not only is avoiding neighborhood projects and games, but does nothing but sit in a lounge chair drinking beer and grilling sausages. In a friendly manner, you lean over and say, "Hey, keep that up and you'll get a heart attack like my grandfather did." Your neighbor responds, "Oh, that just runs in your family—in my family, we process alcohol and cholesterol differently. Remember, I always outran you at the community picnic, and this is the way I've always eaten." You walk away shaking your head, saying, "No, it's not. I remember when he ate health food. I just hope that he doesn't keel over while driving and hurt someone else." Next thing you know, there's a scream as your neighbor has sharp chest pains, and you have to drive him to the hospital. It turns out to be a warning, not an actual heart attack, but the neighbor says, "That's it, I'm changing my lifestyle, going on a diet, running everyday." You wait to see if he can stick to his commitment, knowing that it will be tough, but it is ultimately up to him to pursue his own self-interest.

That neighbor is Japan, and, as argued in this book, it is misguided and ultimately self-destructive macroeconomic policies that have allowed the potential for crisis, a full-scale heart attack as it were, to grow. Up through most of the 1990s, Japanese policymakers insisted that their economy followed a different model and so was not subject to the same dangers from the cyclical swings as were the other OECD economies. The official recession of 1998, the June attack on the yen, and the July upper-house defeat for the LDP constitute the warning chest pains. New Prime Minister Keizo Obuchi and his cabinet have promised rapid response in the form of fiscal stimulus and financial reform, just as your hypothetical neighbor promised to exercise and cut out the fat after being scared by chest pains. The question remains open whether Japan will carry through on the necessary changes to reduce the risk of outright economic crisis.

Japan's economic performance in the late 1990s is ultimately a matter of policy choice. If the Japanese government takes the necessary steps before the risks described in chapter 4 come to pass, Japan can rapidly return to growth; if the government waits too long or chooses not to change its macroeoconomic stance, unprecedentedly severe contraction could hit Japan and then the rest of Asia. The analogy to a person putting himself or herself at risk of heart disease is appropriate—the modification required is some conscious alteration of behavior, but nothing invasive or structural. The condition of the Japanese economy is not one of a chronic or terminal illness, analogous to a cancer, which would require radical chemotherapy or surgery in the form of wholesale structural reform and a long period of pain to bring about potential recovery.[1] Even the much feared long-run economic burdens arising out of the aging of Japanese society are open to change, if faced, by increasing female work-force participation, the birthrate, immigration, or the retirement age (or some smaller amount of each in combination). In other words, even the social security gap can be closed without the sort of outright pain of short-run adjustment that many of Japan's neighbors are having to face or that Japan itself faced in the 1940s and 1950s.

There is sometimes a discomfort with talking about economic policy choices and mistakes as a source of economic outcomes. Implicit in many analyses of Japanese and other nations' economic performance is a sense of determinism. If so much is at stake and there is clear reason for a course of action, how can a mistake be made unless it is the result of political forces that the policymaker cannot control? It is important to remember, however, that we all spend a great deal of time reading, writing, and sometimes lobbying about policy precisely because the discretionary acts of economic policymakers do have implications. Also, what is politically possible is a matter of both assessment and courage on the part of the elected officials in question. There was nothing preordained about the Japanese government's general adherence to fiscal austerity (as described in chapter 2) or former Prime Minister Hashimoto's specific efforts to pass a law putting a limit on budget deficits by 2003, just as there were no absolute political pressures forcing governments in the

---

1. Asher and Smithers (1998) take the opposite view and compare the Japanese situation to a metastasizing cancer that requires long and painful treatment. As discussed in chapters 1 and 3, the sorts of exaggeration of the fiscal problems and sources of economic downturn in Japan required for such a view are unsupported.

1930s to adhere to the gold standard in general, or the decision makers at the US Federal Reserve to mistakenly tighten monetary policy in 1932-33 in particular.[2]

While analogies to the Great Depression come cheap in the East Asia of the 1990s, Japan's mistaken economic policy is the main point of similarity as far as the Japanese economy is concerned. The macroeconomic policy response, or lack thereof, to a financial bubble's bursting has turned a standard downturn into a prolonged recession with a risk of outright financial crisis. The problem remains serious but soluble. The underlying strengths of the economy are being eroded slowly by the downturn, yet the downturn itself is being used as an excuse for claims that the economy is inherently weak. It is this confusion about what the economy is capable of and the potential role for macroeconomic policy, not inherent political deadlock, that is the stumbling block to recovery. This reality has a broader significance beyond the likelihood of Japanese government action—it is important to take the proper long-run lessons from the Asian crisis and Japan's role in it.

There are three primary lessons to be taken from the Japanese economic stagnation and policy's role in it. First, countercyclical policy continues to matter for modern economies, and, under certain circumstances, aggressive discretionary action is appropriate. Macroeconomic failure can occur in every economy, including Japan's, and it is not prima facie evidence of structural collapse. The second is that national economic models do not determine short-run economic performance. Partly because Japan has taken so much credit, much has been made of the Japanese model as an explanation for the outstanding economic performance of Japan and the East Asian region through much of the past three decades. Since the crisis of 1997 and Japan's 1990s stagnation, almost as much has been blamed on this model. This is misguided thinking that traps policymakers into a dangerous sense of all-or-nothing choices at best and, more frequently, into a misguided belief that year-to-year economic outcomes are largely predetermined and equally affecting of all parts of an economy. The third lesson is that the creativity of destruction is overrated. Some claim that Japan must go through recession to cleanse and reform itself for future growth, echoing the calls of the "liquidationists" of the 1930s (such as Hoover's Treasury Secretary Andrew Mellon).[3] These are, frankly, mistaken ideas. Not only are they illogical in economic terms under closer analysis, but they also

---

2. For historical discussions of the role of ideas and decisions in prolonging and deepening the Great Depression, see Friedman and Schwartz (1963), Eichengreen (1992), and Bernanke (1995).

3. See, among others, Nakamae (1998), Asher and Smithers (1998), Ohmae (1998), and Landers and Biers (1997) for claims that Japan must go through painful transformation and that recession can be beneficial in this context. DeLong (1998) gives a historical look at discussions of US fiscal policies in the 1930s.

misassess the relative benefits and costs of structural reform and recession (even if one allows the uncertain political premise that countercyclical macroeconomic policy is somehow in opposition to readjustment).

Countercyclical Policy Continues to Matter

A number of factors have come together to predispose policymakers against discretionary countercyclical macroeconomic policy, monetary or, especially, fiscal.[4] Some of these are recognized realities of policymaking in the 1990s: fiscal or monetary laxity is often punished by free-flowing international capital markets; macroeconomic policy cannot consistently and predictably affect the natural rate of unemployment, the potential growth rate of the economy, or other deep structures of the economy;[5] and there are long and variable lags between when monetary policy is changed and when its effects are felt, and the fiscal-policy process has still longer decision-making and implementation lags, meaning that most business cycle swings have reversed themselves before policy initiatives would work. Some of these are based on more tenuous or even dubious beliefs: the business cycle is dead in the United States or it ceased to apply in Japan; relaxing a monetary rule or a hard budget constraint automatically leads to spiraling inflation or spending through political pressure; and recessions themselves are either the result of optimizing market behavior or the necessary antidote to previous market booms.

Mainstream economists almost universally agree that macroeconomic failures do inherently arise out of the sum of numerous individual decisions in a world of imperfect information, nonhomogeneous products, and nominal rigidities.[6] In other words, if the bulk of products in an economy (including labor) are not perfectly substitutable and measurable commodity goods sold in open, competitive, spot markets, like oil or wheat, then, even if people make the logical decisions, fluctuations in the economy in aggregate can arise out of these "market imperfections." This is particularly true for financial markets, which, as discussed in chapter

---

4. Automatic stabilizers of the sort discussed in chapter 2 are not in question here or anywhere as a useful policy instrument (even if Japan's are less responsive than many other countries').

5. This consciously differs from the slightly more common statement that macroeconomic policy cannot affect permanently the natural rate of unemployment or the potential growth rate. There is mounting evidence from European unemployment and the ongoing American boom of the 1990s, as well as theoretical models of path dependence and hysteresis, that persistent courses of aggregate demand can have lasting structural effects. This is in addition to the related possibility of macroeconomic policy moving economic confidence and the economy between good and bad states as discussed in chapter 4.

6. For a layman's summary of this view, see Krugman (1994, chapter 8). For more technical surveys, see Blanchard and Fischer (1989) and Romer (1996).

4, trade in information that is inherently difficult to verify and use rigid contracts and unique relationships (such as bank loans of fixed nominal debt). This is why much macroeconomic research of the last 15 years has come around to verifying the long-held belief that financial markets and their interaction with monetary policy are a primary source of business cycles and their propagation.[7] The fact that such cycles exist, however, does not mean that economic policy can or should do anything about them.

The economic performance of Japan in the 1990s is the perfect illustration that discretionary countercyclical policy is appropriate under certain circumstances. In short, not only is the business cycle not dead in Japan, it has turned deadly. The usual reasons for avoiding discretionary fiscal policy clearly do not apply. The recession has gone on for so long that there is no danger that the lags of decision making and implementation will outlast the downturn. There is no reason to think that the Japanese economy is anywhere near full employment, so fiscal stimulus would not be a misguided attempt to push unemployment below the natural rate. All information and forecasts point in the same negative direction, so there is no meaningful chance that fiscal policy will provide wasteful support for an upswing already under way. There is no question, given the economic and political events of the summer of 1998, that this would be seen as an emergency measure, one to be reversed when times are better, and not as an opening to an ongoing expansion of government.

Nothing in the experience of arguably excessive fiscal activism in the 1960s and 1970s, and disregard for budgetary discipline in the early 1980s, constituted a disproof that under sufficiently severe circumstances fiscal policy is the necessary response. What was proven is that economic policy-makers should not attempt to fine-tune the economy, smoothing out every business cycle, and that no one should attempt to permanently raise the rate of employment and growth through fiscal stimulus. "Coarse tuning" of the sort called for after seven years of stagnation and now decline in Japan remains important. As Schultze (1992, 213) puts it, discretionary fiscal policy "is suited for the occasional big effort rather than a continually monitored application of force."[8] A driver who ends up risking fender benders and wasting time unnecessarily by darting in and out of lanes in normal traffic should stop such behavior—having improved his day-to-day driving, however, the same driver should not forget about the possibility of passing an obstacle on the freeway in order to avoid a serious accident.

---

7. Bernanke, Gertler, and Gilchrist (1998) review the state of research. Bernanke (1995) and Calomiris (1993) discuss the critical role of financial factors in the Great Depression.

8. Krugman (1994, 32) similarly observes, "But remember that [fiscal expansion] is not by any means an all-purpose policy recommendation; it is essentially a strategy of desperation, a dangerous drug to be prescribed only when the usual over-the-counter remedy of monetary policy has failed."

The willingness to engage in discretionary fiscal policy in a clearly identifiable economic emergency must not be lost in the rush to meet arbitrary budget rules, such as the European Union's post-EMU stability pact or the Japanese government's revised promise to limit budget deficits to 3 percent of GDP by 2005, any more than the driver who normally follows the speed limit must not forgo the possibility of accelerating to well beyond 55 miles an hour in certain rare circumstances for safety's sake. Buchanan and Wagner (1977) influentially argued that myopic voters will be unable to feel the future tax bite of deficit-financed public spending, so removing a strong barrier against budget deficits, even for good countercyclical reasons, will lead to spiraling debt.[9] Yet, as seen in table 2.1, there is no connection between the extent to which (combined discretionary and automatic) fiscal stabilization offsets cyclical swings and the size of a country's government sector. A similar lack of connection exists with the level of government debt.

As representatives of the well-known fiscal-responsibility advocate, the IMF, pointed out, "Keynes' *General Theory* opened the door for the Keynesian practitioners in government to recommend 'functional finance,' that is the use of deficit spending to iron out cyclical fluctuations in the economy. However, sizable and persistent deficit spending only started in the 1970s, when the influence of Keynesianism was waning" (Masson and Mussa 1995, 6).[10] Alesina and Perotti (1995) establish that in the OECD from 1960 to 1990, governments were three times more likely to initiate a loose fiscal policy in recession years than in nonrecession years, meaning that cyclical factors, not boundless political demands, are an important determinant of budget policy. "Conversely, during a recession governments are about 2.5 times *less* likely to carry out a strong adjustment . . . very tight fiscal policies initiated in nonrecessionary years are twice as likely to be successful [i.e., lead to sustained reductions in government debt] than those initiated during recessions" (Alesina and Perotti 1995, 21). The appropriate use of fiscal stabilization, actively pursued only during times of clear and present danger as seen in the persistent Japanese downturn of the 1990s, is clearly supported by cross-national evidence. Countercyclical concerns should not be the everyday concern of policy, but they do still matter and should be given their due when the correct dire circumstances arise.

---

9. DeLong (1998, 83) sympathetically summarizes their argument: "'Cyclical deficit: good, structural deficit: bad' appears to a message that is just a little bit too hard for the political nation to grasp."

10. This is a widely recognized pattern (see, e.g., Blanchard and Fischer 1989, chapter 11; Bordo, Goldin, and White 1998, chapter 1), and should be obvious to anyone who observed the rise of *structural* deficits in the 1980s without concern for the business cycle under the Reagan, Thatcher, and Kohl conservative governments.

National Economic Models Do Not Determine Short-Run Performance

The relative decline of Japanese economic performance against the other members of the OECD in the 1990s, as well as the Asian economic crisis of 1997, have occasioned a reassessment of the "Japanese economic model."[11] Some are ready to pronounce a verdict upon that model, because many of the very things praised—relationship banking, close government-business ties, long-term or lifetime employment, cheap capital through low returns on massive pools of savings—seem to be the sources of the crisis. For some commentators who see the US economy riding high at the moment, there seems to be extra incentive for offering such triumphalism, especially because credit was ascribed to Japan (with some explicit Japanese encouragement) for having been the model that other East Asian economies followed to economic success in contrast to the cautionary example of lagging economic performance in the United States in the 1970s and 1980s.[12]

What should be reassessed instead is the very idea that coherent "national economic models" are determinants of short-run macroeconomic performance. Even the low methodological standard of those economic analysts who are correctly ridiculed for labeling two similar observations a trend cannot be met when discussing the explanatory power of national models: a supposedly unchanging independent variable (Japan's political-economic system) is correlated with opposite outcomes on two observations (growth in the 1980s, stagnation in the 1990s), and the same can be said in reverse for the United States. Clearly, the difference in performance is attributable to something other than the model. As discussed in chapter 1, it is difficult to point to a change in some external factor that made the Japanese economy, or for that matter any other large developed diversified industrial economy, less viable as a whole in the 1990s, unless that factor changed for all of them at once. If, as I have argued, poor macroeconomic performance in Japan in the 1990s was the result of mistaken economic policies, that is, a matter of choice, the national-model concept has no explanatory power for subpotential growth.

Equally important, the idea that there is an identifiable and stable Japanese model does not really apply. For all the concentration of attention upon the *keiretsu* and Main Bank ties of Japanese industry, there are large parts of the Japanese economy that simply do not fit this idealized pattern (e.g., the eminently successful Honda auto and motor company arose

---

11. For the most sober and thorough argument in praise of this model, see World Bank (1993).

12. Krugman (1998b) argues against US economic triumphalism on the basis of a lack of change in the fundamental growth potential of the US economy.

independently of any such *keiretsu* bond). Even before unemployment began to rise significantly in 1997, lifetime employment only applied to a small proportion of the Japanese workforce, primarily older workers at large firms. As reviewed in chapter 3, there is strong evidence that Japanese savers respond to the same sorts of life cycle and precautionary motivations as do savers in the United States and elsewhere.

The deservedly criticized Japanese financial system is more distinctive in degree than type from its Anglo-American counterparts than originally thought. Despite initial evidence that firms with Main Bank ties had longer time horizons for investment and better monitoring and workouts of financial distress (see, e.g., Hoshi, Kashyap, and Scharfstein 1990a, 1990b, 1991), these results proved not to be robust to changes in data sets and time periods.[13] Just as mainstream financial theory would predict (e.g., Myers and Majluf 1984), large Japanese firms that can go directly to capital markets for financing tend to do so at the margin and leave their banking relationships. The different *levels* of bank debt, long-term employment, or savings in Japan than in the United States do reflect a number of real historical and institutional differences between the countries—the fact that these do not represent universal characterizations of *every* entity in the Japanese economy, or determine distinctive *behaviors* at the margin by those entities, means that treating these differences as the basis for using a national model to explain business-cycle swings is misguided.

The demonstrated ability of particular sectors or companies of the Japanese economy to change and adapt further undercuts the idea of a unified national model as an explanatory device.[14] The most articulate and sophisticated proponents of the idea of the national economic model as an explanation for differences in national economic performance work in the political-sociology tradition and tend to view national models as complex integrated systems where the functionality of one segment depends on its relationship with the other segments.[15] If one believes instead that economies are collections of sectoral components (or perhaps even firms and individuals), where one or another can be replaced or altered without throwing off the whole system, the concept of the Japanese economic model as some sort of unified whole begins to break down.

---

13. For evidence supporting this revisionist view, see Hayashi (1997), Gibson (1995, 1997), Horiuchi, Packer, and Fukuda (1988), and Yafeh (1995).

14. This is not a claim that the Japanese economy is a shining example of flexibility, adapts quickly, or has no need for structural reform. It simply suggests that there has been change in parts of the Japanese economy and that reform need not be an "all or nothing" proposition.

15. The originator of this view is Shonfield (1969). A particularly notable and scholarly example of this systemic approach to the Japanese economy is the collection of papers in Aoki and Dore (1994).

While the pace of change in Japan in the 1990s leaves many opportunities for improved efficiency, there is no question that change in some sectors has taken place. On the deregulation front alone, retail stores, oil prices, and telecommunications all have been liberalized to a noticeable degree. There has been extensive movement of industrial production offshore from Japan to East Asia and elsewhere, transforming the nature of employment and corporate governance in the same fashion and for the same reasons as it did in every other rich industrialized economy. There is net emigration as well as (by non-US OECD standards) high labor mobility on the part of skilled and young Japanese workers preferring risk taking to the (exaggerated) possibility of lifetime employment.

Financial liberalization began in 1984, long prior to the current "Big Bang," and those early efforts resulted in significant increases in the issuance of securities (e.g., bonds and commercial paper) as alternatives to bank debt. Banking in general is a declining industry, in Japan as in continental Europe, as both savers and borrowers seek better alternatives (although the process is much further along in the United States). The Bank of Japan was granted independence and a clear price stability mandate, just like most central banks around the world, despite decades of monetary policy run by the Ministry of Finance in pursuit of numerous goals. Again, this is not to say that the Japanese economy has come anywhere close to some ideal of free-market liberalization, but that various attributes of it have altered over time. The "Japanese economic model" has not constrained change in particular sectors, or for individuals, businesses, and households, in the direction of their counterparts in other industrialized economies.

Explicit comparison to the neighboring economies of East Asia underscores the inability of a monolithic Asian economic model to compete with more general economic explanations of macroeconomic fluctuations. Attribution of these economies' decline in performance to following the Japanese model, or lumping together the causes of Japanese stagnation with those of the Asian financial crisis, is a misleading oversimplification. First, what provoked the financial crisis in Asia and the current banking problems in Japan was a series of financial factors familiar to those who saw not only the crises in Latin America but also the banking problems of the United States, France, Spain, and the Nordic countries in the last decade. It was lack of supervision, regulatory forbearance for banks with low net worth, aggressive lending by those weak banks, and debt deflation—all following a monetary policy tightening—that led to banking problems and financial crises; a common set of economic incentives can account for all of these (see chapter 4; Mishkin 1994; Goldstein 1998). It is one thing to say that the macroeconomic effect of a banking crisis is larger in the East Asian economies because of the relatively large role of connected lending or the low level of transparency—it requires a great deal more to say that the crisis is different in *nature*, as claims that recent events reflect coherent Asian versus US national models imply.[16]

Arguments that the United States has benefited from its distinct liberal aspects, especially, I would maintain, in finance and corporate governance are justified, but those are arguments about specific industries and regulations, not about coherent systems or national economic models. It is a matter of adaptation and choice, again, not of an all-or-nothing decision to follow a particular national template. Just as the United States benefited from the adoption of certain Japanese industrial techniques regarding quality, inventories, and worker involvement—and did not have to change its entire "national model" to integrate these components—Japan can benefit from certain financial changes (many of which are already promised in the "Big Bang") without having to change its entire "national model." In fact, as documented in Posen (1998), there is no relationship between the nature of a country's financial system (relationship-based versus arm's length) and its social cohesion (government welfare spending, distributional equity, absence of conflict, etc.), as should be apparent from the mixing and matching of attributes seen in many OECD countries. Not only does the "Japanese economic model" remain as much a mix of good and bad attributes as it ever was, as argued in chapter 1, relying on it to explain short-run economic performance presents a significant conceptual obstacle.

The Creativity of Destruction Is Overrated

Underlying this book's argument has been the assumption that countercyclical macroeconomic policy and structural reform are largely independent of one another. To the extent that there is any relationship between them, it is that in the short run structural reform requires the significant and usually abrupt reallocation of resources (including workers) between sectors, thereby imposing some temporary costs. I have therefore maintained that, for the most part, structural reform in the Japanese economy, as in most economies, can wait for cyclically good or at least not so bad times before being undertaken. In the case of the critical fragility of the Japanese financial system at present, cleanup and reform cannot be postponed, but their short-run reallocative effects should be recognized and, as stated in chapter 5, these effects are an additional argument for accompanying that effort with substantial fiscal stimulus to offset those effects. Further structural reform should be thought of as future opportunities to

---

16. If one were speaking in terms of a formal model, it is one thing to say that the coefficient on a financial shock is higher in Japan than in the United States, but quite another to say that a different model consisting of differing equations and relationships is required to understand the shock's transmission.

Figure 6.1 Japan's output gap, 1987-98

Percentage of potential GDP

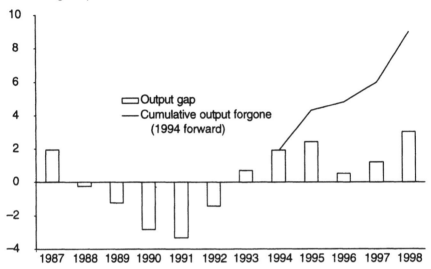

Note: Output gaps are deviations of actual GDP from potential GDP as a percentage of potential GDP. For further details, see Giorno et. al. (1995). Positive (negative) figure implies below- (above-) potential growth. 1998 figure is forecast.

Source: Economic Outlook, June 1998, OECD.

improve the long-run growth potential of the Japanese economy, and their benefits should not be dismissed. But it cannot substitute for appropriate macroeconomic policy in a time of subpotential growth as obtains in Japan in the 1990s (see figure 6.1 for the output gaps, that is, the amount that growth is below potential each year since 1992).

There is an alternative point of view, common both within and outside of Japan, that claims that there is a strong negative connection between structural reform and macroeconomic policy. In this view, the Japanese recession is itself an opportunity to force the reallocation of resources from inappropriate to more profitable uses—in fact, only a sharp recession or even painful crisis is capable of tearing apart the vested interests and old habits that lock up the Japanese economy in inefficiency. The downturn is caused by that inefficiency and efforts to ameliorate it through macroeconomic policy will stymie the necessary reforms and be counterproductive. To cite two of many examples of this mind-set:

> Like a patient suffering from a slowly metastasizing cancer, Japan can opt for a very painful, though probably effective, course of treatment or accept gradual decline under the numbing influence of monetary and financial sedation. . . . Although undoubtedly painful and unsettling, Japan needs a period of almost revolutionary reconstruction (Asher and Smithers 1998, 5).

> [A q]uick fix in the form of economic stimulus or fiscal policy ... meant that
> fundamental problems are momentarily forced into hiding—where they tend to
> grow. Without a proper understanding of underlying conditions, these kinds of
> remedies are at best a palliative, and at worst could hasten the decline they are
> supposed to prevent (Ohmae 1998).

These views, whether their authors realize it or not, are heirs to an intermittent tradition of what has been called "overinvestment" or "liquidationist" thinking. These were very loudly put forward in the late 1920s and early 1930s as an argument for inaction on the part of governments in response to the Great Depression, invoking Joseph Schumpeter's famous phrase, "creative destruction."[17]

The immense rhetorical appeal of such positions, however, does not constitute evidence in their favor, and more direct support for such analyses is difficult to come by. In essence, they require an act of backward reasoning: if an economy is going through a recession that persists, it must be because the economy is suffering from structural stagnation. Because policy inaction or mistakes are equally good candidates for explaining a persistent downturn on the simple basis that it persists and is bad, be it in the 1930s worldwide or in Japan today, other evidence must be brought to bear. The mere existence of structural rigidities in an economy is not sufficient argument because all economies—even the much touted United States of the 1990s—deviate from full efficiency and can benefit from some forms of liberalization. What is required is some reasoning or evidence that the imperfections are procyclical, that is, exacerbated or at least made more resilient by good growth and wiped away more easily if not automatically by recession.

This turns out to be a much harder case to make on the economies than it may appear. If Schumpeter's much more broadly cited and supported insight—that the source of technological progress and economic growth is the entrepreneurial desire for profits—holds, most companies would seek to form temporary monopolies, or at least oligopolies, whether through patents, brand-name identification, relationships with customers, outright collusion, strategic treatment of competitors, or other methods. And this is exactly what happens in the advanced industrial economies including Japan—businesses emphasize market share, identity, brand loyalty, and even anticompetitive behavior, because that is where the profits are (in any perfectly competitive market, remember, profits are competed away to zero because no one's product is different from anyone else's). In labor markets, the same thing occurs—professional guilds try to establish monopolies, skilled workers try to develop specific skills or training that make them particularly valuable to their employer, people attempt to build reputations and relationships, and so on. While this might sound

---

17. DeLong (1998) gives a summary of these in the United States in the period.

like the very sort of rigidity that one would want a recession to wash away, this is actually the engine of economic specialization and development.

These relationships and specializations through the differentiation of products, including the financial information that banks have about customers or the firm-specific training that long-term employees receive, provide benefits that cannot be easily substituted for.[18] A recession is a particularly poor filter for sorting out which relationships and specialized investments should survive and which obstruct reallocation and progress. This is because a recession basically cuts, on the basis of liquidity, across all firms and workers at once. If the markets perfectly rewarded the "right" firms and relationships with liquidity and profitability, there would be no need to purge some of these relationships as obstructive. In short, which firms and relationships get put out of business in a recession is rather arbitrary. This point is established formally in models by Caballero and Hammour (1994, 1996), who show that if workers do not have exactly the right incentives to leave current jobs—meaning they are either too strong in protecting their jobs or too weak to demand the proper investment in their training from firms—the result is a recession characterized by lower job creation than job destruction, a rise in unemployment, and inefficiency.

This is, of course, precisely what we see in economic downturns: not just a short lag until the rise in job creation through reallocation matches the rise in workers losing their jobs (as should be the case if the recession is inducing efficiency improvements), but persistently *higher* job destruction than creation.[19] Despite the possible existence of sclerosis, unemployment and job destruction are wasteful. Other evidence is given in the empirical rejection of Olson's hypothesis (1982) that the rise and decline of a nation's economic growth rates can be explained by whether that nation has recently had a cleansing-out of established interest groups (e.g., Japan and Germany had high growth after the war while the United States and United Kingdom did not because the sclerotic institutions of the former were wiped clean by occupation).[20] The OECD (1997a, 21) reports that "[s]peed of adjustment to regulatory reform can also depend on macroeconomic policy. Excessive macroeconomic fluctuations in the United King-

---

18. See the work of Williamson (1985) on asset specificity.

19. See Davis and Haltiwanger (1990) for the original summary of this evidence.

20. The rejection of Olson's 1982 argument had three parts. First, history does not support the premise that Japanese and German interest groups actually were wiped out by occupation and reconstruction. Second, the cross-national evidence on the number of interest groups has no predictive power when put into standard growth equations of the sort discussed in chapter 1. Third, careful study by political scientists of interest group development and economic growth in members of federal unions, such as US states, rejects the interest group hypothesis as well.

dom in the late 1980s and early 1990s may have delayed the full benefits of structural reforms" for several years.[21]

One can make a *political* argument that policy change will only take place in a crisis, but the *economic* costs of such a course must be made clear. Returning to Japan, it is important to recognize just how serious the costs of a prolonged recession are even in comparison to the benefits of the most radical structural reform. Even if one were to accept the false contention of the liquidationists quoted above that macroeconomic stabilization inhibits structural change—a contention that I strongly reject—there would still be reason for Japan and all reasonably developed and liberal countries to undertake the proper countercyclical policies as opposed to the structural program. As shown in figure 6.1, the cumulative output forgone in Japan just since 1994, when the downturn had gone on long enough to permit thinking about discretionary policy, is now exceeding 9 percent of a year's GDP.[22] According to the OECD (1997a, 18), "More heavily regulated countries, which include some European countries and Japan, can expect to see increases in real GDP levels on the order of 3 to 6 percent after ambitious reform programs."[23] The missed opportunity for Japan of countercyclical macroeconomic policy in the 1990s, in terms of GDP forgone, was on this comparison at least 50 percent greater than the missed opportunity of "ambitious reform." This is not to diminish the importance of political interests in preventing both macroeconomic policy and structural change in Japan, but to say that the stakes of appropriate macroeconomic stabilization policies for Japan are at least as great as those of deregulation.

One can hope that this cost of recession need not be increased in order to persuade Japan to act in its own economic self-interest, as well as that of the world economy. Japanese economic policymakers should restore Japan's economic growth to the rate of which it remains capable. It was mistaken macroeconomic policies, not the Japanese economic model or structural decline, that were the source of Japanese economic stagnation in the 1990s. While the lost output of below-potential growth can never be regained, Japan can achieve rapid growth quickly by following the program offered in chapter 5 or a similar effort at macroeconomic stimulus and financial reform. Regardless of what Japanese economic policymakers decide to do in the late summer of 1998, it is important that students of

---

21. It should be noted that the research and writing of the OECD on deregulation has been one of the intellectual engines of the worldwide push to liberalization, so this is hardly a skeptic's assessment.

22. This is based on the OECD output-gap numbers. For a discussion of various means of estimating this output gap, see chapter 1 and the appendix.

23. While this captures only some of the dynamic benefits of deregulation, the output gap does not capture the hysteresis effects of economic growth, so it is best to compare these numbers directly.

economics and public policy take the right lessons: the business cycle is not dead, but sometimes is deadly; national models do not determine short-run economic performance, macroeconomic policies and corporate decisions do; and, in economic terms, recession-driven economic destruction is simply destructive, so governments should try to do something about it.

Appendix

Latent-Variable Estimation of Japanese Potential GDP[1]

There are several methods available to measure a national economy's potential GDP. Any of these, traced out over time, gives an estimate of the long-run sustainable rate of growth of the economy, that is, the rate at which the economy can expand in line with its productivity improvements and its accumulation of the factors of production (physical and human capital). Because potential growth is by definition unobservable directly, some means must be chosen to filter out the noise of year-to-year swings in output around potential and to identify when the potential shifts. The measure referred to in this paper as the "latent variable" estimate of Japanese potential output follows Kuttner's (1992, 1994) approach to US data and uses a time-series technique known as a Kalman filter to identify the underlying potential growth rate in the measured GDP and inflation data.

This latent-variable approach does not rely on the analysis of the likely paths of factors of production (as the OECD's approach does), nor does it project a growth rate based on the estimated effects of various determinants of cross-national differences in growth rates (as the literature sum-

---

1. I am grateful to Ken Kuttner for his sharing of programs and data, as well as his advice in the preparation of this appendix.

marized in Barro [1997] does). Instead, it takes as a starting point the idea that when the growth rate is at potential, and no positive or negative output gaps have accumulated, the rate of inflation should converge to and then remain steady at some long-run "normal" level.[2] Thus, it works from limited assumptions about how GDP and prices should move and otherwise lets the data tell us the path of potential output. This method has the advantage of allowing the growth rate of potential to vary gradually in response to output and inflation data, which should incorporate changes more promptly than procedures that rely on occasional revisions of underlying data or assumption. If the rates of actual growth in GDP and in prices change rapidly, however, particularly at the beginning or end of the data sample, they may overstate the amount of the shift in potential. That is why it is one of three different methods employed in this book. It is used to give a reliable lower bound on the rate of potential growth and cumulative output gap in 1990s Japan.

Specifying the exact implementation of this technique used here, the movement of output and prices in the economy is modeled as follows. In notation, x is the natural log of real GDP, z is the output gap, x^* is potential output, and π is inflation. The following must hold in this specification:

$$\Delta x_t^* = \mu_t \qquad \text{(equation A.1)}$$

Potential output follows a random walk with time-varying drift.

$$\Delta \mu_t = \eta_t \qquad \text{(equation A.2)}$$

The drift varies as a random walk with shock.

$$z_t = \phi_1 z_{tB1} + u_t \qquad \text{(equation A.3)}$$

The output gap follows an AR(1) process, so the output gap is affected by the previous period's output gap.

$$x_t = x_t^* + z_t \qquad \text{(equation A.4)}$$

Actual observed GDP is the sum of potential output and the gap.

$$\pi_t = \pi_0 + \beta z_{tB1} + \gamma \Delta z_{tB1} + \theta_1 \pi_{tB1} + \theta_2 \pi_{tB2} + v_t \qquad \text{(equation A.5)}$$

Inflation depends on the gap, the change in the gap, and two lags of inflation itself.

In this specification: (1) while the rate of change in potential output (μ) is allowed to vary over time, there is no direct shock to the level of

---

2. Formally speaking, inflation is mean-reverting in this sample in the absence of aggregate demand pressures.

Table A.1 Estimated coefficients from quarterly data on Japanese inflation and output, first quarter 1971 through third quarter 1997

Parameter	Estimate	Standard error	Estimate/ standard error	Probability	Gradient
sigma u	3.4861	0.2485	14.029	0.0000	−0.0000
phi 1	0.9456	0.0344	27.513	0.0000	0.0000
sigma v	2.5478	0.1943	13.114	0.0000	−0.0000
theta 1	−0.0656	0.1505	−0.436	0.3316	−0.0000
theta 2	0.4814	0.0738	6.522	0.0000	−0.0000
gamma	−0.1088	0.1436	−0.758	0.2242	0.0000
sigma uv	−1.2109	0.2730	−4.435	0.0000	−0.0000
beta	0.2463	0.0771	3.196	0.0007	0.0000

potential output included in this model, and (2) the inflation equation is specified in terms of the level of inflation (π), not the change in inflation. These aspects differ from the implementation of this approach on US data in Kuttner (1994), as do some lagged elements of equation A.5, in order to improve the fit to Japanese inflation data, which tended to be mean reverting over the sample.

Table A.1 shows the estimated coefficients that this system of equations yields from quarterly data on Japanese inflation and output from first quarter 1971 through third quarter 1997: note the highly significant estimate of β, that is, the coefficient on the output-gap variable in the inflation equation. This is an indication that the assumed relationship between output gaps and inflation levels used to identify movements in potential output fits the Japanese data very well in this period.[3]

In estimating the model, the condition was arbitrarily imposed that π_0 = 0.5. This says that if the output gap, its change, and inflation shocks are all zero, the inflation rate will tend toward $0.5/(1 - \beta\theta_1\beta\theta_2)$, or about 4 percent at an annual rate (this is what it means for a series to be "mean-reverting"). In an "accelerationist" version, potential output is naturally defined as the level of GDP consistent with no change in inflation. In the nonaccelerationist specification used here, potential output is defined as the level of GDP consistent with inflation at some "normal" level (one could, just as arbitrarily, have picked a π_0 that defined potential as consistent with zero inflation, but that would have been more of a mismatch with long-run Japanese experience). In any event, the choice of π_0 will affect only the estimates of the *level* of potential, not of its *growth rate*

---

3. Using a different econometric specification, Coe and McDermott (1997) also get the result that an output gap model predicts the co-movement of inflation and output very well in Japan and throughout Asia.

(because it affects every period's potential GDP levels the same way), and it is the growth rate of potential GDP in which we are interested.

The standard deviation of the η shock must also be chosen—in this estimation, it is set equal to 0.001. Because this is quarterly data, that corresponds to a shock with a standard deviation of 0.1 percent hitting the quarterly growth rate. This parameter determines the smoothness of the potential GDP series, where a smaller standard deviation implies a smoother development of potential over time (If the standard deviation of the η shock is set to zero, potential GDP is estimated as a straight line, and the potential growth rate is invariant). All time-series based techniques for the filtering of GDP data (e.g., the Hodrik-Prescott filter) require a similar choice of smoothness parameter. As can be seen from figure 1.3, the choice of 0.001 eliminates potential GDP displaying any sort of cyclical variation with the normal business cycles, but it is set a sufficient amount over zero to generate a big kink in potential GDP in Japan in the early 1990s.

Finally, as stated previously, the potential output growth estimated for 1990s Japan by this latent variable method probably *understates* the true level and, thus, the cumulative output gap as well. To make this estimation, the relationship between the output gap and inflation (the coefficients in equation A.5 above) is assumed to be fixed throughout the entire data sample, one which extends back to the higher inflation periods of the 1970s and 1980s. Thus, without significant measured deflation, that is, negative inflation, this method cannot easily generate large (negative) output gaps. As seen in figure 1.2, however, there is reason to believe that some deflation is afoot in the Japanese economy of late, even if CPI inflation does not capture it and the April 1997 tax rise clouds the picture.

Moreover, most macroeconomists believe that in general there is some nominal rigidity of wages and prices, especially near zero inflation. In other words, they believe that changes in wages and prices will remain zero or positive for some time even when subject to forces (such as declining output and rising slack) that at a higher initial level of inflation would lead to wage and price declines. Thus, the existence of a floor on price changes at zero inflation forces this latent-variable technique to lower the size of its output-gap estimate. The approximately 3 percent decline in estimated potential-growth rate generated by this method in less than four years (1988-92) is extraordinarily large by international and historical standards and is difficult to explain except as a statistical artifact of this rigidity. Of course, even on the basis of this lower-bound estimate (worst-reasonable-case scenario) for the potential output growth rate, Japan has built up a sizable cumulative output gap, as noted in chapter 1.

References

Advisory Commission to Study the Consumer Price Index. 1996. *Toward a More Accurate Measure of the Cost of Living: Final Report to the Senate Finance Committee.* Washington: US Government Printing Office (December).

Alesina, Alberto, and Roberto Perotti. 1995. *Fiscal Expansions and Fiscal Adjustments in OECD Countries.* NBER Working Paper, no. 5214. Cambridge, MA: National Bureau of Economic Research.

Alesina, Alberto, and Roberto Perotti. 1996. *Fiscal Adjustments in OECD Countries: Composition and Macroeconomic Effects.* NBER Working Paper, no. 5730. Cambridge, MA: National Bureau of Economic Research.

Alexander, J. Arthur. 1997. The Role of Investment in the Japanese Economy: Past, Present and Future. *JEI Report,* no. 4A (31 January): 9.

Aoki, Masahiko. 1989. The Nature of the Japanese Firm as a Nexus of Employment and Financial Contracts: An Overview. *Journal of the Japanese and International Economies* 3, no. 4 (December): 345-66.

Aoki, Masahiko. 1990. Toward an Economic Model of the Japanese Firm. *Journal of Economic Literature* 28, no. 1 (March): 1-27

Aoki, Masahiko, and Ronald Dore, eds. 1994. *The Japanese Firm: The Sources of Economic Strength.* Oxford: Oxford University Press.

Aoki, Masahiko, and Hugh Patrick, eds. 1994. *The Japanese Main Bank System: Its Relevance for Developing and Transforming Economies.* New York: Oxford University Press.

Asako, Kazumi, Takatoshi Ito, and Kazunori Sakamoto. 1991. The Rise and Fall of Deficit in Japan, 1965-1990. *Journal of the Japanese and International Economies* 5, no. 3 (September): 451-72.

Asher, David, and Andrew Smithers. 1998. *Japan's Key Challenges for the 21st Century: Debt, Deflation, Default, Demography, and Deregulation.* Washington: SAIS Policy Forum Series (March).

Auerbach, Alan J., and Laurence Kotlikoff. 1987. *Dynamic Fiscal Policy.* Cambridge, UK: Cambridge University Press.

Azariadis, Costas, and Bruce Smith. 1998. Financial Intermediation and Regime Switching in Business Cycles. *American Economic Review* 88, no. 3 (June): 516-36.

Balassa, Bela, and Marcus Noland. 1988. *Japan in the World Economy*. Washington: Institute for International Economics.

Ball, Laurence, and Gregory Mankiw. 1995. What Do Budget Deficits Do? *Budget Deficits and Debt: Issues and Options. A Symposium Sponsored by the Federal Reserve Bank of Kansas City*. Jackson Hole: Federal Reserve Bank of Kansas City.

Barro, Robert. 1974. Are Government Bonds Net Wealth? *Journal of Political Economy* 82 (November/December): 128-38.

Barro, Robert. 1997. *Determinants of Economic Growth: A Cross-Country Empirical Study*. Cambridge, MA: MIT Press.

Barsky, Robert B., Gregory N. Mankiw, and Stephen Zeldes. 1986. Ricardian Consumers with Keynesian Propensities. *American Economic Review* 76, (September): 679-91.

Bayoumi, Tamim, and Barry Eichengreen. 1995. Restraining Yourself: The Implications of Fiscal Rules for Economic Stabilization. *International Monetary Fund Staff Papers* 42, no. 1 (March): 32-48.

Bergsten, C. Fred. 1998. Japan and the United States in the World Economy. Paper presented at a conference on Wisconsin-United States-Japan Economic Development, sponsored by Kikkoman Foods, Lake Geneva, Wisconsin (19 June).

Bergsten, C. Fred, and C. Randall Henning. 1996. *Global Economic Leadership and the Group of Seven*. Washington Institute for international Economics.

Bergsten, C. Fred, and Marcus Noland. 1993. *Reconcilable Differences: United States-Japan Economic Conflict*. Washington: Institute for International Economics.

Bernanke, Ben. 1983. Non-monetary Effects of the Financial Crisis in the Propagation of the Great Depression. *American Economic Review* 73, no. 3 (June): 257-71.

Bernanke, Ben. 1995. The Macroeconomics of the Great Depression: A Comparative Approach. *Journal of Money Credit and Banking* 27, no. 1 (February): 1-28.

Bernanke, Ben, and Mark Gertler. 1989. Financial Fragility and Economic Performance. *Quarterly Journal of Economics* 105 (February): 87-114.

Bernanke, Ben, Mark Gertler, and Simon Gilchrist. 1998. *The Financial Accelerator in a Quantitative Business Cycle Framework*. NBER Working Paper, no. 6455. Cambridge, MA: National Bureau of Economic Research.

Bernanke, Ben, and Harold James. 1991. The Gold Standard, Deflation, and Financial Crisis in the Great Depression: An International Comparison. In *Financial Markets and Financial Crises*, ed. by Glenn Hubbard. Chicago: University of Chicago Press.

Bernanke, Ben, Thomas Laubach, Frederic Mishkin, and Adam Posen. 1998. *Inflation Targeting: Lessons from the International Experience*. Princeton: Princeton University Press.

Bernanke, Ben, and Cara Lown. 1991. The Credit Crunch. *Brookings Papers on Economic Activity* 2: 204-39.

Bernanke, Ben, and Frederic S. Mishkin. 1992. Central Bank Behavior and the Strategy of Monetary Policy: Observations from Six Industrialized Countries. In *NBER Macroeconomics Annual 1992*, ed. by Olivier Blanchard and Stanley Fischer. Cambridge, MA: MIT Press.

Bernheim, Douglas B. 1987. Ricardian Equivalence: An Evaluation of Theory and Evidence. In *NBER Macroeconomics Annual 1987*, ed. by Stanley Fischer. Cambridge, MA: MIT Press.

Blanchard, Olivier. 1985. Debt, Deficits, and Finite Horizons. *Journal of Political Economy* 93, no. 2: 223-47.

Blanchard, Olivier. 1993. Suggestions for a New Set of Fiscal Indicators. In *Political Economy of Government Debt. Contributions to Economic Analysis*, ed. by Harrie A. Berdon and Frans A. A. M. van Winden. Amsterdam, London, and Tokyo: North-Holland.

Blanchard, Olivier, and Stanley Fischer. 1989. *Lectures on Macroeconomics*. Cambridge, MA and London: MIT press.

Blinder, Alan. 1987. *Hard Heads, Soft Hearts: Tough-Minded Economics for a Just Society*. Reading, MA: Addison-Wesley.

Bordo, Michael, Claudia Goldin, and Eugene White. 1998. The Defining Moment Hypothesis: The Editors' Introduction. In *The Defining Moment: The Great Depression and the American Economy in the Twentieth Century*, ed. by Michael Bordo, Claudia Goldin, and Eugene White. Chicago: University of Chicago Press: 5-20.

Bordo, Michael, Takatoshi Ito, and Tokuo Iwaisako. 1997. Banking Crises and Monetary Policy: Japan in the 1990s and US in the 1930s. Photocopy. Rutgers University (November).

Bosworth, Barry. 1993. *Saving and Investment in a Global Economy*. Washington: Brookings Institution.

Bosworth, Barry, and Susan Collins. 1996. Economic Growth in East Asia: Accumulation versus Assimilation. *Brookings Papers on Economic Activity*, no. 2: 135-91.

Briault, Clive. 1995. The Costs of Inflation. *Bank of England Quarterly Bulletin* 35 (February): 33-45.

Buchanan, James M., and Gordon Tullock. 1965. *The Calculus of Consent, Logical Foundations of Constitutional Democracy*. Ann Arbor: University of Michigan Press.

Buchanan, James M., and Richard Wagner. 1977. *Democracy in Deficit: The Political Legacy of Lord Keynes*. New York: Academic Press.

Buiter, Willem, and Kenneth Kletzer. 1992. Who's Afraid of the Public Debt? *American Economic Association Papers and Proceedings* 82, no. 2 (May): 290-94.

Caballero, Ricardo. 1990. Consumption Puzzles and Precautionary Savings. *Journal of Monetary Economics* 25: 113-36.

Caballero, Ricardo, and Mohammed Hammour. 1994. The Cleansing Effect of Recessions. *American Economic Review* 84, no. 5 (December): 1350-68.

Caballero, Ricardo, and Mohammed Hammour. 1996. On the Timing and Efficiency of Creative Destruction. *Quarterly Journal of Economics* 111, no. 3 (August): 805-52.

Calomiris, Charles. 1993. Financial Factors in the Great Depression, *Journal of Economic Perspectives* 7, no. 2 (Spring): 61-85.

Calomiris, Charles. 1998. Revitalizing Ailing Banks. *Nikko Capital Trends*, no. 6 (May 3).

Calomiris, Charles, and R. Glenn Hubbard. 1990. Firm Heterogeneity, Internal Finance, and "Credit Rationing." *Economic Journal* 100, no. 399 (March): 90-104.

Cargill, Thomas, Michael Hutchison, and Takatoshi Ito. 1996. Deposit Guarantees and the Burst of the Japanese Bubble Economy. *Contemporary Economic Policy* 14, no. 3 (July): 41-52.

Cargill, Thomas, Michael Hutchison, and Takatoshi Ito. 1997. *The Political Economy of Japanese Monetary Policy*. Cambridge, MA: MIT Press.

Carroll, Christopher. 1997. Buffer-Stock Saving and the Life Cycle/Permanent Income Hypothesis. *Quarterly Journal of Economics* 112, no. 1 (February): 1-55.

Cigno, Alessandro, and Furio Camillio Rosati. 1997. Rise and Fall of the Japanese Saving Rate: The Role of Social Security and Intra-Family Transfers. *Japan and the World Economy* 9, no. 1 (January): 81-92.

Coe, David, and C. John McDermott. 1997. Does the Gap Model Work in Asia? *International Monetary Fund Staff Papers* 44, no. 1 (March): 59-80.

Cooper, Richard, Barry Eichengreen, Gerald Haltham, C. Randall Henning, and Robert Putnam. 1989. *Can Nations Agree? Issues in International Economic Cooperation*. Washington: Brookings Institution.

Davis, Steven, and John Haltiwanger. 1990. Gross Job Creation and Destruction: Microeconomic Evidence and Macroeconomic Implications. *NBER Macroeconomics Annual 1990*, ed. by Olivier Jean Blanchard and Stanley Fisher. Cambridge: MIT Press: 123-68.

DeLong, J. Bradford. 1998. Fiscal Policy in the Shadow of the Great Depression. In *The Defining Moment: The Great Depression and the American Economy in the Twentieth Century*, ed. by Michael Bordo, Claudia Goldin, and Eugene White. Chicago: University of Chicago Press: 67-85.

Dixit, Avinash, and Barry Nalebuff. 1991. Making Strategies Credible. In *Strategy and Choice*, ed. by Richard Zeckhauser. Cambridge, MA: MIT Press.

Dobson, Wendy, and Pierre Jacquet. 1998. *Financial Services Liberalization in the WTO*. Washington: Institute for International Economics.

Dominguez, Kathryn M., and Jeffrey A. Frankel. 1993. *Does Foreign Exchange Intervention Work?* Washington: Institute for International Economics.

Dore, Ronald. 1992. Japanese Capitalism, Anglo-Saxon Capitalism: How Will the Darwinian Contest Turn Out? *London School of Economics Center for Economic Performance Occasional Paper* 4 (October): 2.

Dornbusch, Rudiger. 1976, Expectations and Exchange Rate Dynamics. *Journal of Political Economy* 84, no. 6: 1161-76.

Dornbusch, Rudiger. 1991. Discussion: International Aspects of Financial Crises. In *The Risk of Economic Crisis*, ed. by Martin Feldstein. Chicago and London: The University of Chicago Press.

Drazen, Allan, and Paul R. Masson. 1994. Credibility of Policies versus Credibility of Policymakers. *Quarterly Journal of Economics* 109, no. 3 (August): 735-54.

Driver, Rebecca L., and Simon Wren-Lewis. 1998. *Real Exchange Rates for the Year 2000*. Washington: Institute for International Economics.

Economic Planning Agency of Japan. 1998. English translation of the Ministry of Finance's Summary of Comprehensive Economic Measures (24 April). Tokyo: Economic Planning Agency of Japan.

Eichengreen, Barry. 1992. *Golden Fetters: The Gold Standard and the Great Depression, 1919-1939*. Oxford: Oxford University Press.

Eisner, Robert. 1992. Deficits: Which, How Much and So What? *American Economics Association Papers and Proceedings* 82, no. 2 (May): 295-98.

Elemendorf, Douglas W., and N. Gregory Mankiw. 1998. *Government Debt*. NBER Working Paper, no. 6470. Cambridge, MA: National Bureau of Economic Research.

Evans, George W., Seppo Hankapohia, and Paul Romer. 1998. Growth Cycles. *American Economic Review* 883 (June): 495-515.

Evans, Peter, Harold Jacobson, and Robert Putnam, eds. 1993. *Double-Edged Diplomacy: International Bargaining and Domestic Politics*. Berkeley: University of California.

Feldman, Robert A. 1998. Global Economic Forum. Morgan Stanley. http://www.ms.com/ (various dates).

Fischer, Stanley. 1981. Towards an Understanding of the Costs of Inflation: II. *Carnegie-Rochester Conference Series on Public Policy* 15: 5-41.

Fisher, Jonas. 1996. Comment on Kiyotaki and West in *NBER Macroeconomics Annual 1996*, ed. by Ben Bernanke and Julio Rotemberg. Cambridge, MA and London: MIT Press.

Frenkel, Jacob A. 1991. Discussion: International Aspects of Financial Crises. In *The Risk of Economic Crisis*, ed. by Martin Feldstein. Chicago and London: The University of Chicago Press.

Frenkel, Jacob, and Assaf Razin with Chi-Wa Yuen. 1996. *Fiscal Policies and Growth in the World Economy*, 3rd ed. Cambridge, MA: MIT Press.

Friedman, Benjamin. 1978. Crowding Out or Crowding In? Economic Consequences of Financing Government Deficits. *Brookings Papers on Economic Activity* 3: 593-641.

Friedman, Benjamin. 1988. *Day of Reckoning: The Consequences of American Economic Policy Under Reagan and After*. New York: Random House.

Friedman, Benjamin. 1991. Views on the Likelihood of Financial Crisis. In *The Risk of Economic Crisis*, ed. by Martin Feldstein. A National Bureau of Economic Research Conference Report. Chicago: University of Chicago Press.

Friedman, Benjamin. 1992. Learning from the Reagan Deficits. *American Economic Association Papers and Proceedings* 82, no. 2 (May): 299-304.

Friedman, Benjamin. 1994. How Dangerous is the Deficit? An Exchange. *New York Review of Books* (February 17): 39.

Friedman, Benjamin, and Kenneth Kuttner. 1993. Why Does the Paper-Bill Spread Predict Real Economic Activity? In *Business Cycles, Indicators, and Forecasting*, NBER Studies in Business Cycles, ed. by James Stock and Mark Watson. Chicago: University of Chicago Press.

Friedman, Benjamin, and Kenneth Kuttner. 1994. *Indicator Properties of the Paper-Bill Spread: Lessons from Recent Experience*. NBER Working Paper 4969. Cambridge, MA: National Bureau of Economic Research.

Friedman, Milton, and Anna Schwartz. 1963. *A Monetary History of the United States, 1867-1960*. Princeton: Princeton University Press.

Fukuda, Atsuo. 1996. Main Bank Relationships and Capital Structure in Japan. *Journal of the Japanese and International Economies* 10, no. 3 (September): 250-61.

Gertler, Mark. 1988. Financial Structure and Aggregate Economic Activity: An Overview. *Journal of Money, Credit, and Banking* 20, no. 3 (August) Part 2: 559-88.

Gibson, Michael. 1995. Can Bank Health Affect Investment? Evidence from Japan. *Journal of Business* 68: 281-308.

Gibson, Michael. 1997. More Evidence on the Link between Bank Health and Investment in Japan. *Journal of the Japanese and the International Economies* 11, no. 3: 296-310.

Giorno, Claude, Pete Richardson, Deborah Roseveare, and Paul van den Noord. 1995. *Potential Output, Output Gaps, and Structural Budget Balance*. OECD Economic Studies, no. 24. Paris: OECD.

Goldstein, Morris. 1997. Commentary: The Causes and Propagation of Financial Instability: Lessons for Policymakers. In *Maintaining Financial Stability in a Global Economy*. Jackson Hole: Federal Reserve Bank of Kansas City.

Goldstein, Morris. 1998. *The Asian Financial Crisis: Causes, Cures, and Systemic Implications*. Washington: Institute for International Economics.

Government of Japan. 1998a. Comprehensive Economic Measures. Photocopy. Tokyo: Ministry of Finance (May).

Government of Japan. 1998b. Impact of the Comprehensive Measures. Photocopy. Washington: Embassy of Japan (July).

Greenwald, Bruce, and Joseph Stiglitz. 1988. Imperfect Information, Finance Constraints, and Business Fluctuations. In *Finance Constraints, Expectations, and Macroeconomics*, ed. by Meir Kohn and Sho-Chieh Tsiang. Oxford, New York, Toronto, and Melbourne: Oxford University Press and Clarendon Press.

Haltmaier, Jane. 1996. *Inflation-Adjusted Potential Output*. International Finance Discussion Paper, no. 561. Washington: Board of Governors of the Federal Reserve System.

Hamilton, James. 1989. A New Approach to the Analysis of Nonstationary Time Series and the Business Cycle. *Econometrica* 572 (March): 357-84.

Hamilton, James. 1990. Analysis of Time Series Subject to Changes in Regime. *Journal of Econometrics* 451 (July): 39-70.

Hayashi, Fumio. 1997. *The Main Bank System and Corporate Investment: An Empirical Reassessment*. NBER Working Papers, no. 6172. Cambridge, MA: National Bureau of Economic Research.

Horioka, Charles. 1990. Why is Japan's Household Saving Rate So High? A Literature Survey. *Journal of the Japanese and International Economy* 4, no. 1 (March): 49-92.

Horioka, Charles. 1991. The Determinants of Japan's Saving Rate: The Impact of the Age Structure of the Population and Other Factors. *Economic Studies Quarterly* 42, no. 3 (September): 237-53.

Horioka, Charles. 1993. Saving in Japan. In *World Savings: An International Survey*, ed. by Arnold Heertje. Oxford: Blackwell: 238-80.

Horioka, Charles. 1995. Is Japan's Household Saving Rate Really High? *Review of Income and Wealth* 41, no. 4 (December): 373-97.

Horioka, Charles. 1997. A Cointegration Analysis of the Impact of the Age Structure of the Population on the House Saving Rate in Japan. *Review of Economics and Statistics* (August): 511-16.

Horioka, Charles, and Wako Watanabe. 1997. Why Do People Save? A Micro-Analysis of Motives for Household Saving in Japan. *Economic Journal* 107, no. 440 (May): 537-52.

Horioka, Charles, Horihiro Kasuga, Katsuyo Yamazaki, and Wako Watanabe. 1996. Do the Aged Dissave in Japan? Evidence from Micro Data. *Journal of the Japanese and International Economies* (June): 295-311.

Horiuchi, Akiyoshi, Frank Packer, and Shinichi Fukuda. 1988. What Role has the "Main Bank" Played in Japan? *Journal of Japanese and International Economies* 2, no. 2 (June): 159-80.

Hoshi, Takeo. 1994. The Economic Role of Corporate Grouping and the Main Bank System. In *The Japanese Firm: The Sources of Competitive Strength,* ed. by Masahiko Aoki and Ronald Dore. New York: Oxford University Press.

Hoshi, Takeo, Anil Kashyap, and David Scharfstein. 1990a. The Role of Banks in Reducing the Costs of Financial Distress in Japan. *Journal of Financial Economics* 27, no. 1 (September): 67-88.

Hoshi, Takeo, Anil Kashyap, and David Scharfstein. 1990b. Bank Monitoring and Investment: Evidence from the Changing Structure of Japanese Corporate Banking Relationships. In *Asymmetric Information, Corporate Finance, and Investment, A National Bureau of Economic Research Project Report,* ed. by R. Glenn Hubbard. Chicago and London: University of Chicago Press.

Hoshi, Takeo, Anil Kashyap, and David Scharfstein. 1991. Corporate Structure, Liquidity, and Investment: Evidence from Japanese Industrial Groups. *Quarterly Journal of Economics* 106, no. 1 (February): 33-60.

Hoshi, Takeo, Anil Kashyap, and David Scharfstein. 1993. *The Choice Between Public and Private Debt: An Analysis of Post-Deregulation Corporate Financing in Japan.* NBER Working Paper 4421. Cambridge, MA: National Bureau of Economic Research.

Hutchison, Michael. 1992. *Budget Policy and the Decline of National Saving Revisited.* BIS Economic Papers, no. 33 (March).

International Monetary Fund. 1996. *World Economic Outlook,* May 1996. Washington: IMF.

International Monetary Fund. 1998. *World Economic Outlook,* May 1998. Washington: IMF.

Ishii, Hiroko, and Erika Wada. 1998. Economic Measures, Central and Local Government in Japan. Photocopy. Washington: Institute for International Economics.

Ito, Hiro, and Andrew Z. Zzamosszegi. 1998. *A Cure for Japan's Sick Banks.* Washington: Economic Strategy Institute.

Ito, Takatoshi. 1992. *The Japanese Economy.* Cambridge, MA: MIT Press.

Ito, Takatoshi. 1993. US Political Pressure and Economic Liberalization in East Asia. In *Regionalism and Rivalry: Japan and the United States in Pacific Asia, NBER Conference Report,* ed. by Jeffery Frankel and Miles Kahler. Chicago: University of Chicago Press.

Ito, Takatoshi. 1994. The Role of Demand Management Policies in Reducing Unemployment: Commentary. In *Reducing Unemployment: Current Issues and Policy Options: A Symposium Sponsored by the Federal Reserve Bank of Kansas City.* Jackson Hole: Federal Reserve Bank of Kansas City (August).

Ito, Takatoshi. 1997. Japan's Economy Needs Structural Change. *Finance and Development* 34, no. 2 (June): 16-19.

Ito, Takatoshi, and Tokuo Iwaisako. 1996. Explaining Asset Bubbles in Japan. Bank of Japan *Journal of Monetary and Economic Studies* 14, no. 1 (July): 143-93.

Ito, Takatoshi, and Yukinobu Kitamura. 1993. Public Policies and Household Saving in Japan. NBER Project Report. Chicago: University of Chicago Press: 133-60.

Jenkinson, Tim, and Colin Mayer. 1992. The Assessment: Corporate Governance and Corporate Control. *Oxford Review of Economic Policy* (Autumn): 1-10.

Jonung, Lars. 1979. Kurt Wicksell's Norm of Price Stabilization and Swedish Monetary Policy in the 1930s. In *Pioneers in Economics* 28, ed. by Mark Blaug. Aldershot, United Kingdom: Elgar.

Kapstein, Ethan. 1996. Shockproof: The End of the Financial Crisis. *Foreign Affairs* 75, no. 1 (January-February): 2-8.

Kaufman, George G. 1995. DICIA and Bank Capital. *Journal of Banking and Finance* 19: 721-22.

Kawasaki, Kenichi. 1996. Development of the ERI Compact Model. Photocopy. Tokyo: Economic Research Institute, Economic Planning Agency of Japan.

Kernell, Samuel, ed. *Parallel Politics: Economic Policymaking in Japan and the United States.* Washington: Brookings Institution.

Keynes, John Maynard. 1936. *The General Theory of Employment, Interest and Money.* London: MacMillan.

Kiyotaki, Nobuhiro, and John Moore. 1997. Credit Cycles. *Journal of Political Economy* 105, no. 2: 211-48.

Kiyotaki, Nobuhiro, and Kenneth West. 1996. Business Fixed Investment and the Recent Business Cycle. In *NBER Macroeconomics Annual 1996,* ed. by Ben Bernanke and Julio Rotemberg. Cambridge, MA and London: MIT Press.

Kotlikoff, Laurence, and Willi Liebfritz. 1997. *An International Comparison of Generational Accounts.* NBER Working Paper 6447. Cambridge, MA: National Bureau of Economic Research.

Krugman, Paul. 1991. International Aspects of Financial Crises. In *The Risk of Economic Crisis,* ed. by Martin Feldstein. Chicago and London: University of Chicago Press.

Krugman, Paul. 1994. *Peddling Prosperity.* New York and London: Norton.

Krugman, Paul. 1998a. Japan's Trap. Photocopy. Cambridge, MA: Massachusetts Institute of Technology.

Krugman, Paul. 1998b. America the Boastful. *Foreign Affairs* 77, no. 3 (May-June): 32-45.

Kubarych, Roger. 1998. Japan's Role in the International Trading System: Prospects for Market Liberalization and Economic Reform. Statement before the Committee on Finance, United States Senate. Washington (14 July).

Kuttner, Kenneth. 1992. Monetary Policy with Uncertain Estimates of Potential Output. *Federal Reserve Bank of Chicago Economic Perspectives* 16, no. 1 (January-February): 2-15.

Kuttner, Kenneth. 1994. Estimating Potential Output as a Latent Variable. *Journal of Business and Economic Statistics* 12, no. 3 (July): 361-368.

Landers, Peter, and Dan Biers. 1997. This Will Hurt. *Far Eastern Economic Review* (December 4): 74-77.

Laubach, Thomas, and Adam S. Posen. 1997 *Disciplined Discretion: Monetary Targeting in Germany and Switzerland.* Princeton Essays in International Finance 206 (December).

Laxton, Douglas, and Robert Tetlow. 1992. *A Simple Multivariate Filter for the Measurement of Potential Output.* Bank of Canada Technical Report, no. 59. Ottawa: Bank of Canada.

Layard, Richard, Stephen Nickell, and Richard Jackman. 1994. *The Unemployment Crisis.* Oxford: Oxford University Press.

Lincoln, Edward. 1998. Japan's Financial Mess. *Foreign Affairs* (May-June): 57-66.

Lindsey, Lawrence. 1990. *The Growth Experiment.* New York: Basic Books.

Makin, John. 1996. Japan's Disastrous Keynesian Experiments. *AEI Economic Outlook* (December).

Masson, Paul, and Michael Mussa. 1995. Long-Term Tendencies in Budget Deficits and Debt. In *Budget Deficits and Debt: Issues and Options.* Kansas City: Federal Reserve Bank of Kansas City.

Matsuoka, Mikihiro, and Brian Rose. 1994. *The DIR Guide to Japanese Economic Statistics.* Oxford: Oxford University Press.

McKinsey & Company. 1996. *Capital Productivity.* Washington, DC: McKinsey Global Institute.

Miller, Geoffrey. 1996. The Role of a Central Bank in a Bubble Economy. *Cardozo Law Review* 18, no. 3 (December): 1053-81.

Mishkin, Frederic. 1991. Asymmetric Information and Financial Crises: A Historical Perspective. In *Financial Markets and Financial Crises*, ed. by R. Glenn Hubbard. Chicago: University of Chicago Press: 69-108.

Mishkin, Frederic. 1994. *Preventing Financial Crises: An Integrated Perspective*. NBER Working Paper 4634. Cambridge, MA: National Bureau of Economic Research.

Mishkin, Frederic, and Adam Posen. 1997. Inflation Targeting: Lessons from Four Countries. *Federal Reserve Bank of New York Economic Policy Review* (August): 9-110.

Miyazaki, Isamu. 1997. Prospects for Japanese Economy. *Japan and the World Economy* 9, no. 2 (May): 287-92.

Myers, Stewart, and Nicholas S. Majluf. 1984. Corporate Financing and Investment Decisions When Firms Have Information That Investors Do Not Have. *Journal of Financial Economics* 132 (June): 187-221.

Nakamae. 1998. Three Futures for Japan: Views from 2020. *The Economist* (21 March): 25.

Noland, Marcus. 1993. The Impact of Industrial Policy on Japan's Trade Specialization. *The Review of Economics and Statistics* 75, no. 2 (May): 241-48.

Noland, Marcus. 1996. Trade, Investment, and Economic Conflict Between the United States and Asia. *Journal of Asian Economics* 7, no. 3: 435-58.

Noland, Marcus. 1997. Chasing Phantoms: The Political Economy of USTR. *International Organizations* 51, no. 3: 365-87.

Noland, Marcus, Li-Gang Liu, Sherman Robinson, and Zhi Wang. 1998. *Economic Effects of the Asian Currency Devaluations*. Washington: Institute for International Economics.

Noland, Marcus, Sherman Robinson, and Zhi Wang. 1998. The Global Effects of Japanese Crisis. Photocopy. Washington: Institute for International Economics.

OECD. 1988. *Why Economic Policies Change Course: Eleven Case Studies*. Paris: OECD.

OECD. 1994. Estimating Potential Output, Output Gaps, and Structural Budget Balances. *OECD Economic Outlook* 56 (December): 31-37.

OECD. 1997a. *The OECD Report on Regulatory Reform: Synthesis*. Paris: OECD.

OECD. 1997b. *Implementing the OECD's Jobs Strategies: Lessons from Member Country Experiences*. Paris: OECD.

OECD. 1997c. *OECD Economic Surveys: Japan*. Paris: OECD.

OECD. 1997d. *Aging Populations, Pension Systems and Government Budgets: Simulations for 20 OECD Countries*. Economic Department Working Papers 168. Paris: OECD.

Ohmae, Kenichi. 1998. Five Strong Signals of Japan's Coming Crash. *Washington Post* (25 June): C01.

Olson, Mancur. 1971. *The Logic of Collective Action*, 2nd ed. Cambridge, MA: Harvard University Press.

Olson, Mancur. 1982. *The Rise and Decline of Nations: Economic Growth, Stagflation, and Social Rigidities*. New Haven: Yale University Press.

Ostrom, Douglas. 1997. Prospects for Economic Reform in Japan: Where is the Safety Net? *Japan Economic Institute Report*, no. 37A (October).

Poole, William. 1991. Discussion: Macroeconomic Effects of Financial Crisis. In *The Risk of Economic Crisis*, ed. by Martin Feldstein. Chicago and London: University of Chicago Press.

Posen, Adam S. 1998. Beyond Asia's Fear of Finance. Photocopy. Washington: Institute for International Economics.

Radelet, Stephen, and Jeffrey Sachs. 1997. The Onset of the East Asian Financial Crisis. Photocopy. Cambridge, MA: Harvard University.

Romer, David. 1996. *Advanced Macroeconomics*. New York: McGraw-Hill.

Sachs, Jeffrey. 1997. IMF is a Power Unto Itself. *Financial Times* (30 July).

Sachs, Jeffrey. 1998. Danger in Flogging Japan. *Financial Times* (24 April).

Sakakibara, Eisuke. 1991. The Japanese Politico-Economic System and the Public Sector. In *Parallel Politics: Economic Policymaking in Japan and the United States*, ed. by Samuel Kernell. Washington: Brookings Institution.

Sakakibara, Eisuke. 1998. Moving Beyond the Public Works State. *Japan Echo* 25, no. 1 (February).

Sarel, Michael. 1995. Nonlinear Effects of Inflation on Economic Growth. *IMF Staff Papers* 43 (March): 199-215.

Scharfstein, David. 1996. Comment on Kiyotaki and West. In *NBER Macroeconomics Annual 1996*, ed. by Ben Bernanke and Julio Rotemberg. Cambridge, MA and London: MIT Press: 339-42.

Schelling, Thomas. 1960. *The Strategy of Conflict*. Cambridge: Harvard University Press.

Schelling, Thomas. 1966. *Arms and Influence*. New Haven: Yale University Press.

Schick, Allen. 1996. Fiscal Externalities in US and Japanese Budget Policies. *Maryland/Tsukuba Papers on US-Japan Relations* (March).

Schultze, Charles. 1992. *Memos to the President: A Guide through Macroeconomics for the Busy Policymaker*. Washington: Brookings Institution.

Shapiro, Matthew, and David Wilcox. 1996. Causes and Consequences of Imperfections in the Consumer Price Index. In *NBER Macroeconomics Annual 1996*, ed. by Ben Bernanke and Julio Rotemberg. Cambridge, MA: MIT Press.

Sheard, Paul. 1989. The Main Bank System and Corporate Monitoring and Control in Japan. *Journal of Economic Behavior and Organization* 11, no. 3 (May): 399-422.

Shonfield, Andrew. 1969. *Modern Capitalism*. Oxford: Oxford University Press.

Skidelsky, Robert. 1992. *John Maynard Keynes, Volume Two: The Economist as Saviour, 1920-37*. London: Macmillan.

Stiglitz, Joseph. 1998. Bad Private Sector Decisions. *Wall Street Journal* (4 February).

Stockman, David. 1987. *The Triumph of Politics*. New York: Harper and Row.

Summers, Lawrence H. 1991 Macroeconomic Consequences of Financial Crises. In *The Risk of Economic Crisis*, ed. by Martin Feldstein. Chicago and London: University of Chicago Press.

Takayama, Noriyuki, Yukinobu Kitamura, and Hiroshi Yoshida. 1998. *Generational Accounting in Japan*. Bank of Japan Institute for Monetary and Economic Studies Discussion Paper 98-E-1 (March).

Tobin, James. 1987. *What Does the* General Theory *Itself Say About Policy? Policies for Prosperity: Essays in a Keynesian Mode*. Cambridge, MA: MIT Press.

Ueda, Kazuo. 1990. Financial Deregulation and the Demand for Money in Japan. In *Financial Sectors in Open Economies: Empirical Analysis and Policy Issues*, ed. by Peter Hooper et al. Washington: Federal Reserve System, Board of Governors.

Ueda, Kazuo. 1993. A Comparative Perspective on Japanese Monetary Policy: Short-Run Monetary Control and the Transmission Mechanism. In *Japanese Monetary Policy, NBER Project Report*, ed. by Kenneth Singelton. Chicago: University of Chicago Press.

Vickrey, William. 1992. Meaningfully Defining Deficits and Debt. *American Economics Association Papers and Proceedings* 82, no. 2 (May): 305-10.

Volcker, Paul A. 1991. Discussion: Financial Crisis and the Macroeconomy. In *The Risk of Economic Crisis*. ed. by Martin Feldstein. Chicago and London: University of Chicago Press.

Weberpals, Isabelle. 1997. *The Liquidity Trap: Evidence from Japan*. Bank of Canada Working Paper (February).

West, Kenneth. 1992. Sources of Cycles in Japan, 1975-1987. *Journal of the Japanese and International Economies*, no. 6: 71-98.

Williamson, Oliver. 1985. *The Economic Institutions of Capitalism: Firms, Markets, and Relational Contracting*. New York: Free Press.

World Bank. 1993. *The East Asian Miracle: Economic Growth and Public Policy*. Oxford: Oxford University Press.

Yafeh, Yishay. 1995. Corporate Ownership, Profitability, and Bank-Firm Ties: Evidence from the American Occupation Reforms in Japan. *Journal of the Japanese and International Economies* 9, no. 2 (June): 154-73.

Young, Alwyn. 1995a. *Growth Without Scale Effects.* NBER Working Paper 5211. Cambridge, MA: National Bureau of Economic Research.

Young, Alwyn. 1995b. The Tyranny of the Numbers: Confronting the Statistical Realities of the East Asian Growth Experience. *Quarterly Journal of Economics* 110, no. 3 (August): 641-80.

Zeldes, Stephen. 1989. Optimal Consumption with Stochastic Income: Deviations from Certainty Equivalences. *Quarterly Journal of Economics* 104 (May): 275-98.

Index

falling demand, 25
fiscal austerity, 30
political factors, 144
reversal needed, 5
Australia
estimated pension burden, 79t
major fiscal expansions, 39t
Austria
estimated pension burden, 79t
major fiscal expansions, 39t
average growth forecast, 17
Azariadis, Costas, 88

bad loans problem
banking system reform, 127
cleanup necessary, 66
recapitalization issues, 129-30
shock treatments, 4
balanced-budget rules, 117
Balassa, Bela, 45n, 134n
Ball, Lawrence, 74n, 77
bank inspectors recommended, 130
Bank for International Settlements (BIS)
Basle Capital Accords, 94, 96
Bank of Japan
asset-price bubble, 21
deflationary spirals, 122
discount rates in 1995, 45
inflationary policy, 124
mandate, 151
monetization of deficit, 75
nominal anchor needed, 122-23
restoring liquidity, 109-10
stabilization targets, 9
bank panics
monetary policy, 104-05
reasons for, 95
banking system
bank inspectors, 130
bankruptcies, 104
capital base, 66
Civilian Financial Conservation Corps,
10, 130
cleanup guidelines, 9-10
corporate finance, 151
crises in Europe, 22
current risks, 86
declining, 151
disintermediation, 95
equity values, 94-95
financial reform, 87
fiscal policy, 57n
Japan compared to US or UK, 96
Japan premium, 77

lending policies, 98, 100t
monetization of deficits, 57, 75
overhaul proposed, 114
panics, reasons for, 95
recapitalization opportunities, 127-28,
129
reform measures proposed, 127-35
regulatory practices, 131-32
shareholder dividends, 130
tightening supervision, 94, 95n, 96
willingness of lend, 65
bankruptcies (1984-98), 103t, 104
Barro, Robert, 67n, 160
Barsky, Robert B., 69n
Bayoumi, Tamim, 31n
Belgium
estimated pension burden, 79t
fiscal laxity, 81
major fiscal expansions, 39t
Bergsten, C. Fred, 14n, 43n, 107n, 126,
127, 136n
Bernanke, Ben, 22n, 88, 93, 94n, 105,
123n, 145n, 147n, 156
Bier, Dan, 145n
Blanchard, Olivier, 38, 38n, 67n, 69n,
146n, 148n
Blinder, Alan, 82t
bonds
construction, 35
risk spread, 101t
See also government bonds
Bordo, Michael, 21n, 104, 148n
Bosworth, Barry, 16, 16n, 64, 65n, 68-69
bottom fishing, 123
Briault, Clive, 124n
bridge bank
assessed, 94
credit crunch, 128
Postal Savings system, 134
risk factors, 87
as short-term, 8
brinkmanship, 138-40
Buchanan, James M., 80
budget deficits, 34-41
structural deficit, 37-38, 37t
budgets
for 1996, 50
budget plans (1995-97), 47t-48t
budget policy and cyclical factors, 148
contractionary, 50
government budget balances as share
of GDP, 72t
Ministry of Finance role, 44

success of fiscal restraints, 82
debt, public. *See* public debt
debtor countries, 141
deficit spending
  aging society fears, 70
  budget deficits, 34-41
  costs versus benefits, 70
  debt burden dangers, 148
  deficit reduction law, 80
  direct costs and concerns, 73-78
  effects,
    on interest rates, 56
    on investment, 56
  fiscal stimulus, 41
  funding, 9
  GDP fluctuations, 31
  government liability in 1996, 74*t*
  IMF on, 148
  likelihood of debt repudiation, 75-76
  net debt versus income, 71
  political factors, 81-82
  private savings, 68
  to prompt growth, 73
  public spending, 29
  repealing legislation limiting, 117
  United States, 31
deficits
  government (1988-2003), 37*t*
  legislation limiting, 144-45
  as share of GDP, 73*t*
  structural (1988-2003), 37*t*
deflation
  modest inflation versus, 124
  trends (1984-97), 23-24
DeLong, J. Bradford, 145*n*, 148*n*, 154*n*
demand-led growth, 3
demand management, risks, 10-11
demographic factors
  government debt, 7
deposit guarantees
  savers' confidence eroded, 98
deposit insurance, 130-32
  bank panics, 95-96
  cleanup proposal, 10
  financial crisis, 98*n*
  moral hazard, 65
  refinement proposed, 116
  replenishing funding, 129
Deposit Insurance Corporation
  Financial Emergency Management
    Account, 129
  moral hazard, 133, 133*n*
depression, fears of, 4

deregulation, 151
  pace of change, 15
  potential growth rates, 14
  research by OECD, 156*n*
  waiting for benefits, 5
determinism, 144
devaluations
  threatened, 7, 140
diplomatic pressure, 136-38
direct taxes, 120
  See also consumption tax
discount rate
  detailed (1992-95), 42*t*
  in 1995, 45
discretionary fiscal policy, 44*n*
discretionary income, 121
disinflation, 26
disinformation program on budget, 45
disintermediation, 95
  bank panics, 95
  banking reform, 130
  credit crunch, 128
  dangers, 10
  deposit insurance, 131
  Japanese consumers, 98
  loss of intermediation, 93
  Postal Savings system, 133-34
  reintermediation, 128
  risks of crisis, 104
  threats of, 7
  worrisome trend, 57*n*
disposable incomes, 65
Dixit, Avinesh, 138, 140
Dobson, Wendy, 134*n*
domestic demand, 141
domestic investment patterns, 6-7
Dore, Ronald, 150*n*
Dornbusch, Rudiger, 89*n*, 110, 127*n*
Driver, Rebecca L., 126*n*

economic brinkmanship, 138-40
economic forecasts (1992-98), 49*t*
economic growth
  classical model, 17
  forecasts, 17, 17*n*
  three sources, 16
Economic Planning Agency (Japan)
  economic forecasts (1992-98), 49*t*
  growth estimates, 27*n*
  September 1995 package, 46, 46*n*, 49
economic production decline, 6
Eichengreen, Barry, 31*n*, 137*n*, 145*n*
electricity, bond risk spread, 101*t*

elites
  interest-group deadlock, 2
  sclerosis, 155
Elmendorf, Douglas W., 77
emergency measures, 45, 147-48
estimated pension burden, 79t
Europe, 19t
  banking crises, 22
  coal mining, 15n
  government debt, 35n
  real GDP growth (1992-97), 19, 19t
European Monetary Union, 35n, 117
Evans, George W., 89
Evans, Peter, 137n
excess capacity
  growth rates and, 8
  inflation, 25, 25n
exchange-rate overshooting, 127, 127n
exchange rates
  flexible, and policy errors, 107
  intervention, as short-term remedy, 8
expansion, macroeconomic
  restoring growth rates, 2-4
expansionary fiscal policy. *See* fiscal
  expansions

factors of production, paths of, 159
Feldman, Robert A., 44n
female labor-force participation
  proposed, 80
FILP. *See* Fiscal Investment and Loan
  Program (FILP)
financial crisis
  lack of confidence, 88
  risks of, 86, 92-105
Financial Emergency Management
  Account, 129
financial intermediary
  financial crisis and, 92-93
  tasks, 92
financial markets
  monetary policy link, 147
  purpose of, 92
financial reform
  cleanup proposal, 9-10, 114, 115
  fiscal stimulus, 66, 66n
  focus, 87
  measures proposed, 127-35
fiscal expansions
  advantages, 115
  advocated, 113
  effectiveness in 1995-96, 55
  factors affecting, 58

as failed effort, myth of, 53
major, in OECD countries, 39t-40t
proposed program, 8-9
September 1995 program effects, 57
fiscal impulse size, 38
Fiscal Investment and Loan Program
  (FILP)
  government-directed lending program,
  43
  Postal Savings system, 134, 135n
  surpluses and net debt, 71
fiscal policy
  capital demand, 64-65
  effectiveness, 55-56
  limited countercyclical role, 30-31
  long-term, 7
  savings behavior effects, 66-70
fiscal stimulus, 56-66
  assessed, 29-30
  capital flows, 65
  contraction, 30
  discretionary, 147-48
  as initial step, 58
  multiplier effect, 117
  previous failure, 5
  success of, 6
  to prompt growth, 73
  See also stimulus packages
Fischer, Stanley, 67n, 69n, 124n, 146n,
  148n
Fisher, Jonas, 21n, 22, 22n
foreign direct investment (FDI) (1984-98),
  108t
foreign pressure, 137
France
  estimated pension burden, 79t
  government cyclical stabilization
  (1970-95), 31, 32t
  government liabilities (1996), 74t
  major fiscal expansions, 39t
  net debt, 71
  structural deficit size, 38
Frenkel, Jacob, 67n, 107
Friedman, Benjamin, 74n, 101n, 121n
Friedman, Milton
  financial crisis and collapse, 88n
  Great Depression, 145n
  monetizing the deficit, 123
  permanent income hypothesis, 69
Fukuda, Shinichi, 150n
fundamentals
  analyzed, 16
  confidence in the economy as, 89

Romer, David, 67n, 68n, 89, 146n
Rosati, Fruio Camillio, 69
Rose, Brian, 61n
Roseveare, Deborah, 153t

Sachs, Jeffrey, 64, 88n, 125
Sagawara, Sandra, 52
Sakakibara, Eisuke, 41n, 44, 134n
Sakamoto, Kazunori, 82, 82t
Sam Spade brinkmanship, 138-39
Sarel, Michael, 124n
saver's liquidity premium, 63
savings
    cycle of saving, 58
    emergencies and hard times, 69
    excessive, 8
    financing fiscal expansion, 57
    fiscal stimulus, 56-57
    incentives needed, 104, 114
    interest rate pressures, 59
    liquidity demands, 60
    liquidity trap, 62-64
    need to increase incentives, 10
    paradox of thrift, 58-59
    patterns, 6-7
    precautionary hoarding, 66-70
    precautionary motives, 58n, 69
    radical shift, 23
    rates of, 16, 63t
    Ricardian saving, 66-70
    types of (1980-97), 97t
    yen depreciation, 109
savings rate
    defined, 60, 60n
    disposable incomes, 65
    private (1984-96), 63t
    sources of, 68
Scharfstein, David, 104, 150
Schelling, Thomas, 138n
Schick, Allen, 44, 45, 81, 82, 134n
Schultze, Charles, 66, 147
Schumpeter, Joseph, 154
Schwartz, Anna, 88n, 145n
securities, 151
self-insurance
    labor markets, 33, 34
    younger savers, 67
self-interest of Japan
    additional benefits from US, 140-41
    outside pressures, 137
    policy shifts, 3
    reversal of austerity, 5
    United States and, 136
Shapiro, Matthew, 125n

Shonfield, Andrew, 150n
short-term debt, 121
Skidelsky, Robert, 59n
Smith, Bruce, 88
Smithers, Andrew, 71, 144n, 145n
social safety net
    compared to G-7, 33
    consumption, 34
    deposit guarantees, 132
social security
    burdens of aging society, 5
    estimating pension burden, 79t
    savings rates, 68
    surpluses and net debt, 71
social-welfare spending, of OECD, 33
Spain
    estimated pension burden, 79t
    major fiscal expansions, 40t
stabilization measures
    centrality, 4, 86-87, 148
    importance, 11
stagnation, policy role, 145-46
stealth austerity, 29-30, 41-45, 119
Stiglitz, Joseph, 88n
stimulus packages
    actual amounts, 29-30, 44
    April 1998, 51-54
    contractionary policies, 41
    detailed (1992-95), 42t
    elements of proposed, 117-18
    front-loading public works spending,
      43
    goals analyzed, 28
    as initial step, 58
    Japan's policies examined, 41-45
    larger scale, 30, 38
    patterns, 25
    proposal, 113-16
    September 1995 success analyzed,
      45-51
    short-term debt to fund, 121-22
    structural deficit and, 37
    tendency to overstatement, 41-45
Stockman, David, 118n
stocks, as share of total savings, 97t
Strategic Impediments Initiative, 15
structural budget balance, 37n
structural deficit
    in comparative perspective, 38
    as share of GDP, 73t
    size, 37-38, 37t
structural reforms
    business cycle, 156

minimal approach, 8
negative link to macroeconomic policy, 153-54
postponeable, 152-53
potential growth rates, 14
short-run contractions, 14n
stabilization vis-à-vis, 4-5, 157
UK as example, 156
as unnecessary, 13-14
US as example, 156
Summers, Lawrence H., 93, 110n, 139
surplus rate
defined, 60, 60n
seasonally adjusted (1994-98), 64t
Sweden
estimated pension burden, 79t
inflation targets, 123
major fiscal expansions, 40t

Takayama, Noriyuki, 79n
Tankan survey
banking lending to firms, 98, 98n, 100t
credit unavailability, 98, 98n, 100t
financial position of firms (1983-97), 102t
liquidity ratio in manufacturing, 102, 103t
target-zone literature, 108-09
tax cuts
1998 package, 41n
consumption tax, 50, 51
income, permanent, proposed, 114, 117-21
income tax cut of December 1997, 52-53
proposed program, 8
shortcomings of small, 8
temporary income tax, 50
tax increases
government bonds, 67
savings rises, 66-67
tax policy
tax smoothing, 74
tax revenues in 1995, 46
tax system
business and financial tax-code changes, 52n
consumption tax, 50
Tetlow, Robert, 26n
thrift, paradox of, 58-59
confidence in the economy, 87
Tobin, James, 59n, 61, 63t
total factor productivity (TFP), 16
tough love strategy, 137

trade balance (1984-98), 107t
trade protection, 139
trade surpluses, 141
trade threat and response cycle, 106-07
trade war possibility, 140
triumphalism, 149, 149n
Tullock, Gordon, 80
Turkey
growth forecasts, 17n

Ueda, Kazuo, 81n, 121n, 124n
underutilized capacity
evidence of, 55-56
fiscal expansion and, 57
unemployment
expansionary fiscal policy, 69
hidden, 33, 34
Japanese approach, 33
lifetime employment, 150
new graduates, 90, 91t, 92
output gap, 8
public spending, 33
structural reforms, 156
United Kingdom
estimated pension burden, 79t
government cyclical stabilization (1970-95), 31, 32t
government liabilities (1996), 74t
major fiscal expansions, 40t
net debt, 71
real estate property bust, 22
structural deficit size, 38
structural reform, 156
United States
balanced-budget rules, 117
brinkmanship in Cold War, 238
competitiveness improvements, 15
deposit insurance, 132
diplomatic opportunities, 116
estimated pension burden, 79t
government cyclical stabilization (1970-95), 31, 32t
government liabilities (1996), 74t
Japanese industrial techniques, 152
major fiscal expansions, 40t
net debt, 71
positive cooperation with Japan, 116
real GDP growth (1992-97), 19, 19t
risks of brinkmanship, 139-40
role in Japan's recovery, 135-42
savings and loan crisis, 21-22, 129-30
structural deficit size, 38
structural reform, 156
trade deficit with Japan, 106-07

Other Publications from the Institute for International Economics

WORKS IN PROGRESS

The US - Japan Economic Relationship
C. Fred Bergsten, Marcus Noland, and Takatoshi Ito
China's Entry to the World Economy
Richard N. Cooper
Economic Sanctions After the Cold War
Kimberly Ann Elliott, Gary C. Hufbauer and Jeffrey J. Schott
Trade and Labor Standards
Kimberly Ann Elliott and Richard Freeman
Leading Indicators of Financial Crises in the Emerging Economies
Morris Goldstein and Carmen Reinhart
Prospects for Western Hemisphere Free Trade
Gary Clyde Hufbauer and Jeffrey J. Schott
The Future of US Foreign Aid
Carol Lancaster
The Economics of Korean Unification
Marcus Noland
International Lender of Last Resort
Catherine L. Mann
A Primer on US External Balance
Catherine L. Mann
Foreign Direct Investment in Developing Countries
Theodore Moran
Globalization, the NAIRU, and Monetary Policy
Adam Posen
Behind the Open Door: Foreign Enterprises in the Chinese Marketplace
Daniel Rosen
Measuring the Costs of Protection in China
Zhang Shuguang, Zhang Yansheng, and Wan Zhongxin

DISTRIBUTORS OUTSIDE THE UNITED STATES

Australia, New Zealand, and
Papua New Guinea
D.A. INFORMATION SERVICES
648 Whitehorse Road
Mitcham, Victoria 3132, Australia
(tel: 61-3-9210-7777; fax: 61-3-9210-7788)
email: service@dadirect.com.au
www.dadirect.com.au

Caribbean
SYSTEMATICS STUDIES LIMITED
St. Augustine Shopping Centre
Eastern Main Road, St. Augustine
Trinidad and Tobago, West Indies
(tel: 868-645-8466; fax: 868-645-8467)
email: tobe@trinidad.net

Japan
UNITED PUBLISHERS SERVICES, LTD.
Kenkyu-Sha Bldg.
9, Kanda Surugadai 2-Chome
Chiyoda-Ku, Tokyo 101, Japan
(tel: 81-3-3291-4541; fax: 81-3-3292-8610)
email: saito@ups.co.jp

Canada
RENOUF BOOKSTORE
5369 Canotek Road, Unit 1,
Ottawa, Ontario K1J 9J3, Canada
(tel: (613) 745-2665
fax: (613) 745-7660)
http://www.renoufbooks.com/

India
VIVA BOOKS PVT.
Mr. Vinod Vasishtha
4325/3, Ansari Rd.
Daryaganj, New Delhi-110002, INDIA
(tel: 91-11-327-9280 fax: 91-11-326-7224)
email: vinod.viva@gndel.
globalnet.ems.vsnl.net.in

Visit our website at:
http://www.iie.com

E-mail orders to:
iiecon@pmds.com